# colloquium slavicum

## Beiträge zur Slavistik

Herausgeber
Heinrich Kunstmann, Universität München
Vsevolod Setchkarev, Harvard University

Band 6

jal-verlag · würzburg

Norman W. Ingham

# E. T. A. Hoffmann's Reception in Russia

jal-verlag · würzburg
1974
ISBN 3 7778 0117 8

CC

© jal-verlag, würzburg 1974
Composed by: Irmgard Kottmann, Würzburg
Printed by: repro-druck „Journalfranz" Arnulf Liebing, Würzburg
Printed in Germany
ISBN 3 7778 0117 8

To My Mother and Father

# Contents

# Preface

When Ernst Theodor Amadeus Hoffmann died in Berlin on the 25th of June 1822 at the age of 46, he was an author all but unknown outside his own country.* The first English translation of one of his literary works appeared in 1824,[1] and in France — although he was mentioned in print by 1826 — no translation was published until 1828 and his name became widely known only in the following year.[2] Hoffmann's discovery by the French had his general European fame as a result. The French translations by Loève-Veimars were, for example, eventually rendered into Spanish (the *Cuentos fantásticos* of 1839).[3]

Interestingly enough, the distant Russians were among the earliest to print any works of E. T. A. Hoffmann in translation. The first was published in their country in 1822, at the very time when its author lay on his deathbed in Berlin. In 1830 Russia saw the beginning of a veritable cult of Hoffmann which lasted for more than a decade, passing through several phases. Hoffmann was extensively translated, read and discussed during that time, and his literary manner left its mark on some of the works of Russian writers. Michel Gorlin in his article "Hoffmann en Russie" (1935)[4] went so far as to claim that Hoffmann has been over the years the most influential German author in Russia:

> De tous les écrivains allemands c'est incontestablement Hoffmann qui a exercé l'influence la plus profonde sur la littérature russe. On a vénéré Goethe, on a adoré Schiller, mais on a été ensorcelé, on a été envoûté par Hoffmann. On l'a aimé et on l'aime encore aujourd'-hui d'un amour très vif, très intime et qui passe quelquefois de l'admiration à la haine. Pouchkine, Gogol, Dostoïevski, Blok, pour

---

* The present book is, with some revisions, my doctoral dissertation that was submitted at Harvard University in 1963 under the title "E. T. A. Hoffmann in Russia, 1822 – 1845."

ne citer que les plus grands noms, ont subi l'attrait de son génie
mystérieux. Loin de représenter une vogue passagère, il fait partie
de ces écrivains européens qui ont touché au vif même de l'âme
russe.

While Gorlin may have exaggerated slightly, it is true that Hoffmann has
enchanted the Russians of more than one generation and has remained a
favorite foreign author with them down to the present. His reputation
suffered a partial eclipse in the 1840's, but he was brought back into the
limelight again at the end of the century as an idol of the symbolists.

Some information about Hoffmann's literary fate in Russia has been
given in various publications, but no one   has attempted a full study of
this important chapter from comparative literary history. Aside from
Gorlin's article, there are essays by Rodzevič[5] and Levit.[6] Of these
Levit's, which appeared as an appendix to the 1930 Russian edition of
Hoffmann's works, is overall perhaps the best, but of course it is hardly
available outside Russia and inaccessible to those who do not read Russian.
There are valuable observations in histories of Russian literature and in
monographs devoted to Hoffmann's affiliation with specific writers, such
as Gorlin's book on Hoffmann and Gogol'. Studies of the German author's
connections with Puškin, Pogorel'skij, Polevoj and others have also been
compiled, though none of them is wholly satisfactory. Most importantly,
no thorough history of the publishing and criticism of Hoffmann in Russia
has been printed, information on the subject being relegated to footnotes
and bibliographies.

In 1963 Charles E. Passage's book *The Russian Hoffmannists* was
published.[7] In the last months of my work Professor Passage was kind
enough to correspond and meet with me, and we had informal conversations about our mutual interest. However, both our studies were then
too far advanced to allow much, if any, reciprocal benefit from our discussions. The two books were and remain independent productions. In

revising my text ten years later for publication, I have added some reactions to his book, almost entirely in the form of notes. The titles of our two studies reflect the difference in content. Passage was concerned mostly with the possible influence of Hoffmann on Russian writers; the comparative sections of the present book share space with the detailed history of the publishing and criticism of Hoffmann in Russia in the initial period of his reception there, which I view as the more important part of my study. Passage gave very little attention to the latter subject and was largely dependent on secondary sources for his data. Thus there is less overlapping between our books than might at first appear. The greatest duplication comes in the chapters on Pogorel'skij and Polevoj, though even here there are differences of emphasis. Concerning Puškin, Gogol', Odoevskij, Lermontov, Gercen and A. K. Tolstoj our coverage differs more widely. My chapters on Mel'gunov and Olin find no counterparts in Passage; and, on the other hand, he added V. A. Sollogub (a marginal figure) and Turgenev and Dostoevskij (excluded here as outside the chosen time frame).

Regrettably, it must be said that *The Russian Hoffmannists* suffers from an unsatisfactory methodology and inadequate information about Russian literature. Passage tends to see Hoffmann behind every piece of Russian fiction examined, even when he has to admit that the similarity is very vague. Not infrequently a borrowing acknowledged to be doubtful and undemonstrable is later treated as a certainty and then becomes the base upon which a generalization is built. The weakest part of the study is the climactic chapter on Dostoevskij (summarizing Passage's earlier book on the subject[8])), much of which is plainly unacceptable. A comparatist and specialist in German romanticism, Professor Passage was insufficiently informed about Russian scholarship, missing even major works. He seems not to have consulted any Soviet studies that appeared after his dissertation was finished (1941). The lack of information is reflected too in his incorrect assertion that writers like Odoevskij and Pogorel'skij have not been republished in the Soviet period. These faults of *The Russian*

*Hoffmannists* are all the more to be regretted in that they obscure the valid and useful things in the book. In my view, despite the many errors of detail the majority of Passage's general conclusions about affiliations of Russian writers with Hoffmann are correct — with exception of Dostoevskij. [9]

The present book is an effort toward a connected account of E. T. A. Hoffmann's literary reception in Russia during the first period of interest in him there, from the earliest translation in 1822 to the decline of his vogue around the middle of the 1840's. This span is divided into four rather well-defined phases: 1) that of the first translations (1822 — 1829); 2) the period of intense interest in Hoffmann, principally as a fantasist (1830 — 1835); 3) that of the discovery of Hoffmann as a serious artist (1836 — 1840); and finally 4) the years of diminishing attention to him (1841 — 1845). The quality of the translations is discussed, as well as the critical articles, reviews and mentions of Hoffmann that appeared in the literary press, in order to show in what form he was known to the Russians and what public image he acquired. This chronicle of publishing and criticism should need no special justification, since it is relevant both to Hoffmann studies in general and to the history of Russian literature in the nineteenth century. However, the intervening chapters on the possible affiliations of individual Russian writers with him perhaps do deserve comment, inasmuch as investigations of "influence" and the like are no longer as fashionable as they were at one time. It is my position that the study of sources remains a proper and useful adjunct to literary history as long as it does not degenerate into the game of seeking trivia. At the same time, I am aware that the more meaningful connection between a writer and his predecessors may go far deeper than literary borrowings and is something intangible and rarely susceptible of proof. On the other hand, a *typological* comparison of one author with another is often a means towards understanding the individuality of each. I hope that this book avoids most excesses of the comparative method.

The greater part of the research for the book was carried out during a year of study at Leningrad State University (1961–1962). It would have been much facilitated had the Soviet bibliography of Russian Hoffmann translations and criticism been published a little earlier: *È. T. A. Gofman: Bibliografia russkix perevodov i kritičeskoj literatury,* comp. Z. V. Žitomirskaja (M.: Kniga, 1964; hereafter: Žitomirskaja). This is a most useful reference tool containing an apparently exhaustive tabulation of translations, an interesting but far from complete list of critical mentions of Hoffmann and a fragmentary listing of literary works that refer to him or were influenced by him. The book is prefaced with a brief essay on Hoffmann and Russian literature. However, Žitomirskaja includes only one translation from the early period that I did not locate in my own searches (i.e., T33a).

Appended to the present book are complete bibliographies of the Russian translations of Hoffmann (in chronological order, while Žitomirskaja is organized by titles) and the critical articles about him, both covering the period 1822 to 1845.[10)] The collection of occasional mentions of Hoffmann from the press, which are presented in my text, of course cannot claim to be exhaustive; but I believe the material is sufficient to characterize attitudes toward Hoffmann. It has been supplemented to a certain extent by information from published memoirs, correspondence and other sources. References to translations and articles are marked, respectively, (T) and (C) plus the number of the item in the relevant bibliography. For typographical reasons and because the book may be of interest to readers who do not know Russian, the number of quotations in Russian has been kept to a minimum. Most are also given in English, but this was not possible when technical questions about the Russian rendering of Hoffmann's words were being discussed.

14                              Preface

I wish to express my deep gratitude to my thesis supervisor, Professor
Vsevolod Setchkarev, and to Professor Kiril Taranovsky, both of Harvard
University, who lent guidance and encouragement, and my thanks to the
staffs of the Leningrad Public Library, the Library of the Academy of
Sciences in Leningrad, the Lenin Library and the Bibliothèque Nationale
for their assistance. I was indebted to Harvard University and the U.S.
Department of Education for their financial support of my graduate education, and to the Inter-University Committee on Travel Grants and Harvard University for the opportunity to spend a year of study and research
in the Soviet Union.

Norman W. Ingham

Granby, Massachusetts
August, 1973

# I

# The First Translations, 1822 — 1829

## 1

The publishing history of E. T. A. Hoffmann in Russia begins with the appearance in 1822 of a translation of "Das Fräulein von Scuderi" in the *Biblioteka dlja čtenija* (Library for Reading). In this and the following seven years only eight works by Hoffmann came out in Russian translation, the remaining ones being "Spielerglück," "Doge und Dogaresse," "Die Marquise de la Pivardiere," "Datura fastuosa," "Der Magnetiseur," "Die Irrungen" and "Signor Formica." This is an average of merely one per year, and none was published at all in 1824 or 1828. All of these translations appeared in literary magazines, although one was also issued in offprint. Petersburg produced the very first publication of Hoffmann in Russia, but Moscow followed soon and eventually produced the greatest number of translations for the period up to 1845.

"Devica Skuderi" ("Das Fräulein von Scuderi") was offered to the readers of the *Biblioteka dlja čtenija*, literary supplement to the *Syn otečestva* (Son of the Fatherland) — not to be confused with the later magazine *Biblioteka dlja čtenija*, published 1834 — 1865 — in book 3 for May-June, 1822 (Tl). The actual publication was preceded by notices *(ob" javlenija)* in the magazines *Vestnik Evropy* (The Herald of Europe) for January (vol. 122, p. 155) and *Blagonamerennyj* (The Well-Intentioned; no. 1 for 1822, p. 87), which list "Devica Skuderi" among the works to be published by *Syn otečestva* in its supplements for the new year. In neither notice is the name of the author mentioned, and only *Blagonamerennyj* gives a subtitle, "Istoričeskoe proisšestvie veka Ljudovika XIV" (A Historical Happening from the Time of Louis XIV).

In fact the edition of the story itself does not carry the correct name of the author. At the end of the text we find: "K. G. Gofman," which evidently led the compilers of a recent manual of Russian periodicals to state that the *Biblioteka dlja čtenija* included works of "K. G. Gofman" (Hoffmann) among its translations of foreign writers.[11] Can the Russian publishers have mistaken the unfamiliar E. T. A. Hoffmann for another man? Other than a certain Carl Gottlieb Hofmann who published *Gustav III, König von Schweden,* in 1793, we have been unable to discover an author of the period whose initials could have become K. G. in Russian. The bibliographer of the Leningrad Public Library who indexed "Devica Skuderi" concluded that K. G. Gofman was the *translator,* and that is a possible hypothesis, even though it involves a curious coincidence. In any case, it is of interest to us that the very first Russian translation of E. T. A. Hoffmann was published without the author's (correct) name.

A comparison of "Devica Skuderi (Povest' veka Ljudovika XIV)" with Hoffmann's German text shows that this very first translation was quite good and definitely superior to several of those which followed it in Russia. Inaccuracies are very minor. For example, the sentence: "So streng der Vater uns bewachte, mancher verstohlene Händedruck galt als Zeichen des geschlossenen Bundes," becomes: "Kak ni strogo smotrel za nami otec, nam udalos' odnako ž požat' inogda drug u druga ruku — v znak zaključennogo meždu nami serdečnogo sojuza." The translator has not changed the sense here but has added superfluous words and put the whole into unfortunate syntax. The remarkably professional translation of the *Serapionsbrüder* by Bessomykin (1836), to which we shall often refer, is more faithful to the original in rendering this same sentence: "Kak strogo ni nabljudal za nami otec, no častye tajnye požatija ruki služili znakom zaključennogo sojuza."

Evidently Greč was confident that "Devica Skuderi" would find a sizable reading public, because he published — it would seem simultaneously – an offprint which could be purchased separately (Tla). *Blagonamerennyj* carried (in no. 28 for 1822, pp. 76 – 77) under "Knižnye izvestija" a notice of publication of *Literaturnye pribavlenija* (Literary Supplement) to *Syn otečestva* (i.e., *Biblioteka dlja čtenija*), listing "Devica Skuderi" and adding this footnote:

> This last story has also been printed separately. It may be purchased for 2 rubles 50 kopecks, or with postage 3 rubles, in the bookstores of Plavil'ščikov and the Brothers Slenin, and also at the apartment of the editor of *Blagonamerennyj*. Kindly address out-of-town orders to the latter.

The same advertisement informs us that the *Pribavlenija* itself could be had in Petersburg for 17.50. The offprint of the 117-page "Devica Skuderi," issued with a light paper cover, thus became the first separate edition of a Hoffmann work in Russia. Of course the same plates were used for the offprint, and it differs from the version in *Biblioteka dlja čtenija* only in pagination.

The year 1823 saw two Hoffmann translations published in Russia. The first was "O sčastii igrokov" ("Spielerglück"), found in *Vestnik Evropy*, no. 13 (T2). The author is identified ("S. Gofmana" *[*i.e., sočinenie Gofmana*]* ), and the translator gave his name at the end of the text: Vasilij Poljakov. This man was a bookseller and publisher who is credited with originating the idea of miniature editions of Russian classics. He opened his own bookstore in 1838, but the business collapsed twenty years later, and he died in poverty in 1875.[12] Poljakov must have been quite young in 1823 and not primarily a translator. At any rate, the quality of the translation "O sčastii igrokov" does not testify to professional status. By retaining chiefly sentences essential to the action, simplifying the language at nearly all turns, omitting strongly poetic images and the romantic characterization of the hero, Poljakov managed to reduce Hoffmann's sophisticated story to a mere adventure-well-recounted. The result is not Hoffmann. Gone above all are the typical passages which suggest a striving after knowledge of higher powers and designs. For example, this sentence is entirely omitted:

> Die sonderbaren Verkettungen des Zufalls wechseln in dem selt-
> samsten Spiel, das Regiment der höhern Macht tritt klarer hervor,
> und eben dieses ist es, was unseren Geist anregt, die Fittiche zu
> rühren und zu versuchen, ob er sich nicht hineinschwingen kann
> in das dunkle Reich, in die verhängnisvolle Werkstatt jener Macht,
> um ihr Arbeiten zu belauschen.

One has difficulty finding whole sentences which are accurately translated. An example of an abridgment is: "das trostlose Gefühl der auf ewig zer-störten Liebe, die, die schönste Blüte, aufkeimt im jugendlichen Herzen," which becomes in Poljakov's translation simply: "gorestnoe čuvstvo ljub-vi, navsegda razrušennoj." Occasionally there are additions, as for example: "Man sieht Personen, die sonst keine Karte anrühren, an der Bank als die eifrigsten Spieler," which becomes: "Vidim i takix, kotorye, nikogda nebravši prežde kart v ruki, nikogda nedumavši o banke, puska-jutsja igrat', kak revnostnejsie spodnižniki zapisnyx iskatelej fortuny."

Let us examine here one lengthy example of inadequate translation. The third paragraph of Hoffmann's "Spielerglück" is very important for its characterization of the young hero, but we shall see that the most essential parts are omitted in the poorer translations. Here is that para-graph, followed by the rather good translation of Bessomykin, Poljakov's version and, for good measure, the equally unsatisfactory variant of 1831 (T20):

> Von diesem unwiderstehlichen Zauber, von dieser Regel des guten
> Tons schien allein ein junger deutscher Baron — wir wollen ihn
> Siegfried nennen — keine Notiz zu nehmen. Eilte alles an den
> Spieltisch, wurde ihm jedes Mittel, jede Aussicht sich geistreich zu
> unterhalten, wie er es liebte, abgeschnitten, so zog er es vor, ent-

weder auf einsamen Spaziergängen sich dem Spiel seiner Phantasie zu überlassen oder auf dem Zimmer dieses, jenes Buch zur Hand zu nehmen, ja wohl sich selbst im Dichten-Schriftstellen zu versuchen.

(Bessomykin, 1836) No odin molodoj nemeckij baron — nazovem ego Zigfridom — byl soveršenno čužd ètogo neopredolimogo očarovanija, ètogo uslovija, trebuemogo xorošim tonom. Kogda vse ustremljalis' k igročnym stolam, i on lišen byl vsjakogo sposoba, po obyknoveniju svoemu, pol'zovat'sja zanimatel'noju dlja uma besedoju, — on ili predavalsja, vo vremja uedinennyx progulok, igre svoej fantazii, ili, sidja v svoej komnate, bral v ruki tu ili druguju knigu, ili sam prinimalsja za pero dlja opytov to v stixax, to v proze.

(Poljakov, 1823) O sem nepreoborimom očarovanii igry v bank, o six zakonax bol'šogo sveta, odin molodoj nemeckij baron — nazovem ego Zigfridom — ne imel, po vidimomu, nikakogo ponjatija. Kogda vse spešilo k zelenym stolam, kogda ne bylo nikakoj vozmožnosti baronu zanimat'sja naukami, ljubimym predmetom ego upražnenij, on udaljalsja, i v uedinennyx progulkax iskal i naxodil udovol'stvie.

*(Sankt-Petersburgskij vestnik,* 1831*)* Molodoj nemeckij baron, kotorogo my budem nazyvat' Zigfridom, odin tol'ko byl isklučeniem iz sego obščego pravila. Togda, kak drugie predavalis' igre, on uxodil s knigoju v svoju komnatu ili v progulkax naslaždalsja prirodoju, stol' prelestnoju v ètoj očarovatel'noj strane.

It is characteristic that Poljakov in 1823 mistranslated Vertua's dying word as "proigral"; the 1831 version had the correct "vyigral"; and

Bessomykin (1836) was more sophisticated and retained the French word "gagne," just as it is in the German text.

In 1823 the *Biblioteka dlja čtenija* again published a Hoffmann translation — the second of the year. It was "Dož i dogaressa" ("Doge und Dogaresse"), a story from the second volume of the *Serapionsbrüder* (T3). The title page indicated the author ("Povest' soč. Gofmana"), and the translator signed himself at the end as "K — n." As for the quality of the translation, it may be termed adequate. Notes were added to explain Italian verses and phrases. As usual, however, the 1836 version by Bessomykin is still better; it reflects more of Hoffmann's syntax without much apparent offense to Russian usage.

2

As has been noted, 1824 saw no new translations of Hoffmann at all. But the following three years yielded one story each. In 1825 Moscow took over Hoffmann exclusively, none of his stories appearing again in Petersburg print until the year of sudden general interest in him — 1830. In 1825 the *Moskovskij telegraf* (The Moscow Telegraph), which was to include on its pages more translations of Hoffmann than any other magazine, published in its supplements the story "Beloe prividenie" ("Die Marquise de la Pivardiere"; T4). It was, if possible, a still worse distortion of a Hoffmann original than the unfortunate "O sčastii igrokov" which we examined above. The very choice of the title "Beloe prividenie" (The White Apparition) for Hoffmann's neutral "Marquise de la Pivardiere" already reflects the translator's tendency to alter the story. Although his crimes mostly involve additions to Hoffmann's text, he began with a curious omission. In the very first paragraph he left out the clause "da er, ihrer überdrüssig, um eine andere buhlte," thus omitting the motive for the murder in question! The translator supplied a surname for the victim and had her selling flowers instead of *Gartenfrüchte*. (Unquestionably flowers are more romantic.) The Russian version is very free throughout, even in those places where it adheres to the sense of the original.

The opening paragraphs of Hoffmann's story "Die Marquise de la Pivardiere" form a frame set in the salon of the Duchesse d'Aiguillon. Its stylistic success depends on a great economy of words. For example, much information is conveyed in the very first, brief sentence. Count St. Hermine's revelation of the crime is striking precisely because of its abruptness and lack of embellishment, and it comes like a thunderclap after the duchess' haughty pronouncement. In the Russian version this effect is ruined by superfluous interpolated words. The count, who has become "graf St. Žermen," has quite inappropriate expressions put in his mouth. His factual defense of Barré's education is given the crude preface: "Izvinite, gercoginja, čto ja ne soglašus' s vašimi predpoloženijami. Oni krasnorečivy, no edva spravedlivy." And instead of St. Hermine's challenge, "Was könnt Ihr gegen seine Bildung, gegen seine Religiosität einwenden?" the translator credits him with lengthy observation:

> "No bešenye strasti prevozmogli v nem vse; i obrazovanie i
> pravila ne pomogut nam, esli my predavalisja ix stremleniju. V
> ètom slučae, pozvol'te mne dumat', čto prestuplenija samye
> užasnye mogut byt' soveršeny ljud'mi samymi obrazovannymi."

Hoffmann's count lets the facts speak for themselves. A bit further on, his words "man wird es mir, meinem gerechten Schmerz verzeihen, daß ich das Gespräch über Barrés Untat nicht zu ertragen vermag" are expanded by another addition:

> "Ja ne mog ravnodušno slušat' razgovorov o prestuplenii Barre,

kogda dumal o zlodejstve ešče užasnejšem ... I kto že prestupnik?
Osoba obrazovannaja, ljubeznaja – bolee: ženščina!"

Thus the translation anticipates the count's revelation several lines in
advance and ruins the climax of the scene. The premature declaration
that the murderer is a woman also makes the otherwise ironic commiser-
ation of the listeners for the victim's widow (retained by the translator
in the following lines) less apropos. When the count's final words are
quoted, they are padded with the translator's own interpretation:

> "Und," sprach der Graf mit dem ins Innere dringenden Ton der
> tiefsten Erbitterung, "und diese geistreiche tugendhafte Frau, die
> Zierde der ersten Zirkel in Paris, diese war es, die ihren Gemahl
> erschlug mit Hülfe ihres Beichtvaters, des verruchten Charost!"

> Vdrug s novym, sil'nejšim ogorčeniem načal govorit' graf St. Žer-
> men. Ulybka negodovanija pojavilsja na ustax ego. "Da," skazal
> on, "požalejte o dobrodetel'noj, prekrasnoj markize Pivardier. No
> znaete li vy, Mm. Gg., čto èta dobrodetel'naja ženščina – byla
> ubijceju svoego muža! I kto pomogal ej? – Nečestivyj licemer,
> takže obrazec dobrodeteli – duxovnik ee, Šaro. . . ."

The Russian reader was treated to many more such "improvements"
on the translator's part, some minor, some of considerable importance.
The courtroom scene and the ending of the story are particularly
changed. When the marquise shouts her confession of guilt to the court,
Charost is made to say to her in the Russian text, "Vy sami ne znaete,
čto govorite: vy gubite sebja – ja znaju vašu nevinnost'." An entire
dialogue of some length between the marquise and the judge is likewise
inserted.

The main tendency of these crude interpolations is to introduce more
moralizing than Hoffmann intended. At the end of the text, the now

free marquise is made to read a veritable sermon to the Countess d'Aiguillon, none of which is present in the original story:

> "Net!" — skazala markiza — "vy, svetskie ljudi, ne stòite žertv.
> Ja ne vozvraščus' v vaš legkomyslennyj, xolodnyj svet i vtajne ot
> vsex xoču oplakivat' prestuplenie, kotoroe i teper' tjagotit moju
> dušu. Ja terpela besslavie, videla užasy temnicy — no èto malo."

At the very end we are informed that the marquis was tried and condem-
ned — and then entered military service. Clearly there is no basis in the
case for trying the marquis, and this further addition to the dénouement
appears to result from the translator's overeagerness to see that justice
is done all around.

We cannot but conclude that the *Moskovskij telegraf*'s "Beloe prividenie" of 1825 did grave injustice to Hoffmann. However, "Die Marquise de la Pivardiere" is an untypical story, and if a criterion of our
evaluation be how well a translation may have acquainted Russian
readers with the characteristic style of Hoffmann, perhaps the misguided
version of "Spielerglück," distorting or omitting as it did more typical
features, was after all the greater misfortune.

The year 1825 was notable in the history of Hoffmann in Russia
also for the publication of Pogorel'skij's story "Lafertovskaja makovnica" in *Novosti literatury* (Literary News), literary supplement to the
conservative newspaper *Russkij invalid* (The Russian Veteran). It is the
earliest published Russian work which bears clear traces of Hoffmann's
influence. (Pogorel'skij's total literary production is discussed in relationship to Hoffmann in our Chapter II.)

3

Again in 1826 the *Moskovskij telegraf* printed the only new translation of Hoffmann (T5). This time it was "Botanik (Povest', soč.
Gofmana)" (The Botanist, a story by Hoffmann), a translation of
"Datura fastuosa (Der schöne Stechapfel)," and the quality of the
text partly makes up for the fate of "Die Marquise de la Pivardiere."
The translation may be rated adequate; that is, it represents the original
successfully while having numerous minor inaccuracies. The translator
seems to have genuinely misunderstood the German in an instance such
as:

> Ein von dem tiefsten Unmut, von den widersprechendsten Gefüh-
> len bestürmtes Gemüt verschließt gern sich in sich selbst, und so
> geschah es denn auch, daß Eugenius . . .

> Samoe bol'šoe neudovol'stvie, samye protivorečašče dviženija
> trevožimogo rassudka slivajutsja v odno čuvstvo: tak slučilos' i s
> Evgeniem.

In vol. 18 for 1827 (otd. 2, p. 200) the publisher of the *Moskovskij
telegraf*, Nikolaj Polevoj, reviewed the contents of the *Telegraf* for the
first three years of its existence and stated that for translated stories
and excerpts the most important authors had been (in the order he
listed them) Walter Scott, Irving Washington (sic)[13] Zschokke, Hoffmann, Tieck, Goethe, Jacobs, Picard, Clauren, Franklin, Ancillon, Alibert and Ségur.

Hoffmann's name is mentioned a second time in the same volume
of the *Telegraf* in the article "Perevody v proze V. Žukovskogo" (V.
Žukovskij's Prose Translations) (otd. 1, pp. 73–74). The writer gives a
revealing characterization of the history of translations in Russia which
is worth quoting at length .

If we were to undertake to divide into periods the history of translated stories and translated miscellany in our literature, the first period might be assigned to 1760, when our magazines began to be filled with translations (by way of French) from Addison's *Spectator* and imitations of that writer, who in his day was somewhat better known than our contemporary Jouy. Then the Germans came into fashion — Meissner, Wieland, August Lafontaine and others. Karamzin introduced in our country Marmontel, Florian, Genlis. The Germans occupied us very little (with the exception of Kotzebue) in his time, and in 1808 people were translating predominantly Genlis and her fellow Frenchmen. Žukovskij was carried away by the general example. It was around ten years ago that they abandoned the French entirely; the Germans appeared again, only new ones — Zschokke, Hoffmann, Jacobs. Now, it seems, our great inclination is to the English; W. Scott and Irving Washington *[sic]* are our principal figures *(dejstvovateli)*. However, in our times there are essentially no longer any exceptions; the English, French and Germans all have received rights of citizenship.

Farther on, the article offers a principle for translations:

> . . . In general people think that *faithfulness* is the first quality of a translator. We agree, if *faithfulness* is to consist in conveying, so to speak, the *soul* of the original, the qualities of its style, its merits. But one must not think that faithfulness consists in slavish copying. In that case, the most faithful translation will be the least faithful. It is necessary to understand the spirit and properties of both languages, the one into which, and the one from which, you are translating.

In the same year, 1827, it was the *Moskovskij vestnik* (Herald of Moscow) of Pogodin which produced the sole new Hoffmann story. This

organ of the Ljubomudry turned to the German writer in its first year
of publication for "Der Magnetiseur," which appeared in vol. 5 as "Čto
pena v vine, to sny v golove" (T6). The name was suggested by the title
of Hoffmann's first chapter – "Träume sind Schäume." At the end of
the text the author was identified as Hoffmann, and the translator signed
himself with the single letter "V." Smirenskij has proved that the translation was begun by the young poet D. V. Venevitinov, leader of the
Ljubomudry who died tragically this same year. In a letter of January 28,
1827, to an unknown person, Venevitinov wrote, "Voz'mite u Rožalina
moj perevod iz Gofmana i dokončite ego. Povest' slavnaja, lučše vsex u
nas rus/skix/ napečatannyx." The manuscript in Venevitinov's hand-
writing was found and published by Smirenskij in 1934. It is entitled
"Čto pena v stakane – to sny v golove" and breaks off part way through
the story, in the middle of the tale of the Danish major. Thus the greater
part of the translation is someone else's work. Smirenskij theorized that
it may have been completed by Venevitinov's brother Aleksej, who is
known to have done other translations from German.[14] The printed
version of the first part differed in some details from Dmitrij Venevitinov's manuscript.

The quality of "Čto pena v vine, to sny v golove" might be called
good if it were not for some very serious omissions. The principal ones
occur in Alban's letter ("Fragment von Albans Brief an Theobald"),
where the opening lines are altered to the following:

> . . . Tak nazyvaemye *dobrye dela* sut', po *bol'šej časti,* pustoj ob-
> man. Inogda my staraemsja obol'stit' imi drugix; ešče čašče
> staraemsja oslepit' sami sebja ětimi lučami mnimogo veličija. Ja
> preziraju nravoučenija našix babušek: oni tol'ko stesnjajut svobod-
> nye poryvy potoka žizni. Byt' vlastelinom vnešnego, vozvysit' sily
> fizičeskie i umstvennye – vot prjamaja cel' čeloveka. I neuželi v
> tvoej sobstvennoj grudi ne probuždalis' takie čuvstva, kotorye ne

soglasujutsja s tem, čto po odnoj privyčke ty priznaeš' dobrym, nazyvaeš' mudrym? . . .

Hoffmann's phrases are telescoped into simple, direct sentences which miss some of the subtleties. Then the last three dots above, which are actually in the Russian text, account for an omission of about two and one-half pages. And the translator, evidently not content with this cut, felt the need to add even so an apology for Alban: "No ja sliškom mnogo rasprostranjajus' ob ètom (But I am expatiating too much on that)."

The lengthy passage which is thus left out entirely is nothing short of Alban's credo — a rather significant piece of information. "Alle Existenz ist Kampf und geht aus dem Kampfe hervor," says Alban. "In einem fortsteigenden Klimax wird dem Mächtigern der Sieg zuteil, und mit dem unterjochten Vasallen vermehrt er seine Kraft." In the spiritual side of this struggle, he continues, the ultimate means is available — animal magnetism, which can make one "König der Geister."

> . . . Es ist die unbedingte Herrschaft über das geistige Prinzip des Lebens, die wir, immer vertrauter werdend mit der gewaltigen Kraft jenes Talismans, erzwingen. Sich unter seinem Zauber schmiegend muß das unterjochte fremde Geistige nur in *uns* existieren, und mit seiner Kraft nur *uns* nähren und stärken! — Der Fokus, in dem sich alles Geistige sammelt, ist Gott! . . . Das Streben nach jener Herrschaft ist das Streben nach dem Göttlichen, und das Gefühl der Macht steigert in dem Verhältnis seiner Stärke den Grad der Seligkeit.

Admittedly this treatise is difficult and not strictly necessary to the action. It might also not have held the interest of the Russian reader. One wonders, however, whether Dmitrij Venevitinov, had he reached this passage himself, would have omitted it. We should expect him to be interested precisely in the ideas of the German work.

A few more lines of Alban's letter are also left out, and there are short cuts of little consequence in the last chapter ("Aus Bickerts Tagebuch"). The omissions by Venevitinov's follower are all the more unfortunate because the translation otherwise ranks among the most accurate.

The *Moskovskij vestnik*, having printed this version of "Der Magnetiseur" in vol. 5 for 1827, announced the same year in vol. 6 (p. 379) that it would publish in the coming twelve months something more by Hoffmann, along with works of Washington Irving, Zschokke, Jacobs and others. Despite this stated intention, however, the *Moskovskij vestnik* did not offer any Hoffmann in 1828.

In fact, no Hoffmann work appeared at all in Russian in 1828, but the year is memorable for the publication of Pogorel'skij's collection of tales *Dvòjnik, ili Moi večera v Malorossii,* which contains undoubted borrowings from the German author. What is particularly significant is that by this date some Russian journalists were aware of Hoffmann, for at least two reviews of *Dvojnik* refer to him as the source of some of Pogorel'skij's ideas. They must have known the German writer in the original, because the stories in question had not yet appeared in either Russian or French. Equally indicative is the fact that other reviewers showed *no* knowledge of Hoffmann at this point. (See Chapter II for details.)

One of the reviewers of *Dvojnik* − that of the *Moskovskij telegraf* (vol. 20, pp. 358−62) − discoursed at length on contemporary German fiction. His remarks are interesting insofar as they show the attitude of part of the Russian press in 1828:

> It seems to us that the author /Pogorel'skij/ would have done much better to have avoided the manner of composing stories *(povesti)* which has appeared in Germany in recent times. The Germans have written so many of them, in all kinds of genres,

that all genres, it seems, have begun to bore them, and now the German public derives satisfaction only from the strangest play of fantasy or the most intricate interweaving of events. Read Hoffmann, Clauren, (Gustav) Schilling, Schopenhauer; compare the novels of Van der Velde with those of W. Scott, and you will learn the essence of the new German novels and stories. An agile mind can easily find thousands of strange relationships in society and in the human soul. Mix these relationships up together with a mystical tendency, with fatalism, or with various passions, proprieties, beliefs — and before you opens the inexhaustible source of German stories and novels. Because of this, it seems, many German novelists have acquired the habit of writing in this manner, for they (for example Clauren and Schilling) fill up tens of volumes with stories that are in general all alike but in their particulars most varied. . . . One of the consequences of the German way of writing stories is the feeling of sadness which the German stories sometimes bring on, showing as they do man in such a strange aspect that his weakness or vacillations of mind or instability of haughty self-knowledge are revealed too openly. There are sides of man's soul and of society which one should not touch.

Of course these words are not appropriately applied to the basically optimistic and sunny E. T. A. Hoffmann, and they reveal a stereotyped impression of German fiction.

4

Despite its criticism of Hoffmann, in 1829 it was again the *Moskovskij telegraf* — along with the *Syn otečestva* — which printed Hoffmann. The *Telegraf* offered its readers, in vol. 25 for January-February, 1829, "Očarovannyj bumažnik (Povest', soč. Gofmana)" (The Charmed Pocket-book, a story by Hoffmann), a translation of the work "Die Irrungen" (T7). The Russian title must be viewed as slightly naive and inappropriate in the face of Hoffmann's calculated ambiguities. No translation of one of his works thus far had entirely escaped alteration, and "Die Irrungen" was no exception. It is full of minor omissions and abridgments which do not seem to alter the sense appreciably but detract from the overall quality. The cuts are generally not as interesting as others we have examined. The subtitle "Fragment aus dem Leben eines Fantasten" is omitted; the first paragraph of the chapter "Der Zauber der Musik," which is not necessary for the cohesion of plot elements, is left untranslated.

In the same vol. 25 (pp. 396—97) the *Moskovskij telegraf* renewed its disparagement of the German fantastic writers in a review of the translation "Paž gercoga Fridlandskogo; Istoričeskaja povest' " and "Goroskop":

> Zschokke, Clauren, Hoffmann; these are the three progenitors of the recent German stories *(povesti)*. Despite all our respect for these writers, we recognize that they must take a place far behind Germany's first-rate fiction writers. Humor, endearing simplicity, the ability to recount trivialities, picturesqueness of some passages — these are Zschokke's qualities; the ability suddenly to confuse and suddenly to startle one with the unexpected — those are the qualities of Clauren. Hoffmann — strange, uneven, moody *(strannyj, nerovnyj, mračnyj)* — also has incontestable qualities.

The reviewer does not spell out what these qualities may be. He continues that the authors mentioned have managed to capture the German public and that minor writers are rushing to imitate them, abetted by the multiplying numbers of German almanacs. Of the two stories under review he says:

> Both stories translated by Mr. Tilo are proof of our words and of

the fact that the Germans have currently gone astray in their stories. However, German stories are so often translated in Russian magazines that readers can convince themselves of the justice of our opinion. It would seem that in multiplication of stories in Russian we shall not remain long behind the Germans. No Clauren, Hoffmann or Zschokke is yet to be seen among Russian writers, but we can already count a few Tromlitzes, Miltitzes and Spindlers.

So, in 1829 Hoffmann is rated, at least by the *Moskovskij telegraf,* together with Clauren and Zschokke as talented and original but distinctly inferior to the German classics.

The Hoffmann contribution for 1829 by *Syn otečestva* (now merged with *Severnyj arxiv* [ The Northern Archive ] ) was "Sin'or Formika; Povest', soč. Gofmana" ("Signor Formica"; T8). It is gratifyingly faithful to the original throughout, with only the most minor inaccuracies. It is interesting that the translator altered a somewhat irreverent reference to St. John the Baptist. Compare: "Salvators Platon, ja selbst sein heiliger Johannes, der in der Wüste die Geburt des Heilands verkündet, sähe ein klein wenig aus wie ein Straßenräuber"; and: "Samyj Platon Sal'vatora i drugie počtennye muži sedoj drevnosti, im izobražennye, nemnožko smaxivajut na razbojnikov." It may be added that even Bessomykin in his 1836 translation, ordinarily accurate in all details, saw fit to tone down this same sentence: " . . . Svjatoj Ioann, propovedujuščij v pustyne Roždestvo Spasitelja, poxoži neskol'ko na ljudej nedobryx. . . ."

In 1829 Nikolaj Polevoj, publisher of the *Moskovskij telegraf,* began to issue the multivolumed collection *Povesti i literaturnye otryvki* (Stories and Literary Excerpts), consisting, at least in part, of stories reprinted from his magazine. In the preface to vol. 1 (pp. iii–iv) Polevoj refers to the program of the edition:

Translations of the best stories from the works of contemporary

writers — Irving Washington [sic], Hoffmann, Clauren, Zschokke,
Pougens, Jacobs, Alibert, Henrietta Lee [Harriet Lee?], Steffens
— will be the contents.

Hoffmann is also mentioned further on in the preface:

> I think that the works of Washington [Irving], Zschokke, Hoff-
> mann and the others I have named will never grow old for the
> readers. However, it is not for me, but for the public, to decide
> the fate of my selection. To please the public is my wish, and its
> favor will be my reward.

One Hoffmann work, "Die Marquise de la Pivardiere" in the translation
"Beloe providenie" from the *Moskovskij telegraf* of 1825 (above, T4),
was indeed reprinted in the collection *Povesti i literaturnye otryvki,* vol.
5 (1830; see Chapter III).


5


Without any doubt the Russian publishing event of 1829 which had
the greatest importance for the fate of E. T. A. Hoffmann in that
country was the appearance of a translated article by Sir Walter Scott
in the *Syn otečestva i Severnyj arxiv* for October (C1). It traces to a
piece written by Scott as a review of *Serapionsbrüder, Nachtstücke* and
*Leben und Nachlaß* (the latter edited by Hitzig) in 1827. [15] This article found its way into a French edition of Scott in 1829, [16] whence
it was translated into Russian. The Russian version bears the title "O
čudesnom v romane."

Scott opens with a long discourse on the supernatural in fiction, and
he lists several genres in which it had been used — Eastern tales, the
French *contes des fées,* satires (e.g., those of Count Hamilton), anti-

quarian folktales (the Brothers Grimm), romances (La-Motte-Fouqué).
But now, he says, the Germans have invented another genre (we quote
from the original English):

> This may be called the FANTASTIC mode of writing, – in which
> the most wild and unbounded license is given to an irregular fancy,
> and all species of combination, however ludicrous, or however
> shocking, are attempted and executed without scruple.

The supernatural in older genres had its own limits and rules, or it served a higher function (as in *Gulliver's Travels*), but, asserts Scott, in the
new German fantastic school none of this holds. And "the author who
led the way in this department of literature was Ernest Theodore William Hoffmann. . . . " The latter sentence reached Russian readers in
slightly amended form: "The author who stands above all others in this
branch of romantic literature is Ernst Theodor Wilhelm Hoffmann."
The Russian publication of the article was in two serial parts, and the
first broke off with the above sentence. The remaining half deals specifically with Hoffmann, and it became thus the first article on him printed in Russia.

Scott was, of course, of an entirely different temperament and artistic outlook than Hoffmann, and it is not surprising to find that his
review is not very favorable. He concedes the German's talents but considers them misused. His information on Hoffmann's biography seems to
come wholly from the books by Hitzig, and he presents the German's
life and character in a bad light:

> He appears to have been a man of rare talent, – a poet, and ar-
> tist, and a musician, but unhappily of a hypochondriac and
> whimsical disposition, which carried him to extremes in all his
> undertakings; so his music became capricious, – his drawings cari-
> catures, – and his tales, as he himself termed them, fantastic
> extravagances.

The Russian version of this passage is still more condemning, in that it
calls his music "only a coupling of passionate sounds" and his tales a
"muddle" (bestolkovščina).

Sir Walter does not recount the facts of Hoffmann's biography. Instead he attempts an analysis of the German's internal development. He
depicts his sufferings, claims he was at times close to madness and that
he overindulged in wine and tobacco. Following Hitzig's example, he
quotes a long passage from "Spielerglück," without identifying the
work, and treats it as an autobiographical account of Hoffmann's near-
addiction to gambling. Further on, he says:

> We do not mean to say that the imagination of Hoffmann was
> either wicked or corrupt, but only that it was ill-regulated, and
> had an undue tendency to the horrible and the distressing.

(The Russian translation has "samye ljutejšie užasy" for "the horrible
and the distressing.") Fear dominated hope in Hoffmann, says Scott;
he really believed in his own monstrous creations and was scared by
them.

> Hoffmann spent his life, which could not be a happy one, in
> weaving webs of this wild and imaginative character, for which
> after all he obtained much less credit with the public, than his
> talents must have gained if exercised under the restraint of a
> better taste or a more solid judgment.

And what are the better ends to which Hoffmann might have applied
his capabilities? Scott gives us a suggestion of them in deploring the
fact that the German did not write a lengthy and sober account of the
siege of Dresden which he witnessed firsthand in 1813. Says Scott, we
should willingly do without some of Hoffmann's diablerie in order to
have a solid history of that battle!

To exemplify his claims about the German writer, Sir Walter now discusses in considerable detail two stories, "Das Majorat" and "Der Sandmann," retelling the plots and quoting from both at length. The first is to demonstrate Hoffmann's true talent, despite some "wildness of fancy" (in the Russian, "fantastičeskij bred"); the best passages of "Das Majorat" show what Hoffmann *could* do. Scott has no respect for "Der Sandmann," however, and he in fact makes use of it for a bitter attack on the author:

> But we should be mad ourselves were we to trace these ravings any further. . . . . It is impossible to subject tales of this nature to criticism. They are not the visions of a poetical mind, they have scarcely even the seeming authenticity which the hallucinations of lunacy convey to the patient; they are the feverish dreams of a light-headed patient, to which, though they may sometimes excite by their peculiarity, or surprise by their oddity, we never feel disposed to yield more than momentary attention. In fact, the inspirations of Hoffmann so often resemble the ideas produced by the immoderate use of opium, that we cannot help considering his case as one requiring the assistance of medicine rather than of criticism. . . .

This bit of invective was transmitted essentially unaltered into the Russian version.

Drawing once more on Hitzig, Sir Walter recounts Hoffmann's final sickness and suffering, and he concludes the article as follows:

> Hoffmann died at Berlin, upon the 25th June, 1822, leaving the reputation of a remarkable man, whose temperament and health alone prevented his arriving at a great height of reputation, and whose works as they now exist ought to be considered less as models for imitation than as affording a warning how the most fertile fancy may be exhausted by the lavish prodigality of its possessor.

The Russian translation amended the final words to: "a warning of the danger an author undergoes if he surrenders to the frenzy of a foolish imagination."

There can be no doubt that Sir Walter Scott was less than fair to Hoffmann. His claims of the German writer's near madness, fears and addiction to drink – all derived from Hitzig's anecdotes – are exaggerated. His assertion that Hoffmann was a pessimist and described mostly the dark side of things is mystifying to anyone who has read the author's total literary production, for his works on the contrary suggest a hopeful disposition, and their sunniness often conceals any sufferings their author may have been undergoing. In this regard, one should think of the bright stories composed during his last, painful illness. Finally, the implication that the fantastic or supernatural in Hoffmann has no rules or higher purpose is patently unjustified.

And yet this is the light in which Hoffmann was presented in the article, and the image survived two translations to reach the Russian reading public. The minor alterations which we have pointed out only tended to further exaggerate the points. We shall see that for a number of years this particular characterization of Hoffmann and his work dominated most of the references to him in the Russian press.

Sir Walter Scott's article had a great impact in both France and Russia. Despite the fact it is overall a negative evaluation, it made Hoffmann appear to be a highly romantic character and was a good advertisement for him. A long letter of introduction from the illustrious and greatly respected Sir Walter could not fail to attract attention. It is probably not by chance that the large number of translations of 1830 and 1831 included two versions each of "Das Majorat" and "Der Sandmann" – precisely the stories discussed in detail by Scott.

6

On looking back at the decade of the 1820's, we must conclude that the Russian reading public of that time did not know E. T. A. Hoffmann in any real sense. Although translations began to appear relatively early, they were few and generally untypical. Hoffmann was not mentioned in the press up to 1829 as a familiar author (with the exception of those reviews of Pogorel'skij's *Dvojnik*).

It is rather ironic that the conservative magazines *Syn otečestva* and *Vestnik Evropy*, which were usually unfriendly to romanticism, were the first to take up Hoffmann in Russia. They were able to do this because they chose uncharacteristic works for translation. Obviously they viewed Hoffmann at this time as just another source for entertaining stories. They printed straightforward novellas with an element of adventure or mystery ("Das Fräulein von Scuderi," "Spielerglück," "Doge and Dogaresse," "Die Marquise de la Pivardiere"). Typical fantastic features are missing from their selection, with the possible exception of "Signor Formica," where the fantasy is very mild.

Nor did the ideological side of German romanticism come through in the translations. We have noted how elements of the romantic outlook were eliminated by a convenient omission from the *Moskovskij vestnik*'s version of "Der Magnetiseur." And it is doubtful whether the obscure symbolism of "Datura fastuosa" reached its Russian readers, unprepared as they were to expect deeper meanings.

"Die Irrungen," printed in Polevoj's *Moskovskij telegraf,* is the one story which does not fit the pattern of choices. However, for all of its typical mystifications, it is generally considered one of Hoffmann's weakest tales and can be easily taken as inconsequential nonsense, and all the more so when divorced from its continuation, "Die Geheimnisse." The *Telegraf* took an ambivalent stand towards Hoffmann in the

1820's, for it printed his stories while at the same time criticizing him and his fellow Germans in reviews.

Missing from the short list of Russian translations of 1822 to 1829 are the characteristic music stories and artist stories, the great *Märchen*, the two serious masterpieces *Die Elixiere des Teufels* and *Lebensansichten des Katers Murr*. No, seven years after his death, in 1829, the Russians had yet to become really acquainted with E. T. A. Hoffmann.

And then practically overnight the great change came about and the cult of Hoffmann was in being. The years 1830 and 1831 saw a remarkable outpouring of translations and articles, and his name started to be mentioned in all the literary periodicals, not infrequently alongside those of the most popular and respected German authors – Goethe, Schiller, Jean Paul. The facts indicate that Hoffmann's sudden fame in Russia was brought about by the discovery of his works in France, where translations began to appear in abundance in 1829. The article by Sir Walter Scott clearly played a significant role in spreading Hoffmann's name both in France and in Russia. We shall examine the results of these developments in Chapter III. First, it is time to discuss the author of *Dvòjnik,* whose relevant writings fall mostly in the decade of the 1820's.

# II

## Pogorel'skij

### 1

Aleksej Alekseevič Perovskij (1787 — 1836), who published under the pseudonym Antonij Pogorel'skij, was a relatively minor figure among Russian prose writers of his time. Illegitimate son of a nobleman, he belonged to what has been called the "gentlemen's party" in literature. His production, although it contains a number of superior pages, is uneven and gives the impression of a dilettante's writing. As a case in point, his perhaps most ambitious work, the novel *Monastyrka* (The Convent Girl), begins as a charming, somewhat sentimentalized version of provincial life in the Ukraine as seen through the eyes of a young heroine educated in St. Petersburg, while the second part of the book, composed several years later, turned into an inferior adventure novel.

Despite the mediocrity of his writings, Pogorel'skij is notable for being one of the earliest of his generation to devote himself to prose, and indeed Mirsky pointed out that Pogorel'skij was the sole member of his literary party who refrained entirely from poetry. [17] He is of interest here because he was the first Russian author who has been shown to have written under the influence of E. T. A. Hoffmann.

Still today the principal treatment of the biography of A. A. Perovskij is the article by Gorlenko published in 1888. [18] He stated — and all scholars since have repeated — that most of Perovskij-Pogorel'skij's personal papers were long since destroyed on his estate. Hence we are limited in our information about his life. It is known that he was very familiar with the German language, and in fact he lived during 1814—15 in Saxony. E. T. A. Hoffmann himself was in residence in Dresden part of this time. Ignatov conjectured that Pogorel'skij may have read some of Hoffmann's stories while still in Germany, and Kirpičnikov thought that he perhaps even met their author; but these are the merest guesses. However, even with other sources lacking, the extensive parallels between certain of Pogorel'skij's stories and Hoffmann's will speak convincingly for his knowledge of the German writer at least by the 1820's. He certainly read him in the original, because Russian and French translations of the relevant texts did not yet exist.

Pogorel'skij's earliest published story was "Lafertovskaja makovnica" (The Poppyseedcake-Seller of the Lafertov Quarter), printed in *Novosti literatury*, supplement to the semi-official Petersburg newspaper *Russkij invalid*, March, 1825 (kn. 11, pp. 97–134). It was incorporated three years later into the collection of tales which appeared as *Dvòjnik, ili Moi večera v Malorossii* (The Double, or My Evenings in the Ukraine). In 1829 his story *Černaja kurica, ili Podzemnye žiteli: Volšebnaja povest' dlja detej* (The Black Hen, or The Underground Dwellers: A Fairy Story for Children) came out, and in 1830 and 1833 the two parts of the novel *Monastyrka* appeared. This is nearly the whole of Perovskij-Pogorel'skij's literary production. [19] "Lafertovskaja makovnica" seems not to have attracted attention in the periodical press. When the book *Dvojnik* came out in 1828, the reviewers were not very complimentary. They charged the author with lack of originality, and some named Hoffmann as a source. This is the earliest instance in which the debt of a Russian writer to Hoffmann was pointed out in the press.

Pogorel'skij and Hoffmann were the subject of a comparative study by Sergej Ignatov in *Russkij filologičeskij vestnik*, 1914. [20] The article's general thesis — that Pogorel'skij understood the greater German only superficially — is certainly correct, and Ignatov contributed an important description of parallels in Hoffmann for the stories "Lafertovskaja makovnica" and "Pagubnye posledstvija neobuzdannogo voobraženija," although in neither case did he exhaust the subject. The article suffers somewhat from lack of information about knowledge of Hoffmann in Russia up to 1840. He seems to have relied on Degen's undependable study of 1901 [21] and Sakheim's likewise uninformed book of 1908. [22] Incomplete data led Ignatov to say, for example, that "Das Fräulein von Scuderi," "Meister Johannes Wacht" and "Meister Martin der Küfner" were not translated into Russian by 1840, whereas we know that the first was the very earliest translation (1822) and the second actually appeared in 1838 (T39). Ignatov confidently continued that these examples of Hoffmann's "sober" style would never have been accepted by the Russian reading public anyway.

In matters of theory, Ignatov adopted the narrowest definition of literary influence, according to which true "influence" *(vlijanie)* exists only when one writer is in complete harmony with the world-view and literary ideals of another. Other resemblances are either "chance similarities" or "borrowing or imitation." It is natural, then, that Ignatov concludes Hoffmann had no true influence on Pogorel'skij. He tends to minimize the number of similarities in the course of his analysis, while rather inconsistently asserting in his summation that "there are quite a few parallels." Despite the reservations we must have, the article is valuable for its study of some specific borrowings, and any investigation of Hoffmann's impact on Pogorel'skij must start where Ignatov left off.

2

In Pogorel'skij's story "Lafertovskaja makovnica" of 1825 (*Sočinenija,* vol. 2, pp. 175–222), a relatively poor girl named Maša is encouraged by her ambitious mother Ivanovna to get into the good graces of her elderly great-aunt, who lives alone and, while selling poppy-seed cakes during the day, carries on a lucrative trade as a fortune-teller at night and is rumored to be very rich. The old woman turns out to be a witch

in league with unholy powers. She promises Maša her treasures after
death and a fine young husband. When the suitor appears, however,
Maša recognizes him as the witch's cat turned into a man and rejects
him in horror along with the promised treasures.

A resemblance of the tale to Hoffmann has been felt for some time,
and Kirpičnikov suggested in 1890 [23] that the inspiration came from
"Die Königsbraut," in which the vegetable king, a carrot, is unsuccessful
suitor to a human girl. Ignatov correctly rejected this comparison as much
too vague and evidently discovered himself the actual parallel with sections of "Der goldne Topf." Ignatov did not, nevertheless, treat the subject exhaustively in his article, nor has Passage in his book.

In "Der goldne Topf" the girl Veronika, a symbol of the philistine
world, is trying to win as her husband the student Anselmus, whom she
sees principally as a means to position and wealth. It is her relationship
with the witch Liese Rauerin which Pogorel'skij adapted for his own
purposes in "Lafertovskaja makovnica." His Russian witch is described
as vending poppy-seed cakes by day near a gate *(zastava)* outside Moscow,
while old Liese appears on the first page of Hoffmann's story selling
apples and *Kuchen* outside the Schwarzes Tor of Dresden. The vending
is only a cover for other activity, continues Pogorel'skij in the next
paragraph, because at night visitors come to the *makovnica's* house. She
draws them in with her bony fingers and, once they are inside, tells
their fortunes either with cards or with coffee grounds, for a coffee-pot
sits prominently in sight. This paragraph is parallel to the section in the
fifth chapter of "Der goldne Topf," where Angelika Oster tells her friend
Veronika about Frau Rauerin's employment by night. Cards and coffee
grounds are mentioned there, only Angelika says that this fortune-teller
does not use such common methods. (Later in the story the Hofrat
Heerbrand does refer to Liese as a "Kartenlegerin und Kaffeegießerin"
by association with other fortune-tellers.) The coffee-pot in the Russian
witch's room was probably suggested by the one into which Liese turn-

ed herself in order to spy in Veronika's house and later in that of Archivarius Lindhorst. Finally, the statement that the *makovnica* usually predicts good fortunes for people parallels the conclusion of Angelika's account, where she says that on the preceding night Liese gave her good news about the fate of her fiancé in the wars.

Reading further in Pogorel'skij's text, we learn that the fortune-teller was considered a sorceress and witch (*koldun'ja* and *ved'ma*) by her neighbors (Hoffmann's Liese is specifically called *Hexe* a number of times), and it is said that a raven was known to light on her roof (Frau Rauerin also kept a raven). However, we begin to see that there are differences between the two old women. The Russian one is more human than Liese — at least in the beginning. Pogorel'skij sticks to a fairly ambiguous presentation of the supernatural. Let it be said here that Hoffmann's fantastical world of Atlantis, as well as the Archivarius Lindhorst and the complex good and evil magical forces of "Der goldne Topf" were essentially alien to Pogorel'skij and are absent from his story. He applied the borrowed motifs to Russian figures and mingled them with native Russian folk beliefs and traditions. Maša's parents, Onufrič and Ivanovna, have no real counterparts in Hoffmann.

Onufrič, the Russian story continues, made the mistake some years ago of alienating his aunt, the *makovnica*, and now, in his absence, Ivanovna takes Maša one day to reconcile the family with the old woman in hopes the latter will contribute a dowry for the girl. There follow two night encounters between the old woman and Maša, just as there were two meetings between old Liese and Veronika. Pogorel'skij drew from both encounters at will, a fact which Ignatov overlooks in his presentation. On the first night, in the presence of Ivanovna, the elderly fortune-teller aunt takes a liking to Maša and promises to "make her happy" if she will return *alone* the next night not earlier than 11:30. (Liese tells Veronika to return after 11 o'clock on the night of the equinox.)

It should be noted that Maša has pleasant childhood memories of her great-aunt, and Liese was once Veronika's nurse; but in both cases years and their unholy trade have so repulsively disfigured the old women that the girls are now frightened by them. As the second appointment draws near, Veronika gains faith in the witch and loses much of her terror, whereas Maša becomes more afraid than ever. This difference occurs because Pogorel'skij, instead of following Hoffmann's continuation, returns chiefly to motifs from Veronika's first encounter in describing Maša's second meeting. Maša is terrified on this occasion, as Veronika was on originally approaching the witch's house. A cuckoo clock strikes 11 as Maša prepares to leave home, and a church clock tolls 12 as she reaches her goal. (On Veronika's second errand a tower clock struck 11.) The Russian heroine is greeted by the old woman's cat, which meows twelve times to indicate midnight. (Veronika was met by a black cat which meowed twice before they were admitted to the fortune-teller's presence.) Both girls (Maša on the second occasion and Veronika on the first) feel like fleeing at the last moment but are drawn into the room by the "bony hand" of the witch. In each story the old woman soon puts out the light and ignites a smaller one which seems to transform the room in some way. Both Maša and Veronika see the witch's black cat, which swings its tail and purrs.

But now comes the crucial motif which seems to be original with Pogorel'skij. Maša with horror sees that her great-aunt's cat has taken on the appearance of a man in a green uniform! (There is a small possibility that this was suggested by Hoffmann's vision of the promised fiancé, Anselmus, in the bottom of the pot after Liese's black magic in the second encounter.)

Pogorel'skij now continues to take ideas from the second night with old Frau Rauerin. Maša looses consciousness as Veronika did on that occasion. The *makovnica* promises her a worthy bridegroom and gives her a magic key (to the old woman's treasures). In parallel fashion, Liese assures

Veronika of getting the student Anselmus as her husband and hands over to her a medallion containing a magic mirror. Both girls awaken the next day and tend to believe that the events of the night must have been a dream. But Veronika finds the medallion around her neck and is thus convinced that her experiences with the witch actually happened, and Maša is likewise persuaded on finding the key still on a cord about her neck.

Here the close parallel of passages comes to an end. Pogorel'skij's story parts almost completely from Hoffmann's, and only a few more scattered motifs were borrowed.

A watchman comes to Onufrič on the next day to report the death of the old aunt during the night. He says that neighbors saw a storm whirling about the old woman's house, witnessed lights arise from the cemetery and disappear under the house and heard strange noises — whistling, laughter and cries (compare the similar noises heard in Liese's room on the first night).

At more than one point after the death of the aunt, Ivanovna and Maša imagine that they see her ghost; but it is doubtful that this derives from the visions of Liese seen by Veronika (before she even met the witch). Rather it is one of the motifs Pogorel'skij freely invented or took from folk beliefs. The visitations of the ghost increase in frequency when the family moves into the aunt's former house. Pogorel'skij introduces specifically Christian motifs, such as banning of the ghost by prayer and crossing oneself.

Finally the intended fiancé arrives on the scene and introduces himself as the titular councilor Aristarx Faleleič Murlykin. Maša recognizes him to be the witch's cat and rejects him with revulsion. (We might mention that Hoffmann's cat in "Der goldne Topf" is never really humanized, though Liese does call him "Junge" and "Söhnlein.") Knowing now the full intentions of the deceased sorceress — i.e., that she marry the cat — Maša decides to give up the old woman's treasures and throws the key into a well, at which point the black cat likewise disappears beneath the water. At the moment when Maša marries her true-love, one Ulijan, the old house collapses in ruins, and the evil powers are once and for all silenced. Now, of course in Hoffmann's story old Liese is turned back into a turnip by the victorious salamander Lindhorst, and her black cat is killed by Lindhorst's parrot, which furthermore pecks out the cat's glowing eyes. There is, nevertheless, one last similarity with the Russian tale. Veronika gives the pieces of the broken mirror from the magic medallion to the Hofrat Heerbrand, her new fiancé, and tells him to throw them into the River Elbe at midnight from the bridge close to the cross. Thus in both stories the talisman given by the witch is buried under water.

Neither heroine gets the husband intended for her by the old woman, but both are happily married nevertheless. In the German story, Veronika marries Heerbrand, thus getting her wish of becoming *Frau Hofrätin* and entering society. She subsides into the mediocrity into which she tried to draw Anselmus. But the hero, destined from the beginning for higher things, gains Lindhorst's daughter Serpentina as his spouse and enters the magical realm of Atlantis. The Russian heroine Maša is happy to be the bride of pleasant Ulijan and, after her sacrifice of the old aunt's treasures, suddenly discovers that the supposedly poor Ulijan has a wealthy father. Everybody is happy all around. Naturally the irony of Hoffmann's dénouement is foreign to Pogorel'skij. While the German makes fun of the philistine world of Veronika and Heerbrand and exalts Anselmus' life in poetry, the Russian writer shows a mildly moralistic purpose in portraying the rejection of the witch's wealth which had been won by unholy means. But in the end he satisfies his readers by rewarding the heroine with riches anyway. Pogorel'skij's concession to worldly asperations in this detail is ironic when seen against the background of "Der goldne Topf."

In summary, for "Lafertovskaja makovnica" Pogorel'skij borrowed a high number of motifs from Hoffmann's "Der goldne Topf" without absorbing any of the inherent poetry or irony of the original. There seems to be no basis for Ignatov's curious statement (see his article, p. 273) that in this story Pogorel'skij came closer than at any other time to Hoffmann and that he made use of the German romantic concept — strong in Hoffmann — of man's intimate association with nature. That notion is made tangible in "Der goldne Topf" through the land of Atlantis and its inhabitants, all of which, as we have seen, are missing from the Russian story. In justice to the Russian, however, we must say that in "Lafertovskaja makovnica" he successfully assimilated the borrowed German motifs into a unified plan and produced a coherent, genuinely Russian story.

Despite the fact that unrealistic elements are kept at a minimum in "Lafertovskaja makovnica," it is indicative of the attitude of some Russians in 1825 that the editor of the *Novosti literatury* saw fit to follow the text of the tale with a "Razvjazka," a note supplying natural explanations for all the supernatural elements of the story. He cites the heroine's imagination as the source of most of them:

> The well-intentioned author of this Russian story apparently had the purpose of showing to what extent a heated imagination, frightened from childhood years by tales of witches, imagines all objects in a false aspect.

It is interesting, moreover, that the editor said "of this Russian story" *(sej Russkoj Povesti),* evidently to emphasize that it was not just another translation from a foreign source.

3

Pogorel'skij's first work published in independent edition, the *Dvòjnik, ili Moi večera v Malorossii,* of 1828, was a more ambitious project (cf. *Sočinenija,* vol. 2, pp. 5–297). It is a frame story into which four tales have been inserted, one of them being that same "Lafertovskaja makovnica," reprinted from the *Novosti literatury.* The frame is in the form of an intimate narrative of evenings spent on a lonely and quiet estate in the Ukraine, where the author in fact lived in relative seclusion for long periods. On one of these long and boring evenings, the speaker says, he was thinking how fine it would be to have just one good friend and companion with whom to while away the time, when suddenly there entered a familiar-looking man who introduced himself as the landowner's self – his double. In the dialogue which follows, this strange visitor discusses the fact that there is no word for such as he in Russian and proposes to coin the term *dvòjnik* for the German *Doppelgänger* (or *Doppeltgänger*). Since the German word is specifically mentioned, we can be confident of what we should have suspected anyway – that Pogorel'skij had this concept of the double from his readings in German literature. After some initial doubt and uneasiness, Antonij (the narrator) accepts the urbane double as a friend and conversation partner and receives his visits on a series of six evenings. They agree to spend part of the time reading to one another their prose compositions, and four nights are devoted largely to that occupation.

Thus we have the frame in which the stories "Izidor i Anjuta" (attributed to Antonij), "Pagubnye posledstvija neobuzdannogo voobraženija" (read by the double), "Lafertovskaja makovnica" (Antonij) and "Putešestvie v diližanse" (the double) are introduced. The question has been raised as to whether the plan of *Dvòjnik* was not suggested by E. T. A. Hoffmann's *Serapionsbrüder.* Ignatov argued, however, that no direct connection can be made, and he showed that in many ways Pogorel'skij's diverges from the pattern of *Die Serapionsbrüder*. In the latter a reunion of young friends, all of a literary bent, grows into a custom of regular meetings with the specific purpose of reading aloud their own compositions. They are bound together closely by the romantic cult of poetry, friendship and wine, and, above all, they dedicate themselves to the so-called "Serapion principle" in their art. The essence of this credo is the idealistic-romantic idea that the greater reality is that of the spirit and not that of the outer world; and it leads to a literary emphasis on the "fantastic," not merely for entertainment, but because the fantasy proceeds from the inner spirit of sensitive men or results from supposed interworkings of universal forces. This philosophy and atmosphere are not present in *Dvòjnik*. Nevertheless, one should not underestimate the external similarity. The idea of reading one's own stories from manuscript distinguishes *Die Serapionsbrüder* and *Dvòjnik* from most frame stories known in previous literary history, though Pogorel'skij may have taken the device directly from the same source that was Hoffmann's: Ludwig Tieck's *Phantasus*.

While the Serapion Brothers carry on an animated and inspired conversation, Antonij and his double gossip rather uninterestingly. Among other things, the tendency to moralize appears again here. Hoffmann's Brothers debate whether the stories read fit the Serapion principle. The talk of Antonij and the double has the effect of undermining the very stories they have told by discounting and even making fun of the unrealistic elements. For example, after "Lafertovskaja makovnica" the double tells several anecdotes about fortune-tellers in an effort to discredit their powers. The pair on more than one occasion swap ghost stories, which they themselves call mere "anecdotes" and disavow belief in. What could be more unlike the spirit of *Die Serapionsbrüder?*

Is not the phenomenon of the double (*dvòjnik*) itself taken from Hoffmann? But Antonij's double is hardly a serious creation. The author strongly hints that he is only a figment of the imagination, because he is shown

first entering while Antonij is lost in day-dreams ("building castles in
the air"). After the first, stereotyped scare he causes, the double settles
down to become simply an excuse for a dialogue. He is really a second
Antonij, not differing from him in any important respect, except perhaps in a greater experience of the world. Both characters come out for
common sense in the face of the supposed supernatural, although Antonij
is a little more inclined to believe the ghost stories than is the double. In
short, Pogorel'skij's *dvòjnik* is nothing more than a literary trick — and
not a very interesting one at that. Doubles in Hoffmann are of a different nature and have a more serious purpose. In *Die Elixiere des Teufels* they represent contrasting and inimical sides of one personality. In
the tale "Doppeltgänger" the doubles are not out-and-out enemies, but
they are rivals for the hand of one girl, and the confusion of their
identities is crucial to the plot. Hoffmann had no monopoly on *Doppeltgänger,* and there is nothing to show that Pogorel'skij took the concept from him rather than from a broader tradition.

On the second of the six evenings Antonij reads his "Izidor i Anjuta"
— a tale which belongs to sentimental literature, but which has a bizarre
twist at the end (cf. *Sočinenija,* vol. 2, pp. 30—55). Nothing in it
suggests Hoffmann, and it need not concern us here. [24] As usual, the
listener (in this case the double) protests the improbability of the plot.

The third evening is devoted to the story "Pagubnye posledstvija
neobuzdannogo voobraženija" (Pernicious Consequences of an Unrestrained Imagination), long recognized as an adaptation of E. T. A.
Hoffmann's "Der Sandmann." (Pogorel'skij's text can be found in
*Sočinenija,* vol. 2, pp. 81—136.) Ignatov dealt with the comparison in
his article, but his analysis is incomplete and somewhat vitiated by inaccuracies.

"Der Sandmann" is one of Hoffmann's best-known works, despite
certain imperfections in the structure. It is a classic literary treatment of

an *idée fixe*. The hero Nathanael was terrified in his childhood by stories of the "sandman," who according to folk belief puts children to sleep by throwing sand in their eyes. Nathanael's nurse made him into a frightening figure by saying that he took children's eyes away. The little boy identified the sandman with the hateful old lawyer Coppelius who visited his father and was eventually responsible for the latter's death. Now a young student, Nathanael imagines that he has seen Coppelius again in the form of a peddler of optical goods, the Italian Coppola, and he becomes possessed with fears and forebodings.

Pogorel'skij made no use of the sandman, and what were for Hoffmann the guiding motifs — the memory of traumatic childhood experiences and the "inimical principle" embodied in Coppelius-Coppola — play virtually no part in the Russian version. Pogorel'skij drew chiefly from the later part of the story, in which is recounted the love of Nathanael for the mechanical doll Olimpia. Unfortunately, it cannot be said here, as it was for "Lafertovskaja makovnica," that the author successfully absorbed the borrowed ideas. The adaptation in this case is clumsy and leaves several rough corners.

The hero of the reworked tale is a young Russian count named Al'cest, but the setting is Germany. The narrator, a certain "F.," fifteen years older than his friend, is sent at the father's request to accompany the young Al'cest to Leipzig for two years of study. (Nathanael is a student in "G.") Pogorel'skij of course knew Leipzig firsthand.

F. has no true parallel in "Der Sandmann," the narrator of which is a friend of Nathanael but not present at the events of the story. A minor character, the student Siegmund, serves a similar function as F. on some occasions, for he also tries to dissuade the hero from his follies and steps in to rescue him when the worst has happened.

In the Russian version, F. believes he has good reason to be concerned with Al'cest's possible follies, because he knows the boy is possessed of a very romantic character and is prone to dangerous imaginings.

Just one feature of his character disturbed me; Al'cest, endowed with a fiery imagination, had an unconquerable passion for all things romantic, and, unfortunately, people never prevented him from satisfying it. He would burst out in tears at the reading of a touching story; I even saw him more than once in love with the heroine of some novel or other.

Goethe's *Werther* and Rousseau's *Nouvelle Héloïse* are cited as works which help to infuse this dangerous romanticism (we might say sentimentalism). Uncontrolled imagination, taking the place of Nathanael's complex psychological condition, is, then, the moving force of the story.

The Russian narrator, F., notices one day a sudden change in Al'cest, who avoids company and locks himself in his room. On being questioned, Al'cest tells a curious story. He was walking once outside Leipzig when he happened upon two strange men arguing in Spanish and fighting over the figure of a beautiful girl. The Russian broke up the struggle, and the taller man, in a red cape, ran off laughing evilly. From that day forward Al'cest was not able to forget the beautiful girl and has sought her throughout Leipzig. We eventually learn that the tall man in the red cape was one Venturino and the other was Professor Androni, supposed father of the girl Adelina. The scene is clearly adapted from one near the end of "Der Sandmann" in which Professor Spalanzani and Coppelius fight over the doll Olimpia, each arguing that he contributed the most important parts to the mechanism. Pogorel'skij chose to place such a scene at the beginning of his story. Unfortunately, the figure of Venturino, as Ignatov points out, is never explained, and the reader of Pogorel'skij does not ever learn the cause of that early fight. It is one of the undigested borrowings of the Russian tale.

Androni is represented as a professor of mathematics, mechanics and astronomy newly arrived from Naples. Hoffmann's Spalanzani is a professor of physics. Ignatov mistakenly says that the physical description of Androni is close to that of Spalanzani (his article, p. 268). In fact, Pogorel'skij blended in his professor something of both Spalanzani and Coppelius, and his description matches quite closely that of the latter, rather than the former. Both Androni and Coppelius have large noses, fiery eyes, yellowish skin, hissing voices, and wear small black wigs and gray coats. In each case the style of clothing is called "old-fashioned." They also have a similar habit of laughing satanically.

Al'cest has suddenly changed because he discovered that the heavenly girl he had seen the pair fight over is living in the building across the street and he can see her in the window at certain hours. F. soon learns that her "father" is the professor Androni, and both Russians resolve to attend his lectures. Nathanael, on the other hand, first caught sight of the doll Olimpia through an open door on his way to a lecture by Spalanzani. In each case the "girl" is motionless, or nearly so. Al'cest is madly in love with his Adelina from the start, but Nathanael is at first not affected. Indeed, he attributes the fact her father keeps Olimpia locked up to the theory that she is mad. Let us not forget that Nathanael has a sweetheart at home – the faithful Klara who tries to keep him on the path of reason, though losing him finally to Olimpia and insanity. There is no parallel for Klara in "Pagubnye posledstvija."

To follow the German story for a moment: because of a fire Nathanael is forced to move and by chance gets a room opposite the house of Spalanzani and can see Olimpia sitting in her window (cf. Al'cest and Adelina). He is still not interested in her until Coppola returns and sells him a spyglass which seems to enliven all objects – especially Olimpia. Through this catalyst Nathanael falls in love with the doll and becomes driven by his desire to have her. From this point Nathanael and Al'cest find themselves in the same situation.

How could anyone be so stupid as to fall in love with a doll, thinking it a girl? In Hoffmann this is explained by the effect of Coppola's (magic) glass, but in Pogorel'skij we must accept the vague explanation of Al'cest's unrestrained imagination. It is interesting that in "Der Sandmann" most people notice the stiffness of the doll, and some of the more alert students are close to the discovery of the secret. In "Pagubnye posledstvija" nearly everyone is completely taken in by the fraud. F. finally becomes conscious of Adelina's passionlessness and stiffness. One day he chances into the room where the figure of Adelina is lying on a divan as though dead or in a faint. Not even this scene nor the sound of the doll being wound up is enough to awaken the rather dense F. to the truth.

In each of the two stories the professor surprises everyone by giving a ball at which he introduces his "daughter." The two evenings are very similar. Olimpia and Adelina speak little. Olimpia dances stiffly with the ecstatic Nathanael; Adelina performs a Spanish fandango for the guests. The heroes leave believing they have won the love of the ideal girl.

And now come the climaxes of the stories. In Hoffmann's version Nathanael goes one day to Spalanzani's with an (engagement? ) ring for Olimpia, only to enter the room where the professor and Coppelius are fighting over the doll. Coppelius destroys Olimpia and runs out. Nathanael goes mad, is dragged off to the madhouse, and later commits suicide.

The Russian ending is more complex. The companion F. has to be gotten out of the way by the author, so he is sent to Dresden on crucial business and returns to the news that Al'cest has *married* Adelina and moved into his father-in-law's house. The clergyman at the wedding was Venturino! Al'cest runs to F. from his marriage chamber to report that at a touch of vinegar Adelina popped open and paper stuffing came out. F. rushes back with him, and the pair find Androni repairing Adelina with a needle and thread. Venturino destroys the doll. Al'cest picks up the eyes from the floor and runs out to drown himself.

Hence the scene of discovery in "Der Sandmann" has been divided into at least three scenes by Pogorel'skij: 1) the flashback at the beginning which told of the fight of the two evil men over the doll; 2) the bedroom scene with Al'cest's discovery of the truth; and 3) the return of the two Russians at the end in time to witness the destruction of the robot. It is possible that the occasion on which F. found Adelina in an apparent faint also was engendered by this same scene in Hoffmann, for it is likewise a surprise encounter with the doll and foreshadows Al'cest's final discovery.

Surely Pogorel'skij's ending is not satisfactory. Even the blindest passion on Al'cest's part cannot explain why he allows himself to be "married" by Venturino, whom he could hardly fail to recognize. It may even be objected that the author has exceeded good taste in including this wedding. But most importantly, Androni's motivation is obscure.

There is a further borrowed but undigested bit of "Der Sandmann." Why does Al'cest pick up the eyes of the doll? In Hoffmann's version eyes are a kind of leitmotif. At the climax Coppelius throws the doll's eyes at Nathanael's breast, saying, "die Augen dir gestohlen . . . da hast du die Augen!" This is the passage which engendered the one in Pogorel'skij. Ignatov is wrong in asserting that this allusion to eyes in "Sandmann" is only to the incident in Nathanael's childhood. Rather the connection is to be made directly with a prophetic poem composed earlier by Nathanael in which he imagines Coppelius to touch Klara's eyes, causing them to spring against his breast. In any case, Pogorel'skij's use of the eyes makes no sense when divorced from Hoffmann's optical symbolism for the distorted perception of reality.

Al'cest's coat and the eyes from the doll are found by a riverbank, and it is assumed that he has committed suicide. Too late a letter arrives from his father, the old count, urging F. to protect his son from Androni, who he says is an old enemy of his from youthful days in

Madrid. We finally learn thus that a desire to destroy the count's family was the motive behind Androni's deception of Al'cest. In the old feud of Al'cest's father and Androni there may be a connection with the relationship of Coppelius to Nathanael's father, but we shall not insist on it.

Antonij discredits the double's story "Pagubnye posledstvija" for its improbability, just as the double had objected to "Izidor i Anjuta." He protests that no one could be foolish enough to fall in love with a mechanical doll and no robot could be made so convincingly real. To this the double replies:

> "Look at society; how many dolls of both sexes you will meet who do, and know how to do, absolutely nothing but merely to stroll the streets, dance at balls, bow and smile. Despite this, people quite often fall in love with them and sometimes even prefer them to incomparably more worthy people."

This observation seems to be what is behind the unctuous pronouncement of the professor of poetry and eloquence in "Der Sandmann" that the case of Spalanzani's fraud was all "an allegory — an extended metaphor." In any case, Pogorel'skij's rationalizing once again tends to vitiate the effect of his own story.

To show that very successful robots can be built, the double gives examples of several which are supposed to have existed. These include a wooden "Turk" that played chess and defeated several famous players in the capitals of Europe, and a clavichord in Paris which produced human speech. Pogorel'skij may have these ideas from any source, but the Turk cannot fail to make us think of Hoffmann's story "Die Automate," from the *Serapionsbrüder*. Hoffmann's Turk, admittedly, prophesies instead of playing chess. In "Die Automate" there are also automatons operated by keyboard instruments, including one which controls figures playing musical instruments, among which is a flute. Notice that Androni had organs with flutes and F. praised the accuracy of the musical sounds, as did Hoffmann's heroes in "Automate." These parallels are too limited to speak with certainty of a borrowing, but it is possible that Pogorel'skij consciously or unconsciously made use of mechanisms described in "Die Automate."

The fourth evening of *Dvòjnik, ili Moi večera v Malorossii,* opening part two, is devoted to a lecture by the double on types of human intelligence *(um)* and weaknesses or vices *(poroki).* The only point of interest to us here is that the author characteristically emphasizes the importance of "common sense" among strengths of intelligence.

On the fifth night Antonij reads his "Lafertovskaja makovnica." In the dialogue which follows, he mentions the rationalization of the tale which the editor of the *Novosti literatury* had printed, calling it with all apparent seriousness the *razvjazka* of his story. Here of course *razvjazka* is meant in the etymological sense of an explanatory unraveling.

The final evening of *Dvòjnik* sees a reading of the fourth tale, "Putešestvie v diližanse" (Journey in a Diligence; *Sočinenija,* vol. 2, pp. 242–94). It is a sentimental account of a boy who was brought up in the jungle by a motherly ape! The inspiration for the strange plot was recognized by contemporaries to have been the translated story "Žoko" ("Jocko") by Pougens, which was published in Russia in 1825. We may take Ignatov's word for it that the comparison is vague and that only the "humanness" of the ape was borrowed from Pougens. There is no evident connection with Hoffmann.

In the concluding dialogue Antonij chides the double for the odd "originality" of his stories, "which not everyone would like." The double again says that uncontrolled imagination can bring a person to the most insane actions, and he blames the tragedy of "Putešestvie v diližanse" on the ingratitude of the hero. A sermon on ingratitude follows. The book ends with the double fading away and disappearing – we assume for the last time.

An interesting sidelight on *Dvòjnik* is the reaction to it in the Russian press, which we mentioned at the beginning of the chapter. Some reviewers seem not to be aware of Hoffmann in 1828, for they do not detect the borrowings. The *Syn otečestva,* in a generally positive review, [25] gives Pogorel'skij credit for inventing the word *dvòjnik* and adds this explanation: " . . . His *dvòjnik* serves only to present in form of conservation what a person thinks or day-dreams about sometimes when left all alone with himself." There is no mention of Hoffmann. Orest Somov, in his review in the almanac *Severnye cvety* (Northern Flowers), [26] objects to coining a word *dvòjnik* when Russian, he says, already has the perfectly good word *sten'.* [27] Pogorel'skij's double, he continues, is much too pleasant a companion to be a creature from a dream world. Somov finds the stories "almost entirely not new" but, except for "Jocko," does not seem to know the sources. He likes the literary style, noting, however, "a certain desire to exaggerate the passions of man and to seek out in him such feelings as can only be the result of a disturbance of mental capacities." He suggests that a more appropriate title for "Pagubnye posledstvija neobuzdannogo voobraženija" would be "Žalkoe sledstvie blizorukosti" (Pitiful Consequence of Nearsightedness)!

The more liberal *Moskovskij vestnik,* in the person of its reviewer "S. Š." (S. P. Ševyrev), [28] found that the fantasy of "Lafertovskaja makovnica" "does not go beyond the allowed bounds of the wondrous, and all the figures, despite the dusk in which they are wrapped, speak more clearly [ than those of the other tales ] to the imagination and even leave a pleasant impression." Ševyrev, however, wrongly attributes the "double" to Ukrainian legends and does not seem to know Hoffmann in detail, although he states on the basis of a general impression that in two of the stories "we saw a clear imitation of Hoffmann."

The *Moskovskij telegraf*'s reviewer appears to know Hoffmann a little better. [29] He not only traces "Putešestvie v diližanse" to "Jocko,"

as did the others, but he says "Pagubnye posledstvija" is "copied
(spisany) from the similar Hoffmann story." This man states there is
nothing Ukrainian about Dvòjnik and sees little originality in the
whole book. He concurs with others that "Lafertovskaja makovnica"
is the best story but asserts that even here "the sorceress is German,
and not Russian." The journalist finds some originality in the inter-
spersed dialogues, while remarking that the discussions of human intelligence and philosophy must be taken as jokes! Pogorel'skij would
have done better to have avoided the German fantastic manner, says he.
(We have already quoted at length from this reviewer's remarks on contemporary German fiction in Chapter I.)


4


Although Dvòjnik was not very well received by the critics, Pogorel'-
skij followed it up the next year (1829) with publication of another
work — the story Černaja kurica, ili Podzemnye žiteli: Volšebnaja povest' dlja detej (Sočinenija, vol. 2, pp. 347–407). It tells of a lonely
little boy named Aleša who lives in a Petersburg boarding-school. One
day he saves from the cook's ax a black hen which turns out to be the
prime minister of the little people (gnomes or elves) who dwell beneath
the earth. Aleša visits their kingdom and is given as a reward for saving
the hen a magical hempseed which will cause him to know all of his les-
sons perfectly without studying. In the end Aleša looses the seed and
also breaks a vow not to reveal the secret of the little people, who because of his indiscretion are now forced to move.

It was noted even by contemporary reviewers that the main ideas of
this tale seem to be taken from Ludwig Tieck's "Die Elfen." [30] More
than one scholar has sought without substantial success to find parallels
in Hoffmann, and especially in "Nußknacker und Mausekönig." The si-

milarities with the latter are very general and superficial. In each tale
the child hero (Aleša, the girl Marie) saves the life of a being from a
magical world (Aleša saves the hen; Marie, the nutcracker) and by way
of reward is given a tour of the underground kingdom. Here the broad
parallel ends, for the situations and characters (also the magical realms)
are quite different. Very doubtful and inconclusive are comparisons
such as between the battle against the mice ("Nußknacker") and the rat
hunt (*Černaja kurica*), Fritz's soldiers and the knights about which Alĕsa
dreams, the two porcelain dolls of the Russian story and the German
dolls Klärchen and Trutchen.

Ignatov dismisses as unproven a connection here with Hoffmann, although he adds, curiously, that there may be some minor motifs borrowed from "Die Irrungen" and "Das Majorat." What he had in mind from
the latter, totally different story is unclear. "Die Irrungen" has a gray
talking parrot similar to one in *Černaja kurica*. In fact, an almost identical parrot appears also in "Der goldne Topf." Pogorel'skij's parrot is
described as gray with a red tail; Hoffmann's are simply "gray." It is also true, for what it is worth, that in "Der goldne Topf" Lindhorst evidently bestows on Anselmus the ability to copy occult manuscripts without the smallest error even in alphabets he does not know (compare
Aleša's capacity to recite without preparation). But here we are reduced
to conjecturing about trivia.

We must conclude that there is not sufficient evidence to show an
extensive influence of Hoffmann on *Černaja kurica*. And yet Mirsky asserted that the tale owes much to "Nußknacker und Mausekönig." [31]
Surely he had in mind the *spirit* of the stories and not specific similarities. And we ought to be guarded in even attributing a common spirit
to them, for Pogorel'skij's tale lacks much of the psychological insight
and all the irony of the German work, and it is permeated with the
author's usual didacticism, so alien to Hoffmann. Mirsky is probably
right only in the sense that *Černaja kurica* could never have been com-

posed without the tradition of superior stories for children of which "Nußknacker und Mausekönig" forms an important part.

Perovskij-Pogorel'skij's next publication was part one of the novel *Monastyrka* (1830), treating, as we remarked earlier, provincial life in the Ukraine. It is perhaps his most original work. In part two (1833) he went over to the manner of the adventure novel, and the result is less than satisfying. Kirpičnikov has demonstrated that this second part was composed under influence of Ludwig Tieck's novella "Das Zauberschloß," which was first printed in 1830. [32] This borrowing, as well as that from Tieck's "Die Elfen," is important here insofar as it shows Pogorel'skij's continued interest in German literature.

In the early 1830's Pogorel'skij printed part of an unfinished novel with the title *Magnetizёr (Otryvok iz novogo romana)* (The Hypnotist, excerpt from a new novel). The fragment consists of the first chapter and part of a second. The opening describes in great detail a room in a well-to-do merchant house in provincial Russia. The young girl Pašen'ka is at home with her parents Anisim Anikeevič and Gavrilovna. The father is reading about animal magnetism in a Petersburg magazine and asks his daughter whether she heard of the phenomenon while in the capital. Pašen'ka shudders at an unpleasant memory but agrees to tell the story behind it. Four years earlier, when she had recently come out of boarding-school, she was frequently a guest in the Petersburg house of Countess N. A maid in the household was subject to attacks of a strange sickness during which she cried, laughed, talked wildly and ended with convulsions. Gavrilovna interrupts to suggest that the maid was possessed by a demon *(besnujuščajasja)*. Doctors and a sorceress failed to cure the maid, continues Pašen'ka. Then there arrived in the city an Italian marquis from Naples, who was received in the best houses. Hearing of the sick maid Katerina, he asked to see her, and merely by sending a penetrating look at her and taking her by the hand while she was in a fit, he managed to cure her completely of further attacks. Pašen'-

ka was in the room at the time, and the marquis then turned his gaze on her.

> "From his black, flaming eyes he threw his gaze on me. . . . It seemed to me as though that gaze materialized and in the form of a fiery arrow penetrated my heart."

Pašen'ka became weak and afraid and could hardly find strength to leave the room. Since that day, she says, she has moments when she experiences "unbearable melancholy" and "inexpressible despondency." Although she fears the marquis, she somehow has the feeling that only *he* can cure her from this condition. Such a mood comes on her now, and she retires to bed.

The incomplete chapter two is a flashback which begins to relate the youth of Anisim Anikeevič. He was a fairly bright boy and began to make his way early in the commercial world. He became interested in books, which tended to inflame his imagination (again this theme!). Here the text breaks off. Naturally it is very difficult to tell from this fragment how Pogorel'skij intended to shape the whole novel, but there are enough clues to indicate the central predicament — and to identify a source in E. T. A. Hoffmann. (Ignatov did not treat this question; Passage does, but very briefly.)

Animal magnetism, or hypnotism, was a fairly frequent subject in Hoffmann's works. The Russian title *Magnetizër* immediately attracts our attention to the Hoffmann story by the same name — "Der Magnetiseur." However, the situation in Pogorel'skij's work seems clearly to be taken from the later story "Der unheimliche Gast," which was in some sense a reworking by Hoffmann of the material in "Der Magnetiseur." A few motifs appear to be taken by Pogorel'skij from the latter story too, as we shall see. The publication in Russian translation of "Der Magnetiseur" in 1827 and "Der unheimliche Gast" twice in 1831 may have called them to his attention, even if he was previously aware of the German originals.

First of all, there can be little doubt that a main element of the novel was to be the attempt of the mysterious Italian nobleman to seduce the heroine Pašen'ka by means of hypnotism. So much may be easily deduced from the fragment itself, even without recourse to Hoffmann — where a similar design is exercised against the heroines of both "Der Magnetiseur" and "Der unheimliche Gast." The very look of the marquis has cast some sort of spell over Pašen'ka which only he (or his death? ) can remove.

The mysterious figure of Hoffmann's "Unheimlicher Gast" is also precisely an Italian count, and we know that he too comes from Naples (Boleslav knew him there). He uses his hypnotic powers to draw to him the girl Angelika despite the fact that she is in love with the hero Moritz. The count arrives on the scene unexpectedly, and one of his characteristics is his fearsome eyes ("der furchtbare Blick der entsetzlichen Augen"). So there is a decided resemblance of Pogorel'skij's marquis to Hoffmann's count.

In "Der unheimliche Gast" there figures a servant-girl named Marguerite who is secretly in love with Moritz. When it becomes apparent that Moritz will marry Angelika, Marguerite tries to commit suicide by taking opium. She is lying in her room unconscious and having something like convulsions ("und nur zuweilen krampfhaft zuckte"). The count spends some time with her alone, and she becomes completely cured. Surely this scene inspired the cure of the servant-girl Katerina in Pogorel'skij's story. Admittedly the cure is not identical nor as immediate, but there are parallels for the cure by hypnotic gaze and touch of hand in Hoffmann's earlier story, "Der Magnetiseur." There, in a story-within-the-story, the baron recounts his youthful acquaintance with a certain Danish major who had "magnetic" powers and was noted for his burning look ("brennender Blick"). The common folk of the town credited him

with the ability to cure sickness by a touch of the hand or a mere look
("Krankheiten durch das Auflegen der Hände, ja durch den bloßen
Blick heilen"), although he angrily drove away people who came to him
for such cures. In this same story Theobald uses a hypnotic gaze to
help win back Auguste, and Alban causes Maria to recover from an attack of nerves by clasping her hand. It is interesting, moreover, that the
major in "Der Magnetiseur" sometimes had an effect on the young
baron like that of Pogorel'skij's Italian marquis on Pasen'ka. After conversations with the major, the boy says, "Ich fühlte mich krank und
matt zum Umsinken."

All of these similarities show with considerable certainty that in *Magnetizër* Pogorel'skij adapted material from "Der unheimliche Gast" and
the probability that he was aware of "Der Magnetiseur" at the same
time. To the borrowings he added important Russian figures and motifs
— the wholly Russian Gavrilovna and Anisim Anikeevič, Russian Christian customs, such as crossing oneself at the mention of evil and bow-
ing to saints' images. The mysterious subject of animal magnetism has
been thrown together with Russian folk beliefs (e.g., the people "possessed by demons"). How Pogorel'skij would have completed the novel
can only be guessed at. It is particularly difficult to imagine how the
youth of Anisim Anikeevič was to be connected up with the main line of
plot, unless he knew the mysterious marquis in his youth, in which case
there might be something of a parallel in "Der Magnetiseur," where the
father (the baron) tells of his acquaintance with that Danish major. The
diverse directions of the beginning and the problem of imposing the hypnotic theme on a Russian situation perhaps explain in part, we may conjecture, why Pogorel'skij did not complete the text.

5

Antonij Pogorel'skij (A. A. Perovskij) never entirely emerged from a literary tradition older than romanticism, for sentimentalism and rationalism are very much present in his works and common sense is an important component of his approach to experience. His sentimentalism
can be seen in *Monastyrka,* "Izidor i Anjuta" and elsewhere; we observed his rational bent particularly in *Dvòjnik.* If we add to this his
tendency to moralize, we have most of the essential features of his literary manner. However, despite adherence to the older tradition, Pogorel'skij was one of the first serious Russian prose authors to show awareness of the German romantics and to draw upon them in his own
work. We have noted his debt to Hoffmann (and to Tieck). He does
not seem to have understood or been attracted to the essence of their
romanticism but rather viewed the movement as a source for novel
literary devices. From Hoffmann he borrowed many specific motifs,
while absorbing none of the German's world-view, his engagingly optimistic spirit or his irony. It was perhaps inevitable that a clash should
occur when a rationalist made use of fantastic ideas, and indeed it is
part of Pogorel'skij's literary failure that he did not always manage to
reconcile the two elements. A weakness of *Dvòjnik* is the author's ambivalence in using on the one hand fantastic stories and on the other
narrators oriented toward common sense. He had his greatest success
when borrowings were of a general nature (e.g., in *Černaja kurica*) or not
too typically fantastic ("Lafertovskaja makovnica"). These he could adapt
fully to a Russian setting. Unconvincing were those cases where he tried
wholeheartedly to embrace fantastic devices ("Pagubnye posledstvija,"
*Magnetizër*). He was, however, by no means the only Russian writer of
this period who found himself torn between German influences and his
own outlook on things, as we shall see in later chapters.

Pogorel'skij was, then, something of a transitional figure, with one foot firmly in the eighteenth century and the other part way in the door of romanticism. As a purveyor of the German movement he probably was not of great importance. As an intermediary for Hoffmann in Russia he was more significant. Attention was drawn to the German by his imitations, which were themselves not completely without effect on later Russian writers. In some future cases we shall have to distinguish the influence of E. T. A. Hoffmann from that of Antonij Pogorel'skij.

# III

# The Emergence of Fantasy, 1830 — 1835

## 1

At the end of the 1820's the emphasis in native Russian literature began to shift from poetry to prose, the first of the modern novels being produced in 1829. Writers looked to foreign models, such as Sir Walter Scott. The Russians' interest in German literature which arose about the mid-1820's reached a high point in the following decade, and at the same time the 1830's were the period of the important intellectual "circles," which occupied themselves in large measure with philosophical ideas from Germany. Thus in 1830 the atmosphere was right for the reception of a new German fictionist.

The sudden interest in Hoffmann in Russia was triggered by his newly acquired stature as a literary figure in France. Although there were scattered mentions of the German in that country in the preceding years (and three translations in 1828), only in 1829 did Hoffmann achieve French fame. The important literary magazine *Revue de Paris* was founded in April, 1829, and immediately took up the banner of E. T. A. Hoffmann. A series of translations in the *Revue de Paris* between May and December served to make him known to the French public; Hoffmann adherents Loève-Veimars and Saint-Marc Girardin both worked for the journal, and an installment of Sir Walter Scott's article was published in the very first issue. In November, 1829, four volumes of Loève-Veimars' translation *Contes fantastiques* appeared, and this year and the next saw a veritable flood of French translations. A publishing battle arose between Renduel (publisher of Loève-Veimars) and Lefebvre (whose translators were Toussenel and Richard), both houses trying to profit by the new vogue of Hoffmann. These processes were temporarily slowed by the July Revolution of 1830, but interest rose again later in the year. It was the novelty of Hoffmann's fantastical side, seen superficially, which seems to have most attracted French readers at first. (The details of Hoffmann's reception in France can be read in Teichmann's fine book.)

The remainder of Scott's article on Hoffmann, the first part of which appeared in *Revue de Paris*, was published by Loève-Veimars as an introduction to the edition of his translation. It clearly had an important influence in France, as it did in Russia. We saw in Chapter I that a Russian version of the article came out at the very end of 1829 in the *Syn otečestva i Severnj arxiv* and was based on a French translation. Thus it appeared in Russia almost simultaneously with the introduction to Loève-Veimars' edition. We noted earlier that, although the Scotsman deprecated much in Hoffmann's style, he did represent him as a talented and interesting writer. The very two stories discussed by Scott ("Das Majorat" and "Der Sandmann") were both translated *twice* into Russian in 1830–31. Scott's article may help explain the choice of an obscure story from *Die Serapionsbrüder*, "Erscheinungen," for translation early in 1830. However, this tale had also been published in the *Revue de Paris* in 1829, and the Russian adapter used the French edition as his source.

A further indication of Scott's influence is the fact that the Russian translations of 1830–31 drew heavily on the collection *Nachtstücke*, which had been singled out for attention by Sir Walter. (He mistakenly called it "Night Pieces after the Manner of Callot," an error which was faithfully reproduced in the Russian version of the article.) In the years 1830 and 1831 six of the eight stories of *Nachtstücke* were rendered into Russian. But here again it is not clear whether Scott influenced the Russian choices directly or by way of French editions.

Altogether ten translations of Hoffmann were printed in Russia in 1830 and as many again in 1831. A distinct decline followed, for only three translations appeared in 1832, one in 1833 and two in 1835. This is the same pattern experienced by France, where editions of the German declined sharply in number in 1833. For the French also the novelty had apparently worn off, and, moreover, the French government had begun to fight romanticism as synonymous with republicanism.

Discussions of Hoffmann in the Russian press continued after the decline in translations and were common through 1833. But it would be the end of the decade before a reawakening in Hoffmann publishing in Russia would take place.


2


The *Syn otečestva i Severnyj arxiv* quickly followed up its publication of the Walter Scott article with that of a second article on Hoffmann in January, 1830 (C2). Again the source was French — the *Revue de Paris'* article "Les dernières années et la mort d'Hoffmann" by Loève-Veimars. The Russian title was "Poslednie dni žizni i smert' Gofmana (Otryvok)." An editor's footnote on the first page read:

> In the 44th issue of the *Son of the Fatherland and Northern Archive* was included the opinion of Walter Scott about Hoffmann and his works. As a supplement to that published notice, we adjoin the following article written in another spirit. From two different opinions one has a better chance of learning the truth.

Just as Walter Scott, Loève-Veimars seems to have most of his information from Hitzig, although it is known that he was personally acquainted in Paris with Hoffmann's friend Dr. Koreff. He asserts that in the final years Hoffmann found drink more and more necessary and his friends could not keep him away from Lutters Keller *(Ljuterov pogreb)*. The German even began to compose stories in defense of drink, says the writer. Like Scott, the Frenchman recounts an anecdote about Hoffmann awak-

ening his wife in the middle of the night because he was afraid of the
creatures of his own imagination.

In the article there is inserted a long passage from Hoffmann — a
translation of "Die Gesellschaft im Keller," the second part of "Die
Abenteuer der Silvester-Nacht," which is cited as proof of Hoffmann's
preoccupation with drink. The name of the work is not given. Since it
is removed from the context of "Die Abenteuer der Silvester-Nacht,"
some details relating to the other chapters were altered. Thus in the
translation there is no indication of the preceding episode, and the following is added to explain how the hero set out for the tavern:
" . . . And a fever drove me out of the house." Some Berlin street names
are omitted. Interestingly enough, in the Russian version General Suwa-
row has become simply "General S.....," undoubtedly out of respect for
the beloved military hero Suvorov. The ending is slightly confused, and
these sentences which identify the personage as Chamisso's hero are not
translated:

> "Peter Schlemihl — Peter Schlemihl!" rief ich freudig, aber *der*
> hatte die Pantoffeln weggeworfen. Ich sah, wie er über den Gen-
> darmesturm hinwegschritt und in der Nacht verschwand.

The translation is by and large complete and accurate, despite the fact
that it is by way of the French.

The article continues with further anecdotes. Loève-Veimars claims
the above story was written at a time when friends had persuaded Hoffmann to stay away from taverns and drink only at home; his friends met
with him once a week to give him company, and the stories he thought up
at these gatherings were later published as *Die Serapionsbrüder* (this is
straight out of Hitzig). The Frenchman's chronology is a bit inaccurate,
for he states that Hoffmann's best stories came from the later period
and included *Nachtstücke* (actually an early collection). Mentioned in
particular are "Der Sandmann" ("Pesočnye časy"), "Das Majorat"

("Maiorat"), "Die Jesuiterkirche in G." ("Iglija Iezuitov") and "Das Sanctus" ("Sanktus"). All of these stories were translated into Russian in 1830, a fact which may speak for an influence of this article, as well as Scott's, on selections.

The French writer now asserts that the final blow to Hoffmann was the death of his beloved cat Murr! (This of course is also derived from Hitzig.) Hoffmann, says the Frenchman, became more and more an invalid but kept dictating stories ("Meister Johannes Wacht," "Meines Vetters Eckfenster," "Die Genesung" and "Der Feind" are mentioned). We hear the story of how the doctors poured molten metal on Hoffmann's spine, just as we read it in Scott's account. Hoffmann is said to have died while dictating. A physical description of the German is given.

Loève-Veimars concludes with the statement that he merely wanted to give an idea of Hoffmann's stories, not write a critical article. In his opinion, Walter Scott was too harsh.

> It was unpleasant for me to see Walter Scott attack imagination, and it seems to me that one cannot analyze Hoffmann's originality according to rules. And then Walter Scott should not have forgotten that, if there are writers whose gift is stimulated by happiness and wealth, there are others whose road is laid out through all human sorrows and whose imagination cruel fate has fed with terrible sufferings and eternal poverty.

This second article is much more friendly to Hoffmann than that of Sir Walter Scott, and yet, if anything, its author viewed him more superficially. Again, the colorful anecdotes about Hoffmann's addiction to drink, etc., hardly give a fair picture of the man, and "Die Gesellschaft im Keller" serves as a very small start indeed in characterizing his work. Although disagreeing with Scott, the Loève-Veimars article in fact tends to support the same image of Hoffmann as that in Sir Walter's piece. Despite its defects, however, the essay was another advertisement for the German. We have noted that several of the mentioned stories were translated in 1830. It cannot escape our attention, on the other hand, that "Meister Johannes Wacht" did not appear until 1838 and "Die Genesung" and "Der Feind" (cited both by Scott and Loève-Veimars) were not translated into Russian at all in the early period.

3

In 1830 the many mentions of Hoffmann in the Russian press began to appear. The magazine *Moskovskij telegraf*, which had done the greatest service to him in the 1820's, refers to Hoffmann in the first part of 1830 in a review of *Nevskij al'manax* (č. 31, p. 358):

> . . . P. B. Bajskij has collected together in an absorbing story many folk tales about hidden treasures. Some of the details are excellent, although the story as a whole suffers from the usual illness of Mr. Bajskij's stories — there is no general truth *(obščnost');* we miss that which engraves itself on the memory of those who read the Irvings, the Hoffmanns and the Zschokkes.

Discussing another tale, the reviewer remarks: " . . . Mr. Karlgov's story 'Trip to the Island of Rozelmi' is well told and is pleasing for its mysterious, *German* ending." The first comment reflects an appreciation for the deeper human appeal of the writers, and the second remark, curiously, appears to be a reference to superficial romantic devices. Be that as it may, in January or February, 1830, the *Moskovskij telegraf* recognized Hoffmann as a superior craftsman.

In its next volume, March, 1830, the *Telegraf* carried a review of "Bogemskie amazonki" ("Der böhmische Mägdekrieg" by Van der Velde), in which the fantasy of Lewis and Ann Radcliffe is attacked while Hoffmann is placed in an elevated category (č. 32, p. 93): "In fact, we cannot understand how one can translate the novels of Van der Velde while in our country the novels and stories of Goethe, Hoffmann, Zschokke and many other writers genuinely worthy of translation have not been translated."

In the second quarter of 1830 the magazine *Slavjanin* (The Slav), taking a cue from Walter Scott, printed a version of Hoffmann's "Erscheinungen" under the title "Vospominanija osady Drezdena, v 1813 godu" (Recollections of the Siege of Dresden in 1813; T10). This was the last year of existence of the *Slavjanin* (subnamed *Voenno-literaturnyj žurnal* [ Journal of Military Literature ] ), a patriotic magazine which started publishing in 1827 in St. Petersburg under A. F. Voejkov and specialized in military articles and reminiscences. The translator of "Erscheinungen" (a certain Laxman) at the very outset leaves no doubt that the article by Walter Scott in *Syn otečestva* led him to this story, because he uses a passage from the article as a long epigraph. It is the last paragraph of the first installment of the article, greatly abbreviated — that in which Scott asserts that the fantasy of the new German stories exists only for its own sake and has no higher purpose or sense. But Laxman made his version of "Erscheinungen," not from the original German, but from the French translation by Loève-Veimars "Souvenir du siège de Dresden (1813)" which had appeared in *Revue de Paris*, 1829 (reprinted in *Contes fantastiques* with the title "Agafia"). The French adaptation was already a considerable reworking of Hoffmann's story; Laxman added the epigraph from Scott and made some changes of his own. Proof of the French intermediary can be found in passages like this: "aber der Delphin spritzte wunderbaren Lebensbalsam aus den silberblauen Nüstern"; "mais Agafia me couvrit de ses mains bienfaisantes; elle m'entoura de ses voiles mouillés, comme la naïade du fleuve"; "no Agaf'ja blagotvoritel'noju rukoju spasla menja, i upodobljajas' rečnoj najade, obvila menja svoim vlažnym pokryvalom." Like the French text, the Russian version opens with a large cut — the beginning of Anselmus' speech from the words "Herr des Himmels" through "wär' nicht noch der Archivarius Lindhorst gewesen." There are numerous abridgments and some interpolations. The closing is changed by leaving out the information that Agafia was saved and married Anselmus. Rather, the French and Russian versions leave the fate of the old man and the girl in doubt, for we last see them being led away under arrest. Then there is added a sentence to the effect that Anselmus again fell silent and became immersed in his thoughts. At the very end a paragraph is appended in the French and Russian reworkings to recount the end of the siege and the fate of Count Lobau.

At the same time, the Russian has some new twists that are found neither in the German nor the French. "Die so kurz vergangene verhängnisvolle Zeit" ("ce temps si riche en événemens") is explained to Russian readers as "prošedšaja vojna za nezavisimost' Germanii, vojna, stol' bogataja čudesami." The more interesting changes are those that introduce elements of conventional ghost stories or tend to make Anselmus all the more a hopeless dreamer. Thus "irgendeine himmlische Erscheinung" ("quelque apparition céleste") becomes "kakogo-nibud' mertveca v dlinnom savane, ili, po krajnej mere, prividenie." Anselmus' words beginning "Ihr habt es ja alle oft gesagt," which are somewhat more accurately rendered in the French, are given this distorted version in the Russian: "Vy neodnokratno mne govorili, čto kakaja-to tajnaja sila, mnoju upravljajuščaja, besprestanno predstavljaet mne takie sverx"-estestvennye javlenija, kotorym nikto ne xočet verit' i kotorye vy sčitaete mečtoju svoenravnogo moego voobraženija, xotja sii samye javlenija jasno živut pered moimi glazami v fizičeskom mire, kak znamenovanie toj sverx"estestvennoj vlasti, kotoraja v našej žizni obnaruživaetsja vo vsex vidax."

"Vospominanija osady Drezdena" could not serve the purpose for which it probably was intended — to pass on Hoffmann's reminiscences of that event which had been referred to by Scott. Very likely Scott had in mind not so much "Erscheinungen" as "Der Dichter und der Komponist." More important to us, the adaptation of the story greatly misrepresented Hoffmann and could only contribute to the false image of him. The omissions and interpolations (many due to the French translator) undermined the theme of fate, reinterpreted Anselmus as the stereotype of the tragic romantic dreamer and added motifs from second-rate fantastic literature.

*Slavjanin* was not the only periodical to take up Hoffmann for the first time in 1830. The new *Literaturnaja gazeta* (Literary Gazette), under the editorship of A. A. Del'vig and favorable to romanticism, issued at midyear "Pustoj dom" ("Das öde Haus") from *Nachtstücke* (T11). The translation by V. Langer appears complete and faithful throughout, although not ideal. Langer seems a little less credulous of visionary powers than Hoffmann. Compare: "Ich kenne jemanden, dem jene Sehegabe, von der wir sprechen, ganz vorzüglich eigen scheint," with: "U menja est' odin znakomyj, kotoryj tverdo uveren, čto odaren sposobnostiju imet' čudesnye videnija."

"Erscheinungen" in *Slavjanin* and *Literaturnaja gazeta*'s "Das öde Haus" were the only Petersburg translations in 1830. The remaining items for that year appeared in Moscow. The *Moskovskij vestnik* of M. P. Pogodin published about midyear "Zaxarij Verner," a translation of the passage about Zacharias Werner from part four of the *Serapionsbrüder* (T12). A footnote acknowledges it was taken from the French version in *Le Globe*, which was greatly abridged. [33] The text is preceded by a long note, reading in part as follows (as in *Le Globe*):

> Our readers already know about Werner, a writer with a sick imagination, whose life was so sad and disturbed, and who in his last years wandered in strange dreams which his ailing reason tried vainly to dispel; whose last works represent a kind of unshapely and vague phantasmagoria; and who, being the poet of Protestant-

ism, suddenly became a Jesuit in Venice and died bequeathing
his pen to the treasury of the Virgin in Mariagella. Another writer
with almost as gloomy an imagination and whose moral destiny
(*naznačenie*) greatly resembled the fate of Werner, the illustrious
Hoffmann, was his true friend. We find in the second part of
*Fantastic Stories,* which came out recently, an article with the
title "Zacharias Werner," in which Hoffmann reveals some circumstances of Werner's life and indicates the germ of the fatal idea
which led him to the loss of his reason.

The note continues to set the scene of the conversation among the four
friends, without, however, mentioning the Serapion Brothers as such. The
translation actually opens with the paragraph beginning "Cyprian war in-
dessen schweigend aufgestanden." Cyprian's characterization of Werner's
career becomes interpreted as applying specifically to his sanity:
" . . . der mit wahrhafter hochstrebender Genialität begann, aber plötz-
lich, wie von einem verderblichen Strudel ergriffen, unterging, so daß
sein Name kaum mehr genannt wird," the last part of which was translated: "no kotorogo um, zaslonennyj mračnymi tučami, rasstroivalsja
bolee i bolee."

In the section where Cyprian recounts the central conflict of Werner's
play "Kreuz an der Ostsee," an important sentence is omitted, i.e.: "Und
was diese toten Gebilde zum Leben entflammt, es ist das Feuer, das der
satanische Prometheus aus der Hölle selbst stahl." Everywhere the word
"Serapionsbrüder" is either untranslated or replaced, as with "moi druz'-
ja." Several passages are omitted or abbreviated. Theodor is made to say
that he cannot even guess how the unfinished play might have ended,
while in the original he tells his friends precisely that he has an idea of
how the close might have been. Omitted entirely is a long section in
which Ottmar tells how Werner came to write the play and discusses some
technical points. Farther on, the thesis of an argument is left out, i.e.,
the sentence: "Man sagt, daß der Hysterismus der Mütter sich zwar nicht

auf die Söhne vererbe. ...." At the end of the French-Russian abridgment
there is this footnote: "When Hoffmann wrote this article, Werner was
living in a Jesuit home."

The many alternations made this translation unsatisfactory; but this
time they were owed more to the French translator rather than to the
Russian. It is clear from the introductory note that the editor saw
the text as giving evidence of Werner's insanity and of the notion that
the ideas of his imagination contributed to it. By extension a similar
view of Hoffmann is implied. We should not forget that in 1830 the
*Moskovskij vestnik* was under single control of Pogodin, for, of the
leading Ljubomudry earlier associated with it, Venevitinov was dead, and
Kireevskij, Rožalin and Ševyrev were out of the country.


4


The *Moskovskij telegraf*'s first Hoffmann text for 1830 was "Maiorat"
("Das Majorat"), which appeared in installments beginning with the July
volume (T13). The text contains a number of minor inaccuracies which
do not seem to alter the sense. It may be termed adequate to good, while
by comparison the later translation in *Sankt-Peterburgskij vestnik* (Saint Petersburg Herald, 1831; T21) is far inferior. "Das Majorat" was one of the
two stories analyzed by Walter Scott in his article printed in 1829.

*Vestnik Evropy,* having published Hoffmann as far back as 1823, returned to the German for two more stories in 1830, its last year of publication. The first (T14) was "Sanctus" (title given in Latin letters) in
nos. 19–20 (October). This was the first translation of "Das Sanctus," a
story from *Nachtstücke,* and in quality it belongs to that middle group
of adequate translations which give an impression of the original without
being accurate in details. As so often, whole passages are abbreviated.
An example of an abridged sentence is: "Ferdinand begnügte sich, die

Wälle zu beschießen und die Ausfälle der Belagerten zurückzutreiben,"
which becomes simply: "Ferdinand mešal rabotam osaždennyx." The
entire last paragraph is reduced to: "Spustja nedelju posle sego Bettina
garmoničeskim golosom pela Pergolezovu: Stabat mater." The translation
was evidently made from Loève-Veimars' version, which ends: "Huit jours
après, Bettina chantait d'une voix harmoniense le *Stabat mater* de Pergo-
lèse."

Some of the Russian magazines of the period had small supplements,
often containing notices of Paris fashions, including prints, and occasionally light social satire. In 1830 and 1831 the *Moskovskij telegraf* had as
its supplement the satirical *Novyj živopisec obščestva i litteratury* (New
Painter of Society and Literature). The issue for November, 1830, included the piece "Sumasšedšie i nesumasšedšie" (The Mad and the Sane).
One of the writer's themes is the old saying "Ignorance is bliss" – only
those are unhappy who recognize their misfortune. He tells that a certain friend of his, blind from birth, is a peculiarly happy man. ". . . He
often mixes up all ideas and conceptions. On such an occasion he is
like an intelligent child who, knowing something – having noticed something – develops on that small basis his own ideas and conceptions, confuses time and space and creates such monstrosities and oddities that
they resemble the fantastic figures *(lica)* of Hoffmann and Jean Paul"
(p. 360). Someone once bet this blind man that he could not tell an insane person from a sane one. As a test he was taken on one evening to
a rich man's drawing room and to an insane asylum, and afterwards he
was unable to tell which was which by comparing the conversations he
heard! The piece ends:

> That's our entire conversation. Now isn't it true that the blind
> man is sometimes strange and eccentric *(originalen)* like a Hoff-
> mann tale? Really, how ridiculous not to be able to distinguish
> madness from intelligence! It would seem that that is so easy to
> do . . .   (p. 370).

Hoffmann is of course quite incidental to the point of the story, but it is clear that by this date the writer assumed Hoffmann to be well enough known so that such a reference would call forth a common response in his readers. The focus is on the fantastic personages of Hoffmann's stories, which are represented as "monstrosities and oddities" that mystify without having any real sense or purpose. We detect here the impact of Scott's characterization of Hoffmann's fantasy.

The *Vestnik Evropy* also helped to spread the notion of Hoffmann's eccentricity. It printed a second translation in 1830, the "Kremonskaja skripka" (Cremona Violin) of November (T15). The original is a passage from the first part of *Die Serapionsbrüder* untitled by the author but usually called "Rat Krespel" by editors. The publisher of *Vestnik Evropy* (Kačenovskij) placed this footnote on the first page:

> The stories of that eccentric Hoffmann *(čudak Gofman)* are known in general under the name of *fantastic* stories, and justly so. We hope to print an article translated from a foreign journal, in which the character of the works of this strange writer is defined.

(The article referred to, "O fantastičeskix povestjax Gofmanna," appeared the next month; see below.)

In the text of "Kremonskaja skripka" Hoffmann seems to come through despite numerous small inaccuracies, most due to the fact that the translator, V. Praxov, worked from Loève-Veimars' "Le violon de Crémone" instead of the original German text. [34] For example, "ein nicht eben bedeutender regierender Fürst" is promoted to "un souverain qui n'était pas peu puissant en Allemagne" – "odin iz ves'ma značuščix v Germanii vladetelej." (Bessomykin's rendering, 1836, avoids such errors.) "Rat Krespel" was surely chosen for Russian publication because it lent strength to the current concept of Hoffmann's eccentricity. Indeed, Krespel may be the biggest "original" in Hoffmann's works.

A final Hoffmann offering for 1830 by the *Moskovskij telegraf* was "Domovoj-pesočnik" ("Der Sandmann"), printed in November and December (T16). We should remember that "Der Sandmann" was one of the two stories discussed in detail by Walter Scott. Parallel passages show that this imprecise translation was made from Loève-Veimars' "L'homme au sable"; mistakes and changes of emphasis were due primarily to the Russian translator, as at the end of this section:

> Sie hat mir einen sehr tiefsinnigen philosophischen Brief geschrieben, worin sie ausführlich beweiset, daß Coppelius und Coppola nur in meinem Innern existieren und Phantome meines Ichs sind, die augenblicklich zerstäuben, wenn ich sie als solche erkenne.

> Elle m'a adressé une épître remplie d'une philosophie profonde, par laquelle elle me démontre explicitement que Coppelius et Coppola n'existent que dans mon cerveau, et qu'ils sont des fantômes de mon *moi* qui s'évanouiront en poudre dès que je les reconnaîtrai pour tels.

> Ona prislala mne otvet, ispolnennyj glubočajšej filosofii, posredstvom koej ona jasno dokazyvaet, čto Koppelius i Koppolo [sic] suščestvujut tol'ko v moem voobraženii i čto oni sut' sobstvenno moi prizraki, kotorye pogubjat menja, esli ja budu verovat' v nix.

In another place a key sentence is shortened in the French and then further simplified in the Russian, to the extent of naively altering the impression. Compare: "Hast du, Geneigtester, wohl jemals etwas erlebt, das deine Brust, Sinn und Gedanken ganz und gar erfüllte, alles andere daraus verdrängend? " with: "Qui n'a un jour, senti sa poitrine se remplir de pensées étranges? " and "Komu inogda ne prixodili v golovu strannye mysli?"

5

The third and last of the foreign articles on Hoffmann published in
Russian translation in 1829 and 1830 was "O fantastičeskix povestjax
Gofmanna" (On Hoffmann's Fantastic Stories) in *Vestnik Evropy*, December, 1830 (C3). The publisher deemed it necessary to put this footnote at the opening of the article:

> This Hoffmann was a native German, and one should not con-
> fuse him with the French writer of the same name — a composer
> of excellent reviews who also died in recent years.

The Frenchman in question was François-Benoît Hoffmann (1760 —
1828), a talented and respected collaborator in the *Journal des Débats*,
and some of whose articles had been translated in Russian magazines.
His *Oeuvres complètes* were published in Paris in 1828.

Another note indicates that "O fantastičeskix povestjax Gofmanna"
was translated from French by V. Praxov (who also did the "Kremonskaja skripka" included in the preceding volume). It is taken from a review (*Journal des Débats*, May 22, 1830) of Loève-Veimars' translation
*Contes fantastiques* of 1829–30. Teichmann thinks to have proved that
the review, which appeared with the signature "Cs.," was the work of
Philarète Chasles, who is known to have signed himself that way. This
hypothesis is strengthened by the fact that the review opens with a
quote from Jean Paul, whom Chasles was to translate later in the year.
Teichmann further infers that Chasles' preoccupation with Jean Paul
may explain his disparagement of Hoffmann in the article. (See her
book, pp. 47–48.)

The long quotation from Jean Paul treats the world of fantasy as an
escape from an unhappy life. Chasles says that the German national
character strangely mixes a leaning toward fantasy with a bourgeois desire for physical satisfactions. At first  he maintains that Hoffmann never

quite lost control of his sanity. "His reason, undergoing extreme danger, wavered but did not fall into the abyss." Hoffmann, according to Chasles, stood on the edge of the precipice looking down and drew the figures he saw there, with lively color and astonishing charm, "which, however, does not conceal the obvious incongruities."

> . . . On the one hand he transformed the ideal into the material; on the other, the images created by painting and musical sounds acted on him as though like infernal or heavenly forces. . . .

The Frenchman terms Hoffmann an "idealist-anthropomorphite" and a "dreamer-metaphysician":

> this man accustomed to confusing a plant with a human being, a sound with an image, a marble statue with a living being, a superb colored canvas with the model from which it was done, a thought with an organic being and an organic being with a thought.

Among Hoffmann's building blocks he mentions "golden-winged sylphs, mysticism, supernaturalism, all the creations of the most recent psychology and Eastern cabalism." The German, we are reminded, found both pleasure and inspiration in alcohol.

In an only slightly more instructive part of the article Chasles declares Hoffmann's feeling for art was very strong but led him at times to desperation, for he saw that there was a bound beyond which the artist cannot adequately express himself. Hence the idea in some stories (e.g., "Ritter Gluck") that the true work of art only exists in the artist's mind, while he can give us in the finished product merely a weak reflection of his thought. The plight of the artist in "Die Jesuiterkirche in G." is discussed, and the works "Artushof," "Ritter Gluck," "Don Juan" and "Zacharias Werner" are pointed out as containing "the same inimitable feeling for the arts, the same rapture produced by their sorcery."

But the writer goes on to assert that the ecstatic experience of art drew Hoffmann away from the material world and led him to a sad state of derangement (*gorestnoe pomešatel'stvo;* in the French, *déraison*). "Vlastitel' blox" ("Meister Floh") is referred to as "something still stranger." On the other hand, "Das Fräulein von Scuderi" and "Meister Martin" are cited as stories taken from real life and almost lacking the fantastic coloring of "Callot's imitator." Chasles admits he prefers "Meister Martin" to all the fantastic stories, but he shows a somewhat inconsistent attitude, saying next that Hoffmann's forte was, after all, fantasy, and recommending that everyone read "Der Sandmann." In that story, he asserts, the German was satirizing his own stupidities. Finally, an even stronger irony is attributed to "Razmyšlenija Kota Murra, peremešannye s biografieju kapel'mejstera Krejslera" *(Lebensansichten des Katers Murr . . . )*.

The article overall is more constructive than Scott's despite a certain lack of sophistication and some blind spots. Philarète Chasles, in discussing the artist stories, opened the possibility of a deeper significance in Hoffmann than Scott had been prepared to admit. The French article must be considered positive in that respect, and yet, on the other hand it too helped to spread and perpetuate the current image of that "eccentric," Hoffmann.

At the very end of 1830 the expiring *Moskovskij vestnik* printed one last Hoffmann text — "Ezuitskaja cerkov'" ("Die Jesuiterkirche in G."; T17). The translator, identified only by the initals V. D., gave a very free rendering of the original German, allowing abbreviations. As an example, consider the following passage and its treatment by V. D.:

> Dem Berthold war es so, als habe der Malteser nur dem, was in seiner Seele gärte und brauste, Worte gegeben; die innere Stimme brach hervor — "Nein! Alles dieses Streben — dieses Mühen ist das ungewisse, trügerische Umhertappen des Blinden, weg — weg mit

allem, was mich geblendet bis jetzt!" — Er war nicht imstande, auch nur einen Strich weiter an dem Bilde zu zeichnen. Er verließ seinen Meister und streifte voll wilder Unruhe umher und flehte laut, daß die höhere Erkenntnis, von der der Malteser gesprochen, ihm aufgehen möge.

Kazalos', čto v samom dele čužezemec probudil v Bertol'de taivšeesja v nem čuvstvo. On ne mog prodolžat' kartiny, ostavil učitelja svoego, i v smuščenii iskal duxa, prizvannogo Mal'tijcem.

To the chronicle of Hoffmann publishing in 1830 must be added the fact that in that year Nikolaj Polevoj reprinted the story "Beloe prividenie" ("Die Marquise de la Pivardiere") in vol. 5 of the collection *Povesti i literaturnye otryvki* (T18). It was taken from the *Moskovskij telegraf* of 1825 (see T4). This volume of the collection bears censor's approval of May 5, 1830.

6

The large number of translations of Hoffmann in Russia in 1830 was at least duplicated if not exceeded in the following year, and casual references to him in the press certainly did increase in 1831, indicating that his name was becoming better and better known. If in the preceding year Moscow had produced nearly all of the translations, in 1831 St. Petersburg shared this work about equally with the old capital.

It was in 1831 that P. Volkov made an abortive attempt to turn out in Petersburg a magazine of translated foreign literature. Unfortunately, only two issues of the *Žurnal inostrannoj slovesnosti i izjaščnyx xudožestv* (Magazine of Foreign Literature and Fine Arts) appeared. Their contents included installments of "Ignac Denner: Povest'" ("Ignaz Den-

ner"), a story from E. T. A. Hoffmann's *Nachtstücke,* and one of the
darkest he wrote (T19). Evidently it was to be printed in four parts, because the two installments cover the first half of the story. The translation breaks off after the burial of Andres' younger child, the last lines
being a rendering of "In dumpfem düsterem Schweigen hatten sie die
Arbeit vollendet und saßen nun vor dem Hause in der Abenddämmerung,
den starren Blick in die Ferne gerichtet." The text has some very minor
inaccuracies but can be considered overall good and perhaps even ranks
in quality with the translation of the *Serapionsbrüder* of Bessomykin
(1836). For this reason it is especially a shame that the remainder was
not printed.

In 1831 there was founded another new magazine which was destined
to survive several years and play an important role in Russian literary life.
This was *Teleskop* (The Telescope) published in Moscow, 1831–36, by
N. I. Naděždin. The *Teleskop* will be of interest to us for its part in the
history of E. T. A. Hoffmann's fortune in Russia. Indeed, in the very
first volume (January-February) the German is mentioned. In the course
of a review the journalist gives a tribute to Hoffmann's craftsmanship:

> In the large picture [i.e., the novel] the inadequacies and failures of
> the parts are swallowed up in the effect of the whole; but in the
> fragmentary essay [i.e., the short story or *novella*] the whole should
> proceed from parts in which everything is in the open, everything
> is obvious, and therefore everything requires expressiveness in mean-
> ing and perfection in the finishing. That is the stumbling block at
> which even the genius of Walter Scott faltered, and if the Hoffmanns,
> Tiecks and Claurens have not always tripped up on it, that alone
> renders them a well-earned patent to immortality. (p. 348)

At the beginning of 1831 the *Syn otečestva* carried a translation of an
article by Menzel on Schiller and Goethe (vol. 17, p. 405). Wolfgang Menzel (1798–1873) was an influential Stuttgart critic, anti-romantic and

particular enemy of Goethe. Discussing the romantic (i.e., fantastic) element in German literature, he says in the translated article that after the
Reformation this feature survived only in some secular genres – magic
operas, tales, knightly romances.

> To this later were attached the stories of spirits and finally the
> mysterious poetry of Werner, the magnetic and diabolical stories
> of Hoffmann and tragedies on the immutability of blind fate.
> Characteristic feature of this entire type is that it seeks the won-
> drous in the *incidents* – in the action – of romantic, dark forces on
> the fates of men. This is the basest type of the romantic. In their in-
> ventions man is a toy, a puppet of a higher force, and the latter
> is itself only a *deus ex machina*. This poetry does not produce its
> effect and becomes ridiculous, because in it the deception is too
> crude, and, like unbelief, it offers all the weapons of derision
> against itself.

A third new magazine of 1831, the *Sankt-Peterburgskij vestnik,* which,
like the *Žurnal inostrannoj slovesnosti,* did not even complete its first
year, took up E. T. A. Hoffmann. In vol. 2 it offered "Sčast'e igroka"
("Spielerglück"; T20). We already referred to this translation and gave a
passage from it for comparison in Chapter I. The translator, who signed
himself "N. Ju.," evidently worked from Loève-Veimars' "Le bonheur au
jeu," which already somewhat shortened passages of the German original.
The Russian version makes more substantial changes. Often Hoffmann's
serious and complex sentences are transformed into brief remarks in a
callous and overly colloquial tone. For example, the section in which it
is told how society came to regard Siegfried as a miser (the sixth paragraph of the story, beginning "Von dieser Geschichte kam man denn
auf Siegfrieds Eigensinn") is reduced thus to a joke:

> Èto zastavilo vsex obratit' vnimanie na xarakter barona, i čto že? vse
> stali nazyvat' ego upornym skupcom. Vsem kazalos' nepojnatnym,
> kak možno, s takim postojannym sčastiem, ne vzjat'sja za karty!

Here is an instance of an apparent misunderstanding combined with overly colloquial Russian phrases: "Ohne daß er es selbst bemerkte, regte sich in dem Innern des Barons die Lust an dem Farospiel, das in seiner Einfachheit das verhängnisvollste ist, mehr und mehr auf. Er war nicht mehr unzufrieden mit seinem Glück. ...." "... I baron, ne znaja, ne vedaja, — bolee i bolee pristrasčalsja v igre, osnovannoj, kak polagal on, na odnom tol'ko sčastii! I točno, baronu grex bylo žalovat'sja na sčast'e!" The following characteristic sentence — completely omitted in the translation of 1830 (see above) — is translated, but with distortion:

> Die sonderbaren Verkettungen des Zufalls wechseln in dem seltsamsten Spiel, das Regiment der höhern Macht tritt klarer hervor, und eben dieses ist es, was unsern Geist anregt, die Fittiche zu rühren und zu versuchen, ob er sich nicht hineinschwingen kann in das dunkle Reich, in die verhängnisvolle Werkstatt jener Macht, um ihr Arbeiten zu belauschen.

> Les singuliers enchaînemens du hasard se développent dans le jeu le plus bizarre, la cohorte des puissances inconnues semble planer au-dessus de vous, il semble qu'on entende le battement de leurs ailes, et l'on brûle de pénétrer dans cette région inconnue pour contempler les rouages de cette machine dont on sent l'influence, et parcourir ces atéliers célestes où s'élaborent les chances de la destinée des hommes.

> Im kažetsja, čto sonmy nevedomyx sil nosjatsja nad nimi, im slyšitsja bienie ix krylij, i v obol'sčennyx serdcax raždaetsja želanie proniknut' v ètu tainstvennuju stranu, želanie sozercat' kruglovrasčenie sudeb, — i proletet' te nepostižimye prostranstva, gde prednaznačajutsja udači i neudači smertnyx.

N. Ju's translation of "Spielerglück," like that of 1823, must be considered unsatisfactory.

In 1831 the *Moskovskij telegraf* continued its association with Hoffmann, contributing translations and mentions. He is referred to twice in vol. 38 (March-April). In a review of Van der Velde (p. 105) the *Telegraf* repeated its plea for translations of better German authors (cf. the 1830 review discussed above):

> Do Russian readers know the novels of Goethe, Tieck, Hoffmann, Jean Paul, Clauren, Zschokke and hundreds of other German novelists of lesser distinction but still great compared with Van der Velde?

Later, in a review of Zagoskin's *Roslavlev,* the *Telegraf* gives a list of worthy foreign authors:

> W. Scott, Cooper, Horace Smith, Lockhart, Manzoni, Alfred de Vigny, Bronikowski and Bernatowicz; Hoffmann, La Motte-Fouqué, Spindler, Clauren, Zschokke, Nodier, Victor Hugo — not all in equal degree — by far not in equal degree — but all are people of remarkable talents   (p. 537).

In April, 1831, the *Teleskop* printed an article on Zacharias Werner ("Zaxarija Verner"; č. 2, pp. 435—70), acknowledged to be taken from the English publication *Foreign Review.* Indeed a piece on Werner appeared in *Foreign Review* in 1828 — in the nature of a review of five books of and about the German, principal among which was *Lebensabriß Friedrich Ludwig Zacharias Werners,* ed. Hitzig (Berlin, 1823). Curiously enough, a comparison shows that, despite the acknowledgment, the article in *Teleskop* is not a translation of that in *Foreign Review.* Only short sections are parallel, the Russian text borrowing merely scattered sentences. For example, the opening sentence of the English article appears, slightly altered, on the fourth page of the Russian piece. It may be that the Russian writer in *Teleskop* had gone to Hitzig's book and drawn material directly from it. In any case, his article is substantially different from that in *Foreign Review.*

In the Russian article we find this passage:

> Under one roof, but on different floors of the same house, lived two children, one of whom was eight years older than the other — *Werner* and *Hoffmann;* both nourished and raised by two unfortunate mothers whose nervous disorders led to madness, they brought into the world the indelible stamp of their upbringing. Their ideas became perverted very early; their youthful brains were unsettled; no habit of order and attention insured their future lives. A certain kind of fantastic ecstasy was imparted to them in the cradle; they took it in with their milk; and neither genius nor successes could cure them.

That passage is not to be found in the *Foreign Review,* nor is the following one, some pages later in the Russian article:

> He [Werner] returned to Warsaw, where he associated himself in the closest way with Hoffmann and Hitzig — witnesses of his persistent eccentricities, for which, however, Hoffmann at least had no right to reproach him.

The article continues that Warsaw had great attraction for people "who are drawn by any momentary impression and who never know how to resist the trials of temptation." Such people were Hoffmann and Werner, asserts the writer, and therefore they tried to prolong their stay in Warsaw as much as possible.

The anecdote about Werner involving the word *Bangputtis* is recounted, and the joke is attributed to Hoffmann himself ("Sometimes the fantastical Hoffmann liked to tease his countryman"). Due credit is given to the passage on Werner in *Die Serapionsbrüder* as the source of the anecdote. (The joke is also told in *Foreign Review,* but the English and Russian texts are not even close to one another in wording.)

The article on Werner in the *Foreign Review* appears to be well informed and sophisticated. The Russian writer who printed in the *Teleskop* borrowed little from it and composed an essentially original and inferior article. He introduced attacks on German "mysticism" and adopted the characterization of Hoffmann, by now accepted in Russia, as half-insane in his life and senselessly capricious in his writings. Hitzig was a stimulus again in this respect. Furthermore, there is a similarity of viewpoint between the Russian piece and one which appeared in the French *Globe* in 1828. [35] That article likewise seems to be partly based on *Foreign Review,* to judge from parallel though not identical passages, but it discusses "German mysticism" as does the *Teleskop* piece. Perhaps the author of the latter had also read the *Globe*. Altogether, the genealogy of these writings on Werner is a puzzle.

The *Sankt-Petersburgskij vestnik,* having already printed "Sčast'e igroka" in 1831 (its only year of publication), followed with another Hoffmann story in nos. 30–33. This time it was "Majorat: Povest'" ("Das Majorat"; T21). A note at the end of the text indicates that it is from the German. The translator signed himself simply "A." (perhaps the publisher of the magazine, E. V. Alad'in? ). Hoffmann is not mentioned as the author!

It is interesting that for its two Hoffmann works the *Sankt-Peterburgskij vestnik* chose stories already translated ("Spielerglück" appeared 1823, and "Das Majorat" 1830), thus causing the only duplication so far. Unfortunately, it must be reported, furthermore, that "Majorat" was as bad a translation as the "Sčast'e igroka" in the same magazine. Omissions and inaccuracies are unusually numerous. The translator leaves some things out, substitutes for others and occasionally expands the text with explanations. Descriptive phrases and sentences are particularly liable to be omitted. But not only inconsequential material is left out. In one place a significant hint of past history was omitted, i.e., the words "ich mußte dabei an die vergangene Zeit und an manches Verwunderliche

denken, was hier sich begab." Left untranslated are the uncle's words to
Daniel's ghost:

"Suche Gnade und Erbarmen vor dem Thron des Höchsten, dort
ist dein Platz! Fort mit dir aus dem Leben, dem du niemals mehr
angehören kannst!"

Another suggestive clue is omitted by not translating that when the baron saw the bricked-up door, turning away quickly, "fuhr er mit der
Hand über die Stirn, als wolle er irgendeine böse Erinnerung verscheu-
chen." The translation continues in this abridged manner. Characteristically, the final paragraph is completely missing. The contribution of
*Sankt-Peterburgskij vestnik* to knowledge of Hoffmann in Russia cannot
be deemed very valuable.

One of two translations of Hoffmann printed by the *Syn otečestva*
in 1831 was "Vybor nevesty" ("Die Brautwahl"), which appeared in the
magazine at midyear (T22) and afterward in an offprint (T22a). The latter carries censor's approval dated August 1, 1831, and differs only in
pagination and placing of titles. The translator signed himself "Ju — č."
It is necessary to relate that "Vybor nevesty" was still another very poor
translation produced by the year 1831. As so often, the major crime was
omissions. In this instance they considerably alter the character of the
work. First of all, the Russian version lacks the subtitle of the story and
the names of the chapters (which are, however, numbered). The adapter
has added his own dedication to "V. I. V — s." Often the effects of
Hoffmann's lively prose are lost, as in "ein seltsames Klopfen, das sich
dicht neben ihm hören ließ, ihn an den Boden festwurzelte," which becomes: "vdrug strašnyj šum, razdavšisja nepodaleku, privlek ego vnima-
nie." A few lines later, pounding on a door ("mein sehnsüchtiges Pochen")
is mistranslated as "bienie moego serdca." The ending of the second
chapter is very much abbreviated. Fouqué's verses are omitted, paragraphs
are shortened, the dialogue of Edmund and the goldsmith is only summa-

rized. The cuts tend particularly to minimize the role of the mysterious goldsmith — and thus of the fantastic element. So in the abbreviated close of the fourth chapter the goldsmith's comment that all will turn out well (indicating his control of the situation) is eliminated. Chapter five is strongly abridged.

The role of the goldsmith Leonhard is very much changed in the key scene in which he presents himself to Albertine. Hoffmann uses a typical transformation:

> Es geschah auch wirklich, daß Albertine nicht im mindesten erschrak, als sie gewahrte, daß das, was sie für den Ofen gehalten, eigentlich der Goldschmied Leonhard war, der sich ihr näherte und mit sanfter, sonorer Stimme folgendermaßen begann . . .

The Russian adaptation excludes the statement of a magical event: "I tak Al'bertina ni malo ne ispugalas', kogda Leonard vnezapno javilsja i skazal ej laskovo . . ." Leonhard's words are then cut to one-third the original length, and Albertine's reaction is distorted. Hoffmann says, "Sie wäre dem alten Goldschmied beinahe zu Füßen gesunken"; the Russian reads: "Al'bertina brosilas' k nogam Leonarda." Leonhard's entire speech revealing himself to be Leonhard Turnhäuser is left out! The final chapter is also condensed; poems are omitted; the closing two pages of the story are summarized in eight short lines. "Vybor nevesty" of 1831 must be termed an unsatisfactory abridgment. By minimizing the part of the goldsmith, the adapter quite changed the character of the tale and eliminated the features typical of Hoffmann. Most of these alterations are also in Loève-Veimars' "Le choix d'une fiancée," and the Russian seems clearly to derive from it, although we have not had an opportunity to make a full comparison.

7

The first *Moskovskij telegraf* translation of 1831 was "Pjatyj i sed'moj večera, iz povesti: Zolotoj goršok" ("Der goldne Topf," excerpt) in the July volume (T23). As the title indicates, only the fifth and seventh evenings (*Vigilien*) are included. These are the two chapters of "Der goldne Topf" which relate the encounters of Veronika with the old witch Liese – the sections on which Pogorel'skij drew in writing "Lafertovskaja makovnica" (see Chapter II).

Subtitles of the chapters are omitted, and the translation is quite free, permitting paraphrases. There is slight evidence of a tendency to add elaborations in the common fantastic style. In particular, the phrase "ließ den vor Erstaunen und Neugierde verstummten Konrektor im Stuhle festgebannt sitzen" becomes: "ostaviv rektora Paul'mana onemevšim ot udivlenija, ot ljubopytstva, i nepodvižno sidjaščim v bol'šix kreslax, kak budto volšebnaja kakaja-nibud' sila uderživala ego v ètix kreslax." At the end of the selection an extra sentence is added: "I nemedlenno otpravilsja rassprašivat' podrobnee u doktora fon-Èkstejna."

The year 1831 saw two translations of Hoffmann's story "Der unheimliche Gast," the first (and more satisfactory one) in the supplement *Literaturnye pribavlenija* of the *Russkij invalid* (T24). The second, in *Syn otečestva,* will be discussed later. V. Tilo is indicated as the translator of the version in *Literaturnye pribavlenija.* His "Tainstvennyj gost' " seems complete and adequately reflects the original; but there are minor inexactitudes and examples of free translation. In the opening scene of the story Marguerite is made to serve tea rather than the German punch. This is accompanied by the following change: " . . . Darum soll euch Mademoiselle Marguerite das gute nordische Getränk bereiten, das allem bösen Wetter widersteht," becomes: " . . . Dlja vas mamzel' Margarita prigotovit drugoj napitok, kotoryj očen' kstati russkie nazyvajut živitelem severnyx serdec; èto lučšee sredstvo ot vsjakoj nepogody." The translation changes Bogislav from a Russian to an Austrian and renames him "Steinbach."

The *Literaturnye pribavlenija* offered a second translation a few numbers later — "Skazka" (T25). It is a brief story from the opening of the fifth section of *Die Serapionsbrüder,* unnamed by Hoffmann but generally called "Nachricht aus dem Leben eines bekannten Mannes." In the translation the short text is slightly cut here and there. Part of the description of the bewitched child is left out, i.e., the words:

> und *[hatte]* keinen Hals. Der Kopf stand ihm zwischen den Schultern, der Leib war runzlicht und geschwollen, die Arme hingen an den Lenden, und es hatte lange dünne Schenkel.

Towards the end of the year we begin to find references to Hoffmann in the *Teleskop* again. In vol. 5 (September-October) there is an article "Vzgljad na prošedšee pjatnadcatiletie nemeckoj literatury" by that same Wolfgang Menzel who was quoted earlier by the *Syn otečestva.* [36] The translator gave his initials as M. Č. In the course of the article Menzel chastizes writers for aloofness from contemporary realities:

> . . . And it happened once that at the time a lot of poetical almanacs were being printed in Leipzig, outside Leipzig a battle of national importance was taking place. Lessing in his time used to brag that he did not read newspapers, and Callot-Hoffmann had such loathing for them that he could not see them. This tendency to dreaminess, this withdrawal from reality, once in high fashion, fortunately no longer exists; and that again comprises a rich acquisition for life, even if art loses from it. (p. 165)

This Menzel article was also translated into French (*Nouvelle Revue Germanique,* vol. 7 *[*March, 1831 *]*, pp. 220–38).

In November-December, 1831, the *Teleskop* published its version of "Der Sandmann" (T26). It was the second translation of the story, which had been given special attention by Walter Scott in the article printed in 1829. The *Teleskop's* "Pesočnyj čelovek" is more accurate than its predecessor and has only small errors. It was reprinted in a *sbornik* (collection of stories) in 1836 (T36).

In 1831 the first fragment of *Lebensansichten des Katers Murr* in Russian was published by the *Moskovskij telegraf.* It could be read in vol. 49 (November-December) under the title "Čerty iz žizni kota Murra i otryvki biografii kapel'mejstera Ioganna Krejslera" (T27). A publisher's note explains the device of alternating Murr's and Kreisler's stories.

> There is no need to add that the brilliant ravings of Murr have an essential connection with Kreisler's life. But we should recall that this fine composition of Hoffmann's is remarkable moreover because it was his last work. The author was finishing it on his death bed. It is to be wished that this novel, which is fully translated into Russian, be also printed in entirety. Our public would receive from it inexpressible pleasure.

The translator is not named, and the fragment seems to be distinct from the version by Ketčer (1840) – the only complete published translation before 1893.

The *Telegraf's* selection appeared in two installments, each of which has one fragment of Murr's story and one of Kreisler's, altogether the first four sections of Hoffmann's text. The translation is good, and the translator managed to find a satisfactory equivalent for Hoffmann's syntax, which proved a stumbling block for many other translators. There are a very few cuts and misunderstandings. The second half of the very first paragraph is omitted; the following rather profound sentence was altered: "Ich glaube überhaupt, daß man sich das Bewußtsein nur angewöhnt; durch das Leben und zum Leben kommt man doch, man weiß selbst nicht wie." In the Russian it reads: "A kak proxodit žizn' i kak načinaetsja ona, ètogo ne znaet nikto."

At the end of this same final volume for 1831 the editor lists some of the important contents of the *Moskovskij telegraf* for the past year, which included "two excerpts from two inimitable compositions of Hoffmann" (p. 507). They were, of course, from "Der goldne Topf" and *Kater Murr.*

The *Teleskop* also mentions Hoffmann in its last volume for the year. He is referred to in a review of Puškin's *Povesti Belkina* (see Chapter IV) and in a note to the Balzac translation "Strast' xudožnika, ili čelovek ne čelovek." The latter reference combines an attack on romanticism with one on the *Moskovskij telegraf:*

> "The Sandman (*Pesočnyj čelovek*)," a story by Hoffmann offered in the foregoing issues of the *Telescope,* presents an interesting and instructive picture of the awful consequences of the excessive tension of German dreaminess. The story offered here forms a curious counterpart to it. In it is drawn with psychological fidelity and poetical vividness a picture of the no less awful workings of the frenzy of French passion. If one compares these two with the portrait of a "Statesman" which was introduced at the end of the last volume of the *Telescope,* where the sad story of English political madness is described so faithfully and vividly, there is composed a complete gallery of madness — of interest for the history of human nature — as it occurs in three major countries of the present enlightened world: England, France and Germany. Whoever may be curious to know what people in our country lose their heads over and involve others in, read the *Moscow Telegraph!*
> — *Publisher.* [37]

The last of the many translations of 1831 was the second version of "Der unheimliche Gast": "Tainstvennyj gost'," in *Syn otečestva,* December (T28). It was made from Loève-Veimars' version, "Le spectre fiancé." At the beginning is a footnote: "This story is completely based on notions of animal magnetism.  . . . It is a satirical picture which had great success in Germany, and especially in Berlin, where they supposed that they even recognized the personages." The note is a translation of two passages in Loève-Veimars' preface to the story (*Contes fantastiques* [Paris, 1830], vol. 4, pp. 151–52), given in inverted order. However, Loève-Veimars' remark about satire applied to the preceding story in his collection, "Le choix d'une fiancée" – "Die Brautwahl"; here it has been falsely attached to "Der unheimliche Gast." Most of the many omissions and elaborations in the Russian text seem to come from the French. Moritz is supplied with a surname (Reinberg); "jeden Donnerstag" becomes "po pjatnicam"; "Geisterseher" is translated simply "mečtatel'" ("un visionnaire"). The Obristin is also given a surname and made a baroness. In both French and Russian the final sentence is omitted: "Gibt es denn noch hienieder eine höhere Seligkeit¹ als diese? " Despite such cuts, no major part of the text is missing.


8

In Moscow in 1832 Ivan Kireevskij began to publish a new magazine called *Evropeec* (The European), of which only two issues appeared. A third was printed but forbidden by the censor because of its liberal sentiments. In the first issue there is a review of *Briefe aus Paris* by Ludwig Börne (Hamburg, 1832). The reviewer, i.a., criticizes the complexity of some German prose.

> However, one must render justice to the Germans that their style *(slog)*, generally speaking, is now becoming much simpler and more natural than it was in the time of Jean Paul and Hoffmann, and the literary taste of the public is becoming stricter and more educated  (p. 118).

It seems to be a fact that Bessomykin's translation of *Die Serapions-*

*brüder* was completed by 1832, although it did not get published *in toto* until 1836. In vol. 44 for 1832 (March) the *Moskovskij telegraf* inserted the following notice in the section "Smes' " under the heading "On the Publishing of New Books" (pp. 150–51):

> *Serapion Brothers (Serapionovy brat'ja)* by Hoffmann. A young Russian scholar living for reason of his work in Revel has translated this book, which is now being printed or will very soon go to press. He has sent us excerpts from his translation; our readers will see them in the coming issues of the *Telegraph* and without any warning from us will determine that the Russian translation is very good. The appearance of one of the best of Hoffmann's works in all of its original beauty will be a veritable holiday for the Russian reading public, for from the French translation they cannot get a full and true idea of the inimitable Hoffmann. Loève-Veimars, the French translator, despite all his art, did not convey Hoffmann as one would wish. As proof let us recall that in translating a few stories from this same *Serapionsbrüder* he left the greater half of the book untranslated, evidently without any cause. He threw out the story which connects the stories and mixed up the translated parts with excerpts from other works by Hoffmann; more than that, of the stories themselves, some he left out, and from others he omitted not only whole pages but even whole episodes. Not according to such a plan did the Russian translator labor. He translated the entire book, completely, just as it is. And we desire such translations, because the time has come to study great writers other than superficially. This book will be interesting not only to those unfamiliar with German but also to those who read it in the original and want to experience in their own language the ideas and images which fascinated them in a foreign world.

Later in the same volume the *Telegraf* began printing an excerpt from

Bessomykin's translation: "Žizn' trex druzej" ("Ein Fragment aus dem Leben dreier Freunde"; T29). A publisher's note stated:

This is an excerpt from the translation of *The Serapion Brothers* about which we spoke in the fifth issue of our magazine. The translation of the entire book will soon be published.

The selection differs only minutely from the final draft which was published in *Serapionovy brat'ja* of 1836. At the end of the excerpt we read: "Revel, December, 1831. From the German, I. Bzsmkn [I. I. Bessomykin]." Bessomykin's version is very accurate throughout.

In 1832 and 1833 there was published in Revel (Tallinn) the periodical *Raduga* (Rainbow). In the second year it became very pious and printed mostly religious tracts, but in 1832 it showed an interest in literature, and especially German literature. It devoted a lot of space that year to Jean Paul, including the publication of some of his letters. *Raduga* also took up the cause of E. T. A. Hoffmann, perhaps encouraged to this by the presence of Bessomykin in Revel. In issue 3 for 1832 *Raduga* published an article entitled "Kratkoe žizneopisanie Gofmana" (A Brief Biography of Hoffmann; C4). In two pages of very fine print an outline of Hoffmann's life, mostly in terms of residences and employment, is given. The article opens with the misinformation that he was born in 1778.[38] All works are cited by German titles: *Phantasiestücke, Die Elixiere des Teufels, Serapionsbrüder, Nachtstücke, Kater Murr, Meister Floh.* The latter two are called his best writings.

The general view of Hoffmann in the article is the current Russian one. For example: "Meanwhile Hoffmann continued to carry on his unbridled life which finally plunged him into an unfortunate illness that ended his days." Anecdotes about his death point to

Hitzig as at least an indirect source. This passage is typical of the vague characterization:

> It is not for man to judge this Titan of the poetical world, this new Raphael. It was destined for Hoffmann, it would seem, by his life and his writings to paint in vivid colors all the hellish attraction of the condition in which lives a man who has melted with all his being in the fire of passions and then turned to glass.

Further on, we encounter:

> The fantastic games of his capricious imagination, exceeding all reality, were compared recently by a German writer with the fantastic games of Hegel's capricious intellect. It would seem one cannot make a more apt comparison.

(The writers of *Raduga* in 1832 generally showed great respect for Hegel.)

This *Raduga* article had a limited circulation and would not in any case have been an important critical contribution. Hoffmann's life is not presented in a well-rounded way (his interest in music is hardly alluded to); there is no penetration of his art. The facts are derived from Hitzig, and the generalizations are somewhat clumsy repetitions of what was said about him already in the press. The reference to a German's comparison of Hoffmann with Hegel, however, shows some awareness of contemporary German writings. Moreover, although the content is not new, the *Raduga* article gives every evidence of having been composed in Russian for this magazine and thus has the honor of being the first "original" article on Hoffmann in Russia which has come to our attention. Indeed, together with Gercen's piece of 1836, it is one of only two *Russian* articles on him in the period up to 1845.

In issue 6 for 1832 *Raduga* printed "Russkij perevod povestej Gofmana" (Russian Translation of Hoffmann's Stories):

The stories of Hoffmann have been translated in Revel by Mr. Bzsomkn [ Bessomykin ]. In a short time they will be published. We print here a small passage from the collection of stories called *Serapion Brothers*.

A brief explanation of the friends' first reunion follows, along with two excerpts from Bessomykin's translation, i.e., the anecdotes about German clubs — the club supplied with an excessive number of by-laws and the club of the postmaster and the customsman (T30). It would be interesting to know what considerations held up publication of Bessomykin's complete text until 1836.

Hoffmann is referred to a couple of times in vol. 47 of the *Moskovskij telegraf* for 1832 (September-October). In a review of a French translation of Tieck (*Oeuvres complètes*, Paris, 1832) we find (p. 405):

> In an article included at the beginning of this issue and written by an intelligent contemporary author,[1] the name of Tieck is placed alongside the great names of German literature — Goethe, Schiller, Jean Paul, Herder. That's what the Germans think of Tieck. . . . It seems to us that Tieck not only does not stand beside the other great names of eighteenth-century Germany, but we will not place him even close to Goethe, Jean Paul, Hoffmann, Herder.

Farther on, in a discussion of Balzac's *Contes bruns,* there is this remark (p. 399):

> The point is, if the substance of your creation originally was contained in your soul, and if your fruit is the result of ardor of soul and heart, you can write *what* you please and as *much* as you please. Hoffmann's apparitions, Jean Paul's madness, Hugo's novels shake the soul and amaze the reader's imagination, despite all their eccentricities.

Nadeždin's *Teleskop,* also in September-October, makes this comment in the section "Letopis' otečestvennoj literatury" (č. 11, p. 101):

> Such is not the true and noble meaning of the *philosophical*
> short story *(povest')* as divined in our times. It *[the short story]*
> presents various aspects of life dispassionately — in their profound
> and undistorted truth, and in that way allows one to see their
> whole, genuine sense, their eternal and independent meaning. Such
> are the short stories of the first-class German writers, in which
> life is presented as a solemn justification of higher philosophical
> ideas, as philosophy in images *(v licax)*. Among them, first place
> belongs incontestably to *Hoffmann* and *Tieck*.

These quotations from the *Telegraf* and *Teleskop* show that by 1832 the apotheosis of Hoffmann in Russia had taken place, for he is now listed alongside the greatest German writers. The passage from *Teleskop* is of particular interest, because it suggests — for about the first time — some understanding of the idealist foundation of German writings. At last Hoffmann's stories are not simply capricious but serve the purpose of presenting life "as a solemn justification of higher philosophical ideas." So convinced does the writer seem of this, that he calls the romantics' very subjective approach a *dispassionate* representation of life.

A final publishing event of interest in 1832 was the appearance of vol. 4 of Nikolaj Greč's collection *Rasskazčik, ili Izbrannye povesti inostrannyx avtorov* (The Storyteller, or Selected Stories by Foreign Authors). The very first story in this volume (T31) is Hoffmann's "Signor Formica," reprinted from Greč's *Syn otečestva i Severnyj arxiv* of 1829 (see T8).

9

The year 1833 saw the publication of Russian works bearing the influence of Hoffmann. Nikolaj Polevoj's story "Blaženstvo bezumija" was first printed in the *Telegraf* for January-February and again in vol. 1 of his works *Mečty i žizn'* later in the year. On the first pages of "Blaženstvo bezumija" he discusses Hoffmann, and in particular "Meister Floh" (see Chapter V).

In January the *Moskovskij telegraf*, in a review of Puškin's *Boris Godunov* (č. 49, p. 123), exclaimed over the large number of great German writings in recent times:

> Not to speak of the immortal and eternal names of Goethe, Schiller, Jean Paul, what a multitude of names there is in all branches of literature! Poetry, the novel, history are brightened with the names of the Müllners, Werners, Kerners, Bürgers, Tiedges, Millers, Heerens, Hoffmanns, etc., etc.

In the same volume there is a review of *Russkie povesti i rasskazy* of Bestužev-Marlinskij (pp. 328–36), in which is said, i.a.:

> . . . Under the name of European writers we mean those creators in mature literatures who have brought the art to its highest point. In short stories they are Jean Paul, Hoffmann, Washington Irving, Zschokke, in part Schiller, Goethe and Walter Scott. . . . Indeed, if of the writers we have named, Jean Paul is distinguished for the immensity of his fantasy, Hoffmann for the marvellous expression of the wondrous in the simplest stories, Washington Irving for his poetic humor, Zschokke for his ability to draw charmingly any picture you please, even so not one of them commands such vitality of imagination as paints every object with gay poetic colors and makes it visible to you, tangible, so to speak intimately familiar *(rodnym),* for you yourself could not imagine it otherwise than as the poet represents it to us.

Marlinskij is given great praise indeed:

> And so this is the place of our writer. In his short stories he is
> equal to the best writers of all times and excels all contemporary
> short-story writers and storytellers. . . .

As long as he writes well, the reviewer continues, it is all the same to
Art whether his subject is modern Russia or old Russia. "Neither Walter Scott, nor Hoffmann, nor Goethe was exclusively a patriot in his
novels."

In 1833 and 1834 the newspaper *Odesskij vestnik* (Odessa Herald)
had a weekly literary supplement, *Literaturnye listki* (Literary Leaflets).
About March, 1833, it carried the story "Don Žuan," a translation of
Hoffmann's "Don Juan" done by M. Ivanenko (T32). The Russian
version omits the subtitle and all references to Theodor but is otherwise reliable. Together with the excerpts from *Serapionsbrüder* published in Revel, this Odessa translation seems to be one of only two in this
period not published in Petersburg or Moscow. It is difficult to estimate
its circulation.

In vol. 50 for 1833 the *Moskovskij telegraf* contained an article by
Polevoj on foreign literature in which he seems to borrow from Victor
Hugo the idea that romantic literature requires "truthfulness of portray-
als (*istina izobraženij*)":

> . . . The romantic needs a profound knowledge of man in the
> real world and elevated philosophy and universality in the world
> of fantasy. For this reason romanticism values the national ele-
> ment (*narodnost'*) so highly and forgives all the unevenness in the
> great creations of Hoffmann, Jean Paul, Goethe and Dante. . . .[39]

Also in this volume, April, 1833 (pp. 522–41), the *Telegraf* carried
"Goffman i Paganini, Soč. Julija Žanena" ("Hoffmann et Paganini" by
Jules Janin). It is a fictional story with Hoffmann as hero. A footnote

states: "Readers familiar with the life and works of Hoffmann will see in this fantastic sketch a true portrait of the great German writer. — *Translator.*" The French story proceeds from the contemporary picture of Hoffmann as a hopeless drunkard and dreamer aloof from life, but its particular theme is that Hoffmann's art was highly personal, penned up inside him, that he did not have a feeling for the public and hence no real feeling for the performing arts. A comparison of French [40] and Russian texts shows that the translator made alterations which do not appear to introduce a new viewpoint but rather amplify the notions of the original. Compare this passage with the expanded translation:

> Ce soir-là je me sentis le besoin de te voir, Théodore, ô mon cher artiste, avide poursuivant du rien, sous toutes ses faces, hardi champion de la couleur, du son, de la forme, de toutes les mani-ères d'être un poëte.

> ... V ètot večer ja čuvstvoval potrebnost' uvidet' moego Teodora, milogo, nevidimogo Teodora, mečtatel'nogo, strastnogo, improvi-zatora, žadnogo presledovatelja vsjakogo *ničto* vo vsex ego vidax, smelogo rycarja cvetov, zvuka, formy i vsex sposobov byt' xudož-nikom. ...

In the second paragraph still more epithets are inserted by the Russian adapter: "blagočestivyj i dobryj, moj bednyj drug — poèt i čelovek čuvstvennyj; on garmonist i živopisec."

The translation compounds Hoffmann's alleged sin of creative pride. He is described by Janin as sitting in a tavern and conducting an opera which he alone hears. "Théodore est le vrai créateur de la symphonie invisible." This sentence was expanded in Russian into: "Teodor, moj Teodor umeet sozdat' vsex ètix ljudej; on bog ix i gljadit na nix kak tvorec; èto on, odin on; vo vsex ètix ljudjax slyšite vy ego, tol'ko ego."

In Janin's story Hoffmann becomes jealous on hearing the great violinist Paganini play; the Russian version puts additional words in the German's mouth: "Odnakož, ja sam velikij xudožnik; ja voobražal sebe opery, kotorye izjaščnee Mocartovyx. . . ." Farther on, the Russian story has a lengthy passage not to be found in the original; the theme is that the invisible, internal life of the artist cannot be fully shared with the public and that we are thus deprived of much poetry.

> Ja ponjal takže, ot čego ja stol'ko ljubil Teodora. Teodor — èto samo Iskusstvo, skrytoe, Iskusstvo ne ponimajuščee sebja, Iskusstvo p'janoe, lenivoe, sebjaljubivoe, odnakož Iskusstvo istinnoe, narodnoe, Iskusstvo, kotoroe preziraet svet i sostavljaet slavu kakojnibud' lavki ili sčast'e kabaka.

In the *Telegraf* version the ending of the story is also changed. Hoffmann returns to his imaginary opera stage in the tavern and gets drunk, while absorbed in his inner music. Janin, rather, makes the Paganini performance an awakening for Hoffmann, who blames his friends for having let him live in ignorance and isolated bliss. The original French story ends with Hoffmann's toast to Paganini: "Honneur à Paganini, le miracle! — A la santé d'Hoffmann, le ménétrier!" (Honor to Paganini the miracle; to the health of Hoffmann the fiddler).

Hoffmann is discussed in the *Telegraf* for April in a review of Odoevskij's *Pestrye skazki* (see Chapter VIII).

In 1833 the *Teleskop* printed a biography of Hoffmann (C5) by the Frenchman Xavier Marmier, which appeared originally in *Nouvelle Revue Germanique* in January. [41] The *Teleskop's* translation in the department "Znamenitye sovremenniki" (Famous Contemporaries) bears the simple title "Goffman." It divides the subject's life into three parts:

> . . . His youth, sad and dreamy, filled with artist's thoughts and internal shocks; his maturity, when he, thrown into the world, was to hobnob with society; and his last years, which recalled

with sarcasm and penetrating satire the people among whom he lived and created his fantastic pictures.

According to Teichmann, Marmier had been sent to Germany by the magazine to study literature at firsthand and learn about Hoffmann, but in his biography of the latter he adhered to the general lines of Hitzig's book. Important dates and places are reported, but no further details of external biography are supplied. Rather the article (in its Russian form) is a very flowery and imaginative account of the supposed trials of Hoffmann's innermost heart and soul. Hippel is called his only true friend in his youth, and his letters to Hippel are quoted. Hoffmann is painted as full of fire, passion, fantasy, inspiration, unsatisfied longing. There are many anecdotes and much guesswork. Typical of the lack of specific facts is the statement: "Meanwhile in Poznan, I don't know how, he gets married." The article attributes Hoffmann's inspiration, as usual, to wine. Stories mentioned are: "Kremonskaja skripka" ("Rat Krespel"), "Don Žuan," "Zapustelyj dom" ("Das öde Haus"), "Maioratstvo," "Sal'vator-Roza" ("Signor Formica"), "Bočar Martin" ("Meister Martin der Küfner"), "Devica Skjuderi," "Pesočnyj čelovek." The article ends in the same anecdotal vein. The author apologizes for not publishing a portrait of Hoffmann, to which the *Teleskop* puts a footnote:

> We intend to carry out this wish by attaching to one of the next issues of the *Telescope* a portrait of Hoffmann in order thereby to perform a double service for our readers. – *Publisher.*

The portrait did not appear.

The *Teleskop* carried in vol. 15 (June, 1833; pp. 494–514) the conclusion of a translated article on German literature in the nineteenth century signed with the Latin initials R. G. It says the following about the subject of our study:

> We must leave a special place to E. T. A. Hoffmann, who for a

long time had an extensive influence and found an innumerable
crowd of imitators! However, the supernaturalism and excessive
tension of his works soon cooled the favor he had found, and
the healthy taste of the nation hastened to shun them.

The author quotes Wolfgang Menzel:

> Hoffmann concluded an agreement with the devil, as a matter of
> fact so that he could introduce the devil and himself into po-
> etry. . . . Hoffmann, just as Werner, was a frenzied man with an
> unbalanced soul. All of his poetry reflects this disorder; or better,
> this disorder, this sickness, comprises its one subject. . . . In the
> art of dissonances and startling effects Hoffmann may be compared
> with Mozart.

Even the hostile Menzel has some praise for Hoffmann's artistry! R. G.
calls *Fantasiestücke* his best work, because it was done at a time when
his imagination was "still fresh." In other words, the thesis of this
section is similar to that of Sir Walter Scott's article – that Hoffmann
was a very talented craftsman whose works were vitiated by excessive
fantasy and whose imagination became spent in his last years.

*Moskovskij telegraf*'s vol. 53 for 1833 (September-October) contains
a couple more references to Hoffmann. In an article on Shakespeare's
*Midsummer Night's Dream* the journalist remarks in passing about the
latest fashionable interests of Russian society women (p. 369):

> . . . The new generation of women laugh at Demoustier and Aimé
> Martin, read Byron and Hoffmann, play Mozart and Meierberg
> [Meyerbeer?], and write – *themselves* write – such novels as
> shake the heads of many lightheaded men.

In another review we find (p. 406):

> . . . Here you have into the bargain hundreds – thousands – of

novels, the wish and intention of which is to arouse strong sensations by representing to us villanous acts, by spilling blood and
uncovering disgusting vices. Those are your Balzacs, Janins, Hugos,
Maturins, Hoffmanns and crowds of their imitators in France, Germany and even Russia, where strong sensations and horrors in
novels are limited to cardboard deceptions, debauched women and
evil landowners or judges.

## 10

The year 1834 marked a low in attention to Hoffmann in the Russian
press. Not only was there no new translation, but it is difficult to find
any reference to Hoffmann at all in the periodicals. This may be account-
ed for in part by the closing of the friendly *Moskovskij telegraf.*

The *Teleskop* for December, 1834 (č. 24) carried a biography of Balzac in its series "Znamenitye sovremenniki." It derives from an article by
˙Sainte-Beuve in *Revue des Deux Mondes* for November 15. In a fairly
accurate rendering of the French passage, the article notes, in discussing
the novel *La peau de chagrin* (p. 492):

> Its beginning is very lively, natural and absorbing, but interest soon
> is lost in a chaos of fantastic lunacies and turbulent orgies. The
> author evidently was under the predominant influence of Hoffmann,
> who at that time was appearing in France.

(Balzac's *La peau de chagrin* was first published in August, 1831, and the
French reviewers at that time drew comparisons with Hoffmann. See
Teichmann, p. 75 ff.)

The next year, 1835, gives some evidence of an upturn of interest in
Hoffmann in Russia, although only one translation was produced. In 1835
was born the magazine *Moskovskij nabljudatel'* (Moscow Observer), des-

tined to be Hoffmann's best friend in Russia during the late 1830's, after the demise of the *Moskovskij telegraf.* During the first years Ševyrev had charge of the literary section; in 1838–39 Belinskij became actual, while non-official, editor of the magazine. Hoffmann is mentioned several times in the very first volume of the *Moskovskij nabljudatel'* in a review of Gogol's *Mirgorod,* which we discuss in Chapter VII. Somewhat later in the year we encounter in *Nabljudatel'* an article "Uprek sovremennoj literature" (A Reproach to Contemporary Literature), which is an excerpt from a French review of *Le nouveaulle Candide* by one Labatère(?) The French reviewer complains that contemporary literature shuns reality and retreats into an imaginary realm:

> It builds a world apart, a world of apparitions and fantasy. . . . How good it is, not having divine worship, to have superstitions – to believe a little in the devil when one barely believes in God, and to turn to the Gospels in reading Hoffmann (č. 3, p. 623).

The *Biblioteka dlja čtenija* for 1835, in vol. 9 (March-April; Smes'), had a piece entitled "Slovesnost' v Germanii" (Literature in Germany). It mentions Hoffmann twice:

> That wizzard Hoffmann *(koldun Goffman)* ended in sickness and suffering a dissipated and even dissilute life adorned with flashes of true genius and feeling. . . .

> . . . Apel and Hoffmann have no successors in the supernatural manner, and Tieck himself . . . often stoops to such fantastic trials of the public's patience that, with all respect for his great talent, it is impossible not to see in them a boring childishness. (p. 131)

This turns out to have been a translation from *Blackwood's* magazine of February, 1835 (vol. 38 no. 232, p. 388).

In vol. 27 of the *Teleskop*, 1835, Belinskij mentioned Hoffmann's name during a review of Gogol': "Byron's heroes are proud types with inhuman passions, desires and sufferings; Hoffmann's creations are fantastic dreams. ..."[42]

Another article on German literature appeared in vol. 12 (September-October; pp. 92–118) of the *Biblioteka dlja čtenija* – "Novejšaja izjaščnaja slovesnost' v Germanii" (Recent Literature in Germany). One section reads:

> Among the story-writers we did not mention Hoffmann, because he cannot be lumped together with anyone else in the world; he is unique and decidedly inimitable. Mr. Jules Janin thought he would imitate that wonderful metaphysical imagination, but in his case something entirely different resulted.[43]

The article continues about Hoffmann's fantasy-world. It calls *Fantasiestücke* his best work and finds imitation of Tieck in *Serapionsbrüder*, together with original ideas. The writer concurs in the notion that Hoffmann wrote too much in his last years.

E. T. A. Hoffmann is mentioned a couple of times in 1835 by *Molva* (Rumor), a supplement to Nadeždin's *Teleskop* which was published 1831–36. We find Hoffmann's name in a review of Puškin's stories (see Chapter IV) and a review of Polevoj's books *Abbaddonna* and *Mečty i žizn'* (see Chapter V).

The 1835 Hoffmann translation *Skazka o ščelkune* ("Nußknacker und Mausekönig") was published in an independent edition (T33). In fact it was the first separate edition of Hoffmann in Russian which was not an offprint from a magazine. The translation has small changes but is adequate and even felicitous in some places. It omits the first subtitle ("Der Weihnachtsabend") and changes the names of the children to Russian ones: Fedin'ka and Maša (Fritz and Marie), Nikolin'ka, Andrjuša, Sereža. Frau Mauserinks is called "Gospoža Myšepryga." Missing is the very last sentence of the story: "Das war das Märchen vom Nußknacker und Mausekönig." (This translation was reprinted in 1843 in *Biblioteka dlja vospitanija;* T53.)

Skazka o ščelkune was reviewed in *Biblioteka dlja čtenija* (1835, vol. 10, Literaturnaja letopis', p. 18) as follows:

> Not long ago we read, in some children's book or other, this clever little tale "redone in the Russian manner." Now someone has had pity on poor Hoffmann and returned him his German caftan, which had been ripped off from him. They have translated the tale complete, without distortions, carefully and clearly, and published it in neat form — three qualities which are rare in children's books.

The earlier version was "Kukla g-n Ščelkuška" (T33a), which we have not seen but which, according to data in Žitomirskaja, was a considerable reworking of Hoffmann's "Nußknacker."

Towards the end of 1835 the *Literaturnye pribavlenija,* supplement to *Russkij invalid,* printed a story entitled "Gofmanskij večer" (A Hoffmann Evening) over the name A. Končeozerskij.[44] Written in a rather crude style, it combines impressions of reading Hoffmann with a "Hoffmannesque" incident. The first-person account opens with: "I am bored!" The speaker sits in his study at evening and tries to select a book for reading, but rejects them one after the other. Balzac is too immoral, Paul de Kock too cold!

> But I won't read such books; instead I'll pick Hoffmann — the mad Hoffmann — and in fact he, it seems, is more intelligent than all writers. But unfortunately I don't always understand him! Do you always understand him?

The narrator continues that one cannot read Hoffmann like other authors. One has to prepare for reading Hoffmann; one must inflame the imagination, excite the blood and become for the time a poet.

So our storyteller puts aside Hoffmann and goes out for a walk in the city, hoping to experience "hot, extravagant *(sumasbrodnye)*, poetic, fantastic impressions." For this purpose he says he will go to a *konditerskaja* (confectionery) to read foreign newspapers! But they are dull, and the faces in the shop are uninteresting — until he drinks some wine. Then he notices a strange little old man, who ventures to start a conversation. The *staricok* has travelled very widely. He begins to seem especially odd when he proclaims that the weather is very good (it is in fact a cold winter night). The two keep drinking past closing hour. Suddenly the little old man jumps up and spins on his left foot like a top for several minutes. The narrator asks him in astonishment if this is a pleasant occupation, to which the old man replies that on the contrary it is "samaja d'javol'-skaja rabota" (a devil of a job).

Turned out of the *konditerskaja,* the two awaken another host and persuade him to serve them wine. The old man now undertakes to tell his life story. Born of German parents in Bohemia, he studied in Jena. His dying father gave him money to go south and experience Italian art and music before he began a career. (Here he interrupts himself to insist the wine they are drinking is Johannesberger.) During his dissipated stay in Italy, the old man fell in love with a certain Lauretta, who made him swear eternal love over a dagger, poison and a magic mirror. But tiring of her, he returned to Bohemia, took to drinking and married Gretchen. From the first night with her he started spinning on one foot and is convinced Lauretta's magic mirror is the cause. Abandoning Gretchen also, the strange little man fled to St. Petersburg, hoping to elude the magic mirror, but that strategem failed. He prophesies the end of Petersburg by flood. When he and the narrator pass a pretty girl on the street he thinks it is Lauretta and calls for help. The watch appears and hauls off the old man, who takes him to be a persecuting magician.

Returning home after this incident, the speaker locks himself in his room with candles and volumes of Hoffmann. He exclaims, "What an enchanting genius of a writer he is!" Having read for some time, he stops to ponder the panorama of the German's works and conjures up a series of fantastic characters from them: "the little old man without a shadow, that queer person without a mirror image, the cat Murr, etc., etc." The next day he awakens in his study with volumes of Hoffmann on his lap.

> No, gentlemen, Hoffmann is the first philosopher and poet of the
> world! You don't believe it? Who imitates him? Everyone who
> wants to make some sort of literary fame. Everyone writes like
> Hoffmann – that is, I meant to say, in the manner of Hoffmann
> For any tailor can sew military uniforms, but only my tailor
> Brunet makes them well, excellently, even with originality!

Our writer closes with the advice that readers buy Hoffmann and burn all other books – with the exception of the one containing the present piece.

"Gofmanskij večer" nicely sums up the Russian attitude toward Hoffmann in the first half of the 1830's, for it is at once enthusiastic and superficial. Only the most radically fantastic features seem to have attracted this Končeozerskij, and merely for their novelty. The incident of the little old man who spins like a top is of course hardly more than a paraphrase of "Die Geschichte vom verlornen Spiegelbilde," to which the writer himself refers. Erasmus Spikher also went to Italy and fell in love with a woman who gained power over him through a mirror (the names Giulietta and Lauretta are even similar), and, returning to a German wife, he found that he was trapped by the magic. Spikher set out on travels to find his mirror image, and the old man of the Russian tale wanders in search of salvation. The use of specific streets and places in Petersburg is like Hoffmann's naming of well-known places in Berlin to make the later fantasy closer to the reader. Such familiar motifs as the Johannesberger

are inserted unimaginatively. The device of spinning like a top is a re-
duction to absurdity of the symbolic theme of the loss of one's shadow
or mirror image. Yet despite the irony and the parody something like a
real love for Hoffmann comes through and lends charm to Končeozerskij's slight tale. And he at least represents Hoffmann to be entertaining
and amusing.


## 11


We have seen that the years 1830 to 1833 were a high point in interest
in Hoffmann on the part of the Russian periodical press. The greatest
number of translations for any period came out in 1830—31 in the wake
of French editions and Sir Walter Scott's article, and mentions of Hoffmann and articles about him were numerous in the periodicals through
the year 1833. The next two years testify to a decline of interest. The
novelty of the new writer and the first fever of publishing were past,
and a new peak would be reached only at the end of the decade.

Among the magazines of the early thirties the *Moskovskij telegraf*
proved to be Hoffmann's biggest supporter. Its translations included
excerpts from the more characteristic works "Der goldne Topf" and *Kater Murr.* The German writer came in for great praise on the pages of
Polevoj's journal, although not all the references to him were unquali-
fiedly positive. After the closing of the *Telegraf,* at the end of this
period, the *Moskovskij nabljudatel'* became Hoffmann's champion. Predictably, the conservative periodicals of the Bulgarin-Greč party found
much to criticize in the works and life of Hoffmann. But their attitude
was ambivalent, because they wished to deprecate romanticism and the
fantastic school, and at the same time they realized that Hoffmann had
drawing power among readers. Thus the *Syn otečestva* printed "Die
Brautwahl" in distorted form (with fantasy eliminated) and published

"Der unheimliche Gast," calling it satire. We have noted the strangely parodoxical references to Hoffmann in the *Biblioteka dlja čtenija*. Naděždin's *Teleskop* also looked somewhat askance at the German fantasist. In 1831 it printed the article on Werner which showed Hoffmann in a bad light, and it quoted the anti-romantic critic Wolfgang Menzel. However, Naděždin did publish "Der Sandmann," and by 1832 he was classing its author among the best of the German prose writers. A number of other periodicals quickly got onto the Hoffmann bandwagon.

The quality of translations in 1830–35 was uneven, but despite many defects the majority of Russian versions managed to convey Hoffmann. The selection included a bit of all types of his stories, some recommended by the foreign articles, others, it would seem, chosen haphazardly. French editions undoubtedly had some effect on the selection, and it is remarkable how many translations were made from French intermediaries where that is not indicated. [45] The rush to publish Hoffmann in this period did not involve responsible and complete editions of his longer works in Russian, but we should not forget that much of the educated public also read him in the multivolume French version by Loève-Veimars.

All articles in Russian on Hoffmann from the first half of the 1830's are either translated or derived from foreign material. There was no original criticism of any length or significance. Some of the passing comments by journalists, beginning as early as 1830, put Hoffmann's name alongside those of Goethe, Schiller and Jean Paul, or in close second place to them. No critic seems to doubt his craftsmanship, and that applies even to the skeptics. It should be added, however, that even at the highest moments of the Hoffmann vogue he was not referred to in the press with as much frequency nor with such universal respect as were the biggest foreign literary names: Scott, Goethe, Byron and perhaps even Jean Paul.

A standard image of Hoffmann the man and the writer quickly formed in Russia under the influence of translated articles (especially Scott's)
which derived their view of him largely from Hitzig. Even his Russian
supporters tended to spread the picture of him as a nearly insane drunkard who lived an unhappy life and wrote, under the influence of wine,
eccentric tales in which the supernatural plays an arbitrary and excessive
role. This image nevertheless had a romantic attraction all its own, and
from time to time even his deprecators were enchanted by that *čudak*
Hoffmann.

The Russians, like the French, did not immediately recognize the true
uniqueness of Hoffmann's works. There was a tendency to associate his
fantastic elements with those of the second-rate genre of horror stories
and to connect his young heroes directly with the tradition of sentimentalism. Hence we have seen ghosts occasionally interpolated in translations of his stories and the expressions *mečtatel'* and *mečtatel'nost'*
(dreamer, tendency to dream) inserted in unlikely places.

In Chapter IX we shall examine the new epoch in publishing and
criticism of Hoffmann which got off to a start in 1836 with the appearance of the complete Russian *Serapionsbrüder* and the sensitive article
by Gercen. We must pause now to consider the reception of E. T. A.
Hoffmann in the early 1830's by particular Russian writers: Puškin, Polevoj, Mel'gunov, Gogol' and Odoevskij.

# IV

## Puškin

### 1

I wanted to sit at least near Puškin. I gathered up my courage and took a place by him. To my surprise he began to talk with me in a very kind manner; he must have been in a good mood. Hoffmann's fantastic tales were translated into French at that time in Paris and thanks to that fact had become known in Petersburg. Here Paris played the main role in everything. Puškin talked of nothing but Hoffmann; it isn't for nothing that he wrote "The Queen of Spades" in imitation of Hoffmann but with more refined taste. I knew Hoffmann by heart; why, in Riga in the happy years of our youth we nearly adored him. Our conversation was animated and lasted a long time. . . .

With these words a certain Wilhelm Lenz (Vil'gel'm Lenc) gave us a glimpse of the fascination with E. T. A. Hoffmann which Petersburg experienced in the early 1830's and which touched even the greatest of Russian authors, Aleksandr Sergeevič Puškin. In his memoirs of 1878 Lenz described his first encounter with the famous Russian, which supposedly took place in the fall of 1833 in the home of Prince V. F. Odoevskij. [46] Even if we account for inaccuracies due to the distance in time, Lenz's words probably reflect a general attitude of the period. But what was the actual extent of Puškin's preoccupation with Hoffmann? And what basis is there for Lenz's assertion that "Pikovaja dama" was an imitation of the German?

A number of scholars have commented on Puškin's relationship to Hoffmann, and it was the subject of a special lengthy study by Sergej

Štejn, *Puškin i Gofman,* published in Derpt in 1927. [47] Our discussion will be principally a critical review of his findings. Štejn began with the words: "The question of Hoffmann's influence on Puškin has never yet been the subject of a special investigation." It must be said that his own study does not serve that goal well. It suffers first of all from numerous long digressions which do not bear on the central problem. He dwells at length on Puškin's friendship with Mickiewicz and on the connection between "The Queen of Spades" and Dostoevskij's *Crime and Punishment.* Hoffmann is forgotten for whole pages at a time (a fact which ironically contradicts the statement in the index that Hoffmann's name appears on nearly every page). Štejn states that Puškin was at the center of his focus, and not Hoffmann. He was clearly more interested in Puškin's make-up as a writer vis-à-vis German romanticism as a whole, rather than exclusively in his debt, if any, to Hoffmann. He discusses possible common interests and attitudes of Puškin and Hoffmann even when there is no likelihood at all of this having resulted from Hoffmann's influence, and even when the results are negative. We learn on the one hand the astounding fact that both Hoffmann and Puškin respected Shakespeare and Walter Scott, and on the other that they differed in their attitudes toward painting, music and children. A number of Štejn's comments are interesting for the light they throw on Puškin but do not contribute to an analysis of his relationship to Hoffmann.

When Štejn actually deals with textual evidence of Hoffmann's impact on Puškin, he is often too superficial, tending to omit real evaluations of alleged parallels. In one place (p. 106) he tells us:

> The analysis of minor similarities *(sbliženija)* between Puškin and Hoffmann could lead us too far afield. On the other hand, such a scrupulous resolution of details into their component parts, detracting attention from the principal and substantive matter, can break up into separate threads the "precious brocade of romantic creation." For that reason we shall confine ourselves in the future

to merely pointing out similarities we have found between individual particulars of Puškin's and Hoffmann's works.

What should be the principal matter of such a study if not to make a
test of the supposed parallels, without which any hypothesis of literary
influence must founder? Following the quoted statement, Štejn gives a
list of alleged minor similarities, to which we shall return later.

Aleksandr Puškin's mastery of the German language is known to have
been slight, and so it is doubtful that he read Hoffmann in the original.
Certainly in his case any extensive acquaintance with the German texts
is precluded. There is ample reason to believe, however, that Puškin read
the German writer in French and Russian translations. At his death he
had in his library a number of volumes of the available French versions
of Hoffmann. These included *L'elixir du diable,* a translation by Jean
Cohen published in Paris in 1829 and falsely attributed to the writer
Spindler. Štejn wonders why Hoffmann's *Elixiere des Teufels,* which he
says was well known at the end of the 1820's, should have been credited
to Spindler. As a matter of fact, not only was the book *not* familiar to
the French public from other sources in 1829, but Hoffmann's name was
not generally known until that year. Teichmann indicates that the mediocre author Spindler had had a small vogue in France, and it is likely that
the translator or publisher thought to sell the book more widely by attributing it to a known author. The *Revue de Paris,* in a note in 1833,
expressed that explanation of the fraud. (See Teichmann, pp. 30, 125
and 201.) Puškin also owned the twelve-volume edition of Hoffmann in
Loève-Veimars' translation (Paris, 1829–33), a two-volume collection
*Contes et fantaisies* (Bruxelles, 1834) by the same translator, and Loève-
Veimars' biography of Hoffmann (Paris, 1833). Finally, Puškin had in his
library the volume of the *Teleskop* for 1836 which contained Gercen's
article on Hoffmann, and the condition of Puškin's copy testifies to attentive reading. [48]

An interesting piece of information is the fact that Puškin became
personally acquainted with the French translator François Adolphe
Loève-Veimars (1801 — 1854). We have had occasion to describe the
successful career of the latter, which found him publishing in several of
the major French journals and turning out separate translations of German authors (see Chapter III). His biography is treated in some detail
by Teichmann (pp. 191–98). According to her, about 1833 Loève-Veimars gave up his role as translator. He wrote a series of articles about
French statesmen and in his last years became a diplomat himself. In
1836 he was sent on a mission to Russia, the purpose of which is not
entirely clear. Apparently it was intended that he use his prestige as a
literary figure to win friends for France. In any case, he certainly did
enter some of the leading circles of St. Petersburg and met Russian
writers. It would seem to have been through Prince Vjazemskij that he
became acquainted with Puškin. An interesting result of that acquaint-
anceship was a translation into French of eleven Russian folksongs which
Puškin prepared at Loève-Veimars' request. It is inconceivable that in
their meetings Puškin and Loève-Veimars would not have discussed Hoffmann, the translation of whose works was the principal source of the
Frenchman's fame in Russia. On the other hand, we must not overesti-
mate Loève-Veimars' direct role in calling Puškin's attention to Hoffmann,
for after all their meeting took place only in the last months before Puškin's death.


2


Štejn and others have contended that early evidence of Puškin's knowledge of Hoffmann is the fragment of an unfinished poem which they supposed to date from the early 1820's. However, since Štejn's time the manuscript has been refound and the poem redated to about the autumn of
1833. The text, which contains several alternate readings and is in no

sense final, may be interpreted as follows (see *Literaturnoe nasledstvo*, vol. 58 *[ 1952 ]*, pp. 279–86):

> *[*V golubom*]* nebesnom pole
> Svetit Vesper zolotoj –
> Staryj dož plyvet v gondole
> S dogaressoj molodoj.
> *[* Vozdux poln *]* *[* dyxa<n'ja lavra>*]*,
> . . . . . . . morskaja mgla,
> Dremljut flagi buče<ntavra>,
> *[* Noč' bezmolvna i tepla *]*.

It is generally believed that the poem was to be about Marino Faliero, a fourteenth-century doge of Venice. That much is almost certain, because the venerable Faliero did take a young bride and appears beside her in modern literature. Three literary sources may have suggested the subject to Puškin: Hoffmann's "Doge und Dogaresse," Byron's tragedy *Marino Faliero, Doge of Venice* (1820) and Casimir Delavigne's play *Marino Faliero* (1829). Puškin's acquaintance with Byron and Delavigne is well established. On the other hand, Hoffmann's story had been printed in French and in a Russian translation of 1823 (*Biblioteka dlja čtenija;* T3). Which was Puškin's source of inspiration?

The poem sets a scene which has the doge and his young wife travelling in a gondola at night or at dusk. There is no such scene described in Byron's play nor in Delavigne's. Indeed, in their formulations the relationship between elderly doge and young wife plays a minor part compared with the political plotting. In Hoffmann's "Doge und Dogaresse," on the other hand, there is a very memorable passage which describes the crossing of the doge and his wife on a quiet evening from St. Mark's to the Island of San Giorgio by gondola. The hero of the story, Antonio, is also in the boat, disguised as a gondolier. The triangle of elderly doge, young dogaressa and amorous hero is accompanied in the dialogue by a thematic contrast between youthful love (Antonio and the dogaressa) and duty and fame (the doge). While the doge talks of his symbolic marriage to the sea and recounts the military victories of the Republic, men's voices are heard singing in the distance: "Ah! senza amare / Andare sul mare / Col sposo del' mare / Non può consolare." In the darkness the dogaressa repeats in a whisper, "Senza amare − senza amare − non può consolare," and begins to weep. The girl starts to realize what she has given up in marrying the old doge.

Aside from the general content, some details of Puškin's lines suggest Hoffmann more than Byron or Delavigne. The ceremonial boat of the doge (*bučentavr;* Italian *bucintoro*) is not mentioned in Byron's play at all and is alluded to only once in passing by Delavigne (III:iii). In the latter the doge is made to say, "Compare nos affronts: autour du Bucentaure, / Quand vos cris saluaient mon règne à son aurore, / Je marchais sur des fleurs, je respirais l'encens. . . ." In Hoffmann's "Doge und Dogaresse" the bucintoro is mentioned several times, and it plays an important role in the opening scene, where Antonio saves the doge from the bucintoro during a sudden storm. It is described in this manner:

> Von San Clemens her schwamm der Bucentoro, den adriatischen Löwen in der flatternden Flagge, mit tönendem Ruderschlage daher wie ein kräftig beschwingter goldner Schwan. Umringt von tausend Barken und Gondeln, schien er, sein fürstlich kühnes Haupt erhoben, zu gebieten über ein jubelndes Heer, das mit glänzenden Häuptern aufgetaucht war aus dem tiefen Meeresgrunde.

Such a haughty picture of the ceremonial boat is implied by one of the variants which Puškin wrote down and then rejected: "Bučenavra gordyj flag." It is somewhat puzzling how Puškin envisioned the doge in a mere gondola, with the bucintoro in the same scene. However, in Hoffmann's story the bucintoro is referred to also in the section describing the night passage to San Giorgio. The doge explains to his wife the significance of the ceremony in which he wedded the sea by throwing a ring from the bucintoro. Whether Puškin was thinking of this connection or not, it is clear that the content of the verses "V golubom nebesnom pole" could derive only from Hoffmann — not Byron or Delavigne.

3

In his memoirs A. I. Del'vig described the literary gatherings of the time, mentioning that Mickiewicz used to improvise stories for whole evenings at a time, "mostly fantastic stories in the manner of the German writer Hoffmann" (Štejn, p. 7 ff). He added that A. A. Del'vig and Puškin competed with Mickiewicz in this pastime. A. P. Kern recalled an occasion when Puškin recounted a tale about "a devil who rode in a cab on Vasil'-evskij Island." A collaborator in the *Moskovskij vestnik*, Vladimir Pavlovič Titov, listened to Puškin's story and later wrote it down from memory and published it (with the poet's permission) in the almanac *Severnye cvety* (1828) under the pseudonym "Tit Kosmokratov." [49] Del'vig quotes a letter written by Titov in which he claims that he took the text to Puškin and that the latter made corrections.

Some scholars, including Štejn and Passage, have taken all this to mean that the story "Uedinennyj domik na Vasil'evskom" (A Secluded Little House on Vasil'evskij Island) from *Severnye cvety* is essentially a composition of Puškin's and ought to be reckoned with as such. This is a subject which must, however, be approached cautiously. Puškin cannot have taken very seriously an improvisation for which he evidently had no intention of claiming authorship (it would seem he willingly gave it to Titov). We can hardly depend on it that Titov was able to set down a verbatim text of what Puškin had said, and any person in such a situation would tend to remember and emphasize the features which most attracted him at the time. Furthermore, we dare not attach too much importance to the "corrections" made by Puškin in the written text, for much depends on his attitude. It is possible that once he was ready to relinquish the tale he did not try to reconstruct his version for Titov but only made scattered suggestions for improving what the latter had written down. Nevertheless, it is enlightening that Puškin did improvise something similar to this story.

Or was it completely an improvisation? Štejn notes that there is extant a sketch for a story by Puškin which reads as follows:

Moscow in 1811.
Old woman, two daughters — one innocent, the other romantic . . .
    Two friends visit them.
One debauched, the other V. b.
V. b. loves the younger girl and wants to ruin the young man. He
    gets him money, takes him everywhere . . . Nast. — widow,
    etc.
Night. Cabdriver; young man quarrels with him. Older daughter
    goes mad from love of V. b.

Štejn believes that this program, thought to date from 1822, relates to "Uedinennyj domik," and he deciphers "V. b." as "Varfolomej bes" — i.e., the infernal villain of this tale. The details indeed seem to imply a connection, although the scene of "Uedinennyj domik" is Petersburg, not Moscow, and the old woman in the case has only one daughter. If we accept the relationship of this sketch to the story under consideration, and if the dating of the former to 1822 is correct, we must conclude that Puškin had the essentials of the tale in mind for several years and did not invent the whole thing from air on an evening in 1828.

The hero of "Uedinennyj domik na Vasil'evskom" is the young Pavel, who has fallen into bad company and given himself over to a dissolute life. One of his friends is a certain Varfolomej — a tempter of distinctly supernatural origins, who is leading Pavel to ruin. The hero has a sweet young cousin Vera living with her mother in an isolated house on Vasil'-

evskij Island. At times Pavel thinks he loves the simple and pure girl, but he is constantly distracted by his debauched life. Varfolomej meets Vera and seeks to win her love, thereby angering Pavel. At the same time he introduces the hero to high society, where Pavel falls in love with an enchanting countess. She seems to return the interest and finally agrees to a secret rendezvous, from which, however, the hero is constantly called away by someone knocking at the door. He leaves in pursuit of the mysterious personage and eventually takes a cab which drives him to places he does not even recognize. The cabdriver turns around and reveals himself to be a skeleton! The cab bears the apocalyptic number 666. Pavel is saved by crossing himself.

Vera's mother murdered her husband some years before, and the knowledge of this gives Varfolomej a power over her. When she dies, he causes her ghost to return and instruct Vera to marry him. An appeal to God saves the girl. Varfolomej disappears in smoke and flame, and the house burns to the ground. When all is over, Vera retires to a convent and soon dies there; Pavel settles in the country. Two famous lines from the story are Varfolomej's warning to Pavel ("Potiše, molodoj čelovek; ty ne s *svoim bratom* svjazalsja") and the concluding sentence: "Otkuda u čertej èta oxota vmešivat'sja v ljudskie dela? "

"Uedinennyj domik na Vasil'evskom" clearly owes much to current stories of the supernatural and is testimony of their popularity even in the most sophisticated literary circles. But what, if any, is its debt to Hoffmann? The predicament of Pavel is reminiscent of situations in two of his stories — "Datura fastuosa" and "Abenteuer der Silvester-Nacht."[50] In each case the hero falls in love with a beautiful and worldly woman who is being employed as an instrument of his ruin. In "Datura fastuosa" she is actually called a countess. In that story the villain Fermino Valies, a renegade Spanish monk and agent for the Jesuits, tries to win power over the young Eugenius through his love for Gabriela. In "Abenteuer der Silvester-Nacht" (to be precise, in the chapter "Die Geschichte vom

verlornen Spiegelbilde") Erasmus Spikher is brought to fall in love with
the seductress Giulietta, who proceeds to deprive him of his mirror
image (sometimes identified in folklore with the soul). Behind her activities lurks the mysterious Doctor Dapertutto. Both of the Hoffmann
heroes have proper objects for their affections who become forgotten
by them in their passion for the temptresses — Erasmus Spikher his
"liebe fromme Hausfrau" and Eugenius the pure and loving young girl
Gretchen (compare Pavel's Vera).

To that extent there is a similarity between the German stories and
the Russian tale. One may add that in Hoffmann's plots murders are
used to get a hold over the heroes (in "Silvester-Nacht" the killing is
actually carried out by Erasmus), while in "Uedinennyj domik" a murder committed by the old mother (not the hero) gives the villain power
over her. Furthermore, Pavel is made jealous by a "kosnonogij's" attention
to the countess, in much the same fashion as Erasmus becomes jealous
of the Italian. Also, it may be said that there is some resemblance of
Pavel's ride in the cab to Spikher's ride in a carriage after the killing.
Erasmus suddenly discovers that his companion is the infernal Dapertutto, while Pavel finds that his driver is Death. There is a difference between "Datura fastuosa" and "Die Geschichte vom verlornen Spiegelbilde" in that the former contains no supernatural elements (only the description of the Spaniard's garden comes close to fantasy), while the
latter is fantastic and highly stylized. Dapertutto is an ambiguous agent,
but it is strongly hinted that he belongs to Hoffmann's gallery of
villains from another world. In spirit, Puškin's improvisation comes
closer to "Silvester-Nacht," but its supernatural features are even more
clearly defined than those in Hoffmann.

The parallels we have cited are adequate to demonstrate that the
plot of Puškin's improvisation is in a real sense "Hoffmannesque," but
they are nevertheless too vague to prove conclusively that the central
situation derives from particular scenes in Hoffmann. "Datura fastuosa"

was available in an adequate translation since 1826 (T5), but "Abenteuer
der Silvester-Nacht" had not yet been translated either into Russian or
French. Furthermore, we must not forget Puškin's early "program" for a
story which already indicates the essentials, including the villain. On the
other hand, the countess was apparently added later, and it is precisely
her role which is most Hoffmannesque. It is of course conceivable that
a friend familiar with the German text could have recounted "Silvester-
Nacht" to Puškin.

Equally interesting about "Uedinennyj domik" is its *dissimilarity* to
Hoffmann. The evil forces of the Russian story are essentially traditional
Christian ones. No doubt is left by Titov that Varfolomej is the Devil —
or one of his agents dealing in human souls. He is properly frightened by
prayer and the sign of the cross and eventually disappears in fire and
smoke. The figure of Death in the cab and the apocalyptic number 666
are suggestive of the conventional horror story based on Christian motifs.
Hoffmann rarely went in for such things. There are of course exceptions,
such as the tale of Barbara Roloffin (called by editors "Nachricht aus
dem Leben eines bekannten Mannes"). These conventional elements are
hardly a part of the two stories we have mentioned, although the simple
Gretchen of "Datura fastuosa" fears that Valies is "der Teufel."

Curiously enough, the supernatural elements in "Uedinennyj domik"
are more reminiscent of Pogorel'skij than Hoffmann. We know for a
fact that Puškin read and liked "Lafertovskaja makovnica" (1825), for
he said as much in a famous passage from a letter to his brother (March
27, 1825), and he mentions "Pogorel'skij's mailman" (i.e., Onufrič) in
"Grobovščik." It is distinctly infernal powers which play a role in both
Pogorel'skij's story and Puškin's improvisation. In each case it is their
purpose to ensnare an innocent young girl by inducing her to marry a
creature from the supernatural world (the cat; Varfolomej). In both
stories a deceased female relative comes back as a ghost to insure that
the marriage will take place. (The deaths of the two old women in iso-

lated houses were accompanied by supernatural phenomena.) When the young heroines learn the nature of the fiancés intended for them, they reject them resolutely and turn to God for help. Their firmness of faith saves them, the infernal suitors are banned and disappear, and the old houses associated with the ghosts are destroyed spontaneously.

We of course cannot insist that Puškin had these ideas from Pogorel'-skij, but the parallel is extensive enough to be almost compelling. The least we can say is that in the pair of stories the very elements which are not Hoffmannesque are similar in kind; that is, Puškin and Pogorel'-skij employed the same fantastic vision, into which they incorporated ideas from Hoffmann.

It is impossible to know to what extent Puškin considered "Uedinen-nyj domik" Hoffmannesque. Del'vig's testimony that the Russian improvisers believed they were using Hoffmann's manner may not apply specifically to this tale. One could wish that texts of other improvisations had been written down. Because of limited publishing, knowledge of Hoffmann in Russia in 1828 was far from balanced. If one takes "Uedinennyj domik" as a typical improvisation, it would appear that Puškin and his friends were intrigued by the novelty of fantasy in general and tended to merge Hoffmann with the conventional "chiller."

The view that "Uedinennyj domik na Vasil'evskom" was basically German and in the style of the common horror tale is found in the review of the story by the magazine *Galateja* (č. 1, 1829, pp. 272–73):

> The author, obviously having studied all the German ravings of this type from the last quarter of the past century, thought to bring Satan out on the stage here in Russia too and attract readers with ungainly devilry. Let us say frankly that his endeavor and his invention are of the most unsuccessful.

The reviewer goes on to criticize the story from all aspects.

4

Sergej Štejn and others have maintained that E. T. A. Hoffmann's "Don
Juan" helped determine Puškin's view of that legendary lover as seen in
the drama *Kamennyj gost'*. Veselovskij, for example, had this to say:

> Molière and Mozart inspired the poet *[ Puškin ]* to rework the
> legend about Don Juan; it attracted him many years before the
> composition of *The Stone Guest,* but the idea took its final form
> under the influence of the original interpretation of it *[ the legend ]*
> in the fantastic study by Hoffmann, who explained it in humane
> terms as the tireless and fruitless search for true happiness and
> the ideal woman. [51]

*Kamennyj gost'* was written chiefly in the fall of 1830; its final revision
came in 1836. As a practical matter it was quite possible for Puškin to
be familiar with Hoffmann's "Don Juan" by the time of composition, for
French translations had appeared in the popular *Revue de Paris,* September 13, 1829, and in vol. 8 of Loève-Veimars' edition, released March 18,
1830 (Teichmann, pp. 237–38). The first Russian version appeared in
1833 in a periodical with small circulation (see T32).

The conception of Puškin's Don Juan is indeed reminiscent of Hoffmann's. However, the evidence from the texts is limited and inconclusive;
Štejn fails, despite his efforts, to make a completely convincing case.
Puškin's general interest in Hoffmann and the likelihood that he received
French translations of "Don Juan" in the months immediately preceding
composition of his drama lead one to think that the similarity of interpretations is not accidental, but it is possible that Puškin could have arrived at this conception of Don Juan independently.

Let us examine now the numerous small parallels (*sovpadenija*) which
Štejn thought to find between motifs in Hoffmann and Puškin. He cites
Sakheim's comparison [52] of the novel *Dubrovskij* with Hoffmann's

"Das Majorat," pointing out that Sakheim really presents no evidence of a parallel. Then Štejn adds his own observation: "But doubtlessly there is a certain something in common between these works, for in each is described a persistent struggle of two families for possession of land." Furthermore, he suggests that one also compare Hoffmann's "Die Räuber." None of this can be taken seriously. The comparison with "Das Majorat" is much too general and vague. Even though the similarity with "Die Räuber" is a little more extensive, as a practical matter it would be impossible to distinguish any influence of the German story from that of Schiller's play, which was the source of Hoffmann's idea. Štejn also refers to Sakheim's remark that Mlle de Scudéry's intercession with Louis XIV is like that with Catherine the Great in Puškin's *Kapitanskaja dočka*. He rejects this parallel, not so much for its vagueness as for the fact that a common source for both can be found in a novel by Scott.

In chapter 12 of his book Štejn lists several minor *sovpadenija* of motifs in Puškin and Hoffmann without evaluating them. He states that "some have to be interpreted as accidental, others as Puškin's reminiscences of Hoffmann, and lastly the third group as due to like personages, images and thoughts occupying the minds of both writers." It would seem that his first and third categories are indistinguishable, and in any case he makes no attempt to say which are which. First of all, the list includes some juxtapositions of very specific motifs. The nutcracker from "Nußknacker und Mausekönig" is said to resemble the squirrel in the tale "Car' Saltan." (A comparison shows that, aside from the fact that they both crack nuts, they have nothing in common.) The motif of Tinte's transformation into a fly ("Das fremde Kind") is likened to Gvidon's changes into mosquito, fly and bumblebee ("Car' Saltan"), although there is nothing to indicate that this is more than a pure coincidence. The circumstances in these cases are entirely different. From the verses of Puškin's beginning "V načale žizni školu pomnju ja . . ." (1830)

Štejn extracted the "obraz veličavoj zeny, nad školoju nadzor xranivšej strogo" and associated it with the figure of the abbess from *Die Elixiere des Teufels*. Again here we are forced to say that the parallel is superficial and not sustained by the context. The figure is probably either invented by Puškin or has an autobiographical basis. (We shall see, however, that there are other indications Puškin had read *Die Elixiere des Teufels*.)

In this same list Štejn likens the "monument with a mysterious inscription" in *Dubrovskij* with the strange mausoleum in Hoffmann's "Das steinerne Herz." However, Puškin's monument (which appears in chapter 13) is not described further, and the only additional similarity is the fact that, like Hoffmann's mausoleum, it awakens the curiosity of a woman visitor. Štejn points to a woman in "Kreisleriana" who sings while accompanying herself on a guitar, and he compares her with Dunja in "Evgenij Onegin." Once again, this appears to be an accidental parallel. The list continues with a reference to attacks on a phrenologist named Franz Josef Gall made by both Hoffmann and Puškin (he is mentioned in *Kater Murr*). Since Gall was a well-known figure in the period it is not surprising that two writers could speak of him independently. Štejn's likening of the learned cat Murr to the "kot učenyj" in the prologue to "Ruslan i Ljudmila" — not justified by any other details — must likewise be assigned to the category of the "accidental." A particularly curious comparison suggested by him is that of the old nurse in "Doge und Dogaresse" with the figure of Puškin's own nurse Arina Rodionovna to the extent she is reflected in his writings. We are inclined to think that since she was a historical personage she had no need of Hoffmann to justify her existence. Finally, Štejn juxtaposes two whole scenes in Puškin with ones from Hoffmann. The first pair is the wedding in "Die Automate" and the wedding in "Metel'." Aside from the fact that they both take place in country churches and that the speaker came upon them unexpectedly, there is no similarity. The second two scenes are the "sudden appearance of the beloved girl" in "Fragment aus dem Leben dreier Freunde" and the last meeting of Aleksej and Liza in "Baryšnja-krest'janka." Here too the parallel is very superficial. We may add here that in still another place (pp. 137–38) Štejn compares Tat'-jana's dream ("Evgenij Onegin") with a vision of Medardus *(Die Elixiere des Teufels)*. Both characters see hideous monsters which are composites of different animals. This is not a great enough similarity to raise the parallel above the coincidental.

In summary, none of the minor comparisons suggested by Štejn reveals sufficient evidence to demonstrate a borrowing of particular motifs by Puškin from Hoffmann. It shows a weakness of Štejn's method that he cited them even while evidently realizing that most of them were coincidences. This irresponsible dealing in trivia is the ultimate *reductio ad absurdum* of the comparative approach.

5

The magazine *Teleskop,* in reviewing Puškin's collection of stories *Povesti Belkina* in 1831, remarked of one of the tales, " . . . 'Grobovščik,' in the Hoffmann manner, is very amusing" (č. 6, p. 121). The hero of the story, the simple coffinmaker Adrian Proxorov, made the mistake of inviting dead clients to his house, and they indeed appeared – to his horror; but it all turned out to be a drunken dream. Needless to say, the ghosts come from the conventional horror story, although here they are treated ironically. "Grobovščik" is generally looked upon as a sort of parody by Puškin of his own *Kamennyj gost',* where Don Juan commits the fatal error of inviting the statue of the commander to supper.

It is difficult to point to anything particularly Hoffmannesque in "Grobovščik," though a certain affinity may be felt with those works of Hoffmann's in which the supernatural powers play tricks on little men (especially "Die Brautwahl"). Such intervention of another world in prosaic lives was a characteristic innovation of the German. It may be that the mischievous activity of the spirits against the simple Proxorov led the *Teleskop's* reviewer (and other readers since) to say the tale is in the "Hoffmann manner." Also, we already know that the current superficial view of Hoffmann attributed to him all types of fantastic writing, including traditional ghost stories. Sergej Štejn hardly discusses "Grobovščik" and does not attempt to draw literary comparisons; Passage rejects the possibility of a source in Hoffmann.

The major mature work of Puškin's which we have yet to examine is the novella "Pikovaja dama" (The Queen of Spades). Written in October and November, 1833, it contains probably the highest number of supernatural motifs Puškin ever put in a serious work, and it has often produced the impression of influence by E. T. A. Hoffmann (cf. Veselovskij). Štejn devoted a long segment of his study to "Pikovaja dama," although by no means all of what he says is relevant here. He discusses the story apart from Hoffmann and also has a long excursus on its connection with Dostoevskij's *Prestuplenie i nakazanie.*

The plot of "Pikovaja dama" is well known. Parallels are to be sought in Hoffmann's "Spielerglück" and *Die Elixiere des Teufels,* both of which treat the gambling theme. In the second work it appears only in an episode – the experiences of Medardus at the prince's court. There can be no doubt of the accessibility of both works to Puškin, since he had them in his library in French translations. Russian renditions of "Spielerglück," though unsatisfactory, also appeared in 1823 and 1831 (T2 and T20).

Hoffmann stated in "Spielerglück" that there are two kinds of gamblers: those who are fascinated by the game itself, i.e., by the twistings of chance, and those who gamble merely as a means to riches. This distinction, which is basic to Hoffmann's view of gaming in both works, is ignored by Štejn, who confuses the passion for the game with the pas-

sion for money. "Spielerglück" presents, as it were, three generations of
gamblers, of which two are particularly interesting here – Siegfried and
Menars. The Germann of "Pikovaja dama" is like both of them in certain
traits. Gambling is stylish in Siegfried's environment, as it is in Germann's
Petersburg, but he abstains from lack of interest. People begin to consider the wealthy Siegfried a miser, and he feels forced to gamble in
order to get rid of that reputation. Having once started, he becomes
fascinated by the "magic" of the game. Menars also abstained from playing, but in his case the reason was poverty. He eventually started gambling out of desperation, hoping that his phenomenal luck in other
things would bring him out of his financial difficulties. Both Siegfried
and Menars have great good luck at first; their every card wins.

Puškin's Germann also does not play, although he admits that the game
fascinates him. Limited money is his reason, as it is Menars'. He explains
to his friends that he cannot afford to "sacrifice the necessary in the hope
of obtaining the superfluous." Puškin tells us specifically that the thrifty
Germann has to take special pains not to be thought niggardly by his fel-
lows (compare Siegfried's plight). Both Germann and Menars get the idea
of enriching themselves and insuring their independence overnight, Germann by means of the three magic cards, Menars by the supernatural luck
with which he is endowed. When this possibility first dawns on them they
have almost identical visions of cards and money:

> Nun erst trat der Gedanke, wie wunderbar das Glück ihn [ Me-
> nars ] an der Farobank begünstigt hatte, lebendig vor seine Seele,
> und träumend und wachend sah er Karten, hörte er das eintönige
> – gagne – perd des Bankiers, das Klirren der Goldstücke!

> Germann zatrepetal. Udivitel'nyj anekdot snova predstavilsja ego
> voobraženiju. On stal xodit' okolo doma, dumaja ob ego xozjajke
> i o čudnoj ee sposobnosti. Pozdno vorotilsja on v smirennyj
> svoj ugolok; dolgo ne mog zasnut', i kogda son im ovladel, emu

prigrezilis' karty, zelenyj stol, kipy assignacij i grudy červon-
cev.

Štejn seems to have overlooked these similar passages.

Thinking of his first successful evening of gambling, Menars says to
himself, ". . . Eine einzige Nacht, wie jene, reißt mich aus der Not. . . ."
His original purpose is to make one large and quick win to rescue him
from poverty. This is also Germann's wish, as he reveals to us in another
connection ("vot čto utroit, usemerit moj kapital i dostavit mne pokoj i
nezavisimost'"). At first Menars does win heavily, and Germann has like
success with his first two cards.

Menars and Germann are examples of the second type of gambler, the
one interested only in the money and not in the game for itself, as we are
clearly told by the authors. (Štejn seems to be mistaken in attributing
to Germann a passion for gambling as such.) Finally, the ultimate down-
fall of both heroes − the loss of all their resources − depends on a
queen! The famous climax of "Pikovaja dama" is paralleled in "Spielerglück" by the scene in which the again impoverished Menars bets his
last treasure − his beautiful young wife:

"Es gilt," sprach der Chevalier dem Obristen ins Ohr, als die neue
Taille begann, und schob die Dame auf den Spieltisch. − Im nächsten Abzug hatte die Dame verloren.

A queen also figures earlier in "Spielerglück" in the play in which old
Vertua loses *his* last possessions to Menars: " 'Die Dame,' sprach der
Alte, und in dem nächsten Abzug hatte die Dame verloren!"

A comparison of "Pikovaja dama" with the relevant passages from
*Die Elixiere des Teufels* produces fewer parallels. Štejn argues that
Medardus and Germann are similar heroes, but his reasoning is unconvinc-
ing. He claims a likeness in character, crimes and the women in their lives.
No doubt there is a limited resemblance of character, for both are capa-

ble of dark and profoundly sinful deeds, and both are guilty, as Štejn indicates, of satanic pride. However, their actual crimes are not the same, nor even of the same magnitude; Medardus is the greater sinner. And their women (Aurelie and Liza) are alike only in their purity.

In *Die Elixiere des Teufels* the emphasis is on the first of the two approaches to gambling defined by Hoffmann. The prince operates the games at his court as a diversion and out of interest in the turns of chance. He does not play himself and reimburses his guests for any losses. Medardus is encouraged to play. He draws a card blindly and wins a large amount, just as did Siegfried and Menars in "Spielerglück" (and Germann with his first two cards). The one motif which brings our attention to the gambling in *Die Elixiere des Teufels* consists in the fact that the card with which Medardus wins is a queen, which he furthermore imagines to take on the features of Aurelie. This of course is reminiscent of the queen of spades in "Pikovaja dama," which also influences the outcome of the game and seems to Germann to bear the face of the old countess.

Štejn mentions a minute detail which he takes as outside proof that Puškin had indeed read *Die Elixiere des Teufels*. In the tale "Baryšnjakrest'janka" from *Povesti Belkina* there is a dog with the name Sbogar, just as there is in Hoffmann's novel. However, the name can easily have been suggested by Nodier's novel *Jean Sbogar*. A group of remaining comparisons drawn by Štejn also cannot be accepted. He tells us that in making the hero of "Pikovaja dama" a German by origin Puškin betrayed the prototype. One is inclined to think instead that this choice was dictated by internal considerations. Elsewhere in Štejn's study it is said that Menars' "derangement" may have suggested to Puškin Germann's end in madness. True, both Menars and Vertua come close to being really unbalanced, but their state should not be confused with insanity. It was Puškin who added that logical outcome for his hero. Finally, we cannot give credence to Štejn's juxtaposition of the old baronesses from "Das Majorat" and the ghost of the aunt in "Fragment aus dem Leben dreier Freunde" with the elderly countess of "Pikovaja dama." The similarities are entirely superficial, and Puškin's countess is thought to have had at least one real-life prototype.

In view of the several rather indicative parallels between "Pikovaja dama" and "Spielerglück," and to a lesser degree *Die Elixiere des Teufels,* even a cautious investigator must conclude that Hoffmann contributed part of the inspiration for Puškin's story. Puškin did not make wholesale borrowings of situations and motifs, as a Pogorel'skij might. Rather he quite transformed ideas for his own purposes and created an original and unique work. Even the fantastic elements are largely Puškin's own. Where they differ from Hoffmann they often show a connection with "Uedinennyj domik na Vasil'evskom." "Pikovaja dama" may be said to be a mature and serious development of the style of the earlier improvisation. As in the latter, the supernatural forces of "Pikovaja dama" are those of Hell. Tomskij remarks that Germann has the "soul of Mephistopheles"; we are told by the author that a "mysterious force" seemed to draw Germann back to the countess' house. In his desperation to learn the secret the hero says to the old woman that if a "pact with the Devil" was involved in obtaining it, he is ready to take the sin on his own soul; drawing a pistol, he calls her angrily an "old witch." All of these conventional motifs are reminiscent of "Uedinennyj domik," but the greatest similarity is in the vision of the countess' ghost and its words to Germann. "I have come to you against my will," she says, "but I am ordered to fulfill your request." Like the old mother in "Uedinennyj domik," evidently the countess was forfeit to the Devil for her sins and must obey his command to return in spirit and lure another person into the snare.

The same lines which connect "Pikovaja dama" to the earlier "Uedinennyj domik" also tie it up indirectly with Pogorel'skij's "Lafertovskaja makovnica." The same fantastic vision pervades the three stories, although the only specific motif common to all is the ghost of an old woman. Curiously enough, part of the instructions of the countess' ghost in "Pikovaja dama" also is an order to marry. In this case, Germann himself is the "demonic" bridegroom. It is problematical whether Liza would marry him after having had the glimpse of his tainted spirit. Čajkovskij in his operatic version had her prefer suicide.

6

What can we say in summary about Aleksandr Puškin's relationship to Hoffmann? It is well established that he had access to the German's works and professed interest in them. Some early verses on Marino Faliero tend to indicate that he had read one of the first Russian translations of Hoffmann. From several sources we know that Hoffmann had a vogue in the circles of Petersburg which Puškin frequented, and that a manifestation of it was the improvising of fantastic tales. One of these attributed to Puškin, "Uedinennyj domik na Vasil'evskom," does indeed include a Hoffmannesque situation, but its essential fantastic vision is not typical of Hoffmann, bearing instead a similarity to the supernatural conception of Pogorel'skij. Efforts to find an influence of the German author in Puškin's *Kamennyj gost'* and "Grobovščik" are inconclusive. In the prose masterpiece "Pikovaja dama" there are evident borrowings from Hoffmann stories which also treat the subject of gambling, while once again the vision of the supernatural world is not Hoffmann's but that of "Uedinennyj domik."

If it were not for "Pikovaja dama" one would be inclined to view Puškin's attraction to E. T. A. Hoffmann as a mere passing episode. But "Pikovaja dama" is a fully mature and serious work written in the last years of the poet's life. That not even here do we see, nevertheless, any acceptance of Hoffmann's romantic world-view and typical kind of fantasy demonstrates that the German's influence on Aleksandr Puškin did not extend far into the realm of ideas.

# V

## Nikolaj Polevoj

### 1

During the entire length of its existence, from 1825 to 1834, the *Moskovskij telegraf* was the Russian periodical most friendly to E. T. A. Hoffmann. The publisher, Nikolaj Polevoj, included on its pages translations of Hoffmann's works as early as 1825, and some of the selections over the years came from the German's most typical works, as, for example, the excerpts from "Der goldne Topf" and *Kater Murr*. It was the *Telegraf* which ventured to print stories with some fantastical elements in the period before 1830, when Hoffmann was not yet widely known. These were "Datura fastuosa" and "Die Irrungen." Although none of the articles about E. T. A. Hoffmann appeared in the *Moskovskij telegraf*, we have noted the numerous enthusiastic remarks about him which Polevoj made in his magazine. The note about *Die Serapionsbrüder* (*Telegraf*, March, 1832) was perhaps the most appreciative. To such an extent was Hoffmann identified with the *Telegraf* that the publisher of the *Teleskop*, Nadeždin, linked them in his attack on German "madness" (*Teleskop*, 1831).

The details of Nikolaj Polevoj's publishing and criticism of Hoffmann are contained in our Chapters I and III. But his activities were not limited to journalism; he also engaged in fiction writing, and it is not surprising that we find traces of Hoffmann in his works of this period. Polevoj was attracted by the theme of the artist's sufferings and used it in his "Blaženstvo bezumija" (The Bliss of Madness) and "Živopisec" (The Painter), and to a lesser extent in "Èmma" and *Abbaddonna*. Rodzevič devoted considerable attention to these works in his article of 1917. They have also been discussed by Ignatov, [53] Passage and others.

Among the works of Nikolaj Alekseevič Polevoj (1796 — 1846) were
*Kljatva pri grobe Gospodnem* (An Oath at the Holy Sepulcher; 1832),
*Očerki istorii russkoj literatury* (Essays on the History of Russian Literature; 1839), *Istorija russkogo naroda* (History of the Russian Nation)
and *Byli i nebylicy* (True Stories and Fables; 1843). His story "Blaženstvo bezumija" was first printed in the *Moskovskij telegraf* of 1833
(č. 49, pp. 52–96, 228–72), and "Èmma" appeared there in the following year (nos. 1–4). Both were reprinted in the four-volume collection
*Mečty i žizn': Byli i povesti* (Dreams and Life: True Tales and Stories;
M., 1833–34). He published the novel *Abbaddonna* in Moscow in 1834,
while an epilogue to it was placed in *Syn otečestva* of 1838 [54] and a
second edition appeared in Petersburg, 1840.


2


The very title of the collection *Mečty i žizn'* is symptomatic of Polevoj's
preoccupation with Hoffmann, as is the name of the included story
"Blaženstvo bezumija," which, moreover, opens with these words:

> We were reading the Hoffmann story "Meister Floh." Different
> impressions quickly went through the mind of each of us as
> Hoffmann, that wild child of fantasy, that mad poet *(poèt-bezumec)*
> who himself was afraid of the apparitions he invented, led us from
> the land of the wondrous into the most ordinary world, from the
> world of magic into a German wineshop, joked, laughed at our ex-
> pectations, deceived us constantly and finally disappeared like a
> dream blotted out by a fast sleep toward morning! The reading
> was finished. Conversations and judgments began.

A certain Leonid has sat silently among the friends listening to the
story, and now, asked his opinion of it, he launches into a philosophical
speech which the ladies claim not to understand. He adds that "Meister

Floh" is like a true story ( *byl'*), for something similar happened to a friend of his.

However, Hoffmann's ending is not the same at all. My poor friend did not fly away into the magical kingdom of spirits but remained on earth and paid dearly for the momentary whims of his frenzied imagination.

Leonid is persuaded to tell the story of his friend, and all draw up their chairs to listen. He describes a summer night on which he became the close friend of a certain Antiox. They happened to meet in a poetic nature setting, and Antiox, in a state of romantic exultation, elected to bare his soul to his new friend.

Antiox opened up for me a new world — a fantastic, wonderful, magnificent world — in which my soul was immersed as it enjoyed oblivion similar to that inexpressibly sweet feeling which we experience when we swim in the ocean or gaze from a high cloud-capped mountain at the low-lying expanses stretching at our feet. Antiox's soul was for me this new, magical world; it [ his soul ] populated for me all of Nature with the wonderful creations of dreams; from its contact, it seemed to me, my soul also began to flash with electrical sparks.

Antiox told his companion that man is a "fallen angel of God" who carries the seeds of Paradise in his soul and may plant them in Nature or in God's greatest creations — a woman's heart and a man's mind. Base passions can spoil man's beautiful soul, but there are higher passions, love and friendship, which become it. (Needless to say, the cult of friendship, love and nature here are very reminiscent of Hoffmann; Antiox also links the arts of poetry, music and painting — a synthesis characteristic of the German.) Antiox became an orphan early in life but was taken in by his wealthy grandfather. He went to Göttingen to study but returned after the old man's death and took over the estate.

Not being able to tolerate society, he locked himself in his study to do research in "magnetism, theosophy, psychology" and other subjects which might throw light on "the secrets of Nature and Man." Antiox's motto is very characteristic of the idealist viewpoint: "Nature is a hieroglyph, and everything material is a symbol of the non-material; everything earthly, of the non-earthly; everything non-spiritual, of the spiritual." Furthermore, great secrets may be accessible to a man under magnetism (i.e., hypnotism).

There arrives in Petersburg a charlatan named Ludwig von Schrecken-feld (Ludvig fon Šrekkenfel'd) who starts to hold "mnemo-physico-magical" evenings, involving "amazing machines, incomprehensible automatons, brilliant physical experiments." Leading artists also provide musical entertainment as variety from magical tricks. But most of all the younger visitors are attracted by a girl whom Schreckenfeld calls his daughter. She plays the harp and piano and also sings. Antiox is persuaded to attend one of these evenings and — falls in love with the girl Adel'gejda. He tells Leonid that he feels he knew her somewhere before but he cannot remember where. Antiox keeps returning to see Adel'gejda, and on one of these occasions he is suddenly enlightened. The greatest bliss, he tells Leonid, is death, which brings man back to the land of his *Urleben.* He once knew Adel'gejda in a "wonderful country" — Italy, where she was sitting on a cliff playing her harp! There is an Oriental legend, says Antiox, that the gardens of Paradise were only made invisible and are accessible to some people.

> "In that invisible country there was a being which now wanders in double form on the earth under the names of Antiox and Adel'gejda. Schreckenfeld, the supposed father of half of me, is an evil demon; he has put Adel'gejda in a spell and given her a separate existence."

Antiox is certain that the evil spell can be broken if he says to the girl, "I love you," and she replies the same.

Understandably, Leonid becomes worried about his romantic friend. But Antiox's relations with Schreckenfeld and Adel'gejda become more familiar. When a drunken officer acts improperly toward her at one of the "evenings," Antiox fights a duel with him and is lightly wounded. Returning he is embraced by her, and Schreckenfeld finds them together. He claims that the girl has been disgraced by this incident and Antiox must marry her. However, the hero is shocked. How can he marry his own soul? Adel'gejda reveals to him that Schreckenfeld had plotted the whole thing in order to get the couple married and obtain Antiox's money. She says she is unworthy of him — but finally pleads that they escape into another world.

> "We shall settle where there are no people, no Adel'gejdas, no Antioxs or Schreckenfelds; where you and I are one; where they breathe love, and life is only joy; where there is neither earth nor sky. My Antiox! *Dahin, dahin (tuda, tuda)*!"

Adel'gejda falls into a fever and is dying. Schreckenfeld's background is recounted. Really her father, he thought to marry her to a wealthy Russian noble in order to pay off his debts. Adel'gejda forgives him and dies; Antiox collapses. By day he merely sits at his desk in a trance; moved to an insane asylum, he continues in this condition for exactly a year, and then, writing down the single word "Adel'gejda," he too dies. Leonid closes with the question, "Were not Antiox's madness and Adel'-gejda's death bliss?"

The three characters Antiox, Adel'gejda and Schreckenfeld and their relationships are taken from sections of the longer and more complex "Meister Floh." The hero Antiox incorporates features of both Peregrinus Tyss and George Pepusch. Like Peregrinus, he is a solitary figure and except one big day every year (his name-day) rarely sees his friends. He only goes out to his work and otherwise sits locked up in his study. Leonid says that everyone respected Antiox but few loved him. On the

other hand, Tyss is more childlike than is Antiox, and his solitariness
results rather from shyness than coldness. The Russian's melancholy and
aloofness connect him with George Pepusch, whose attitude toward
other people is described in similar words. Where Polevoj's hero differs
from both of Hoffmann's he resembles the well-known stereotype of the
romantic dreamer.

Rodzevič demonstrated that Adel'gejda corresponds in part of her
physical description to Hoffmann's Röschen (the eventual fiancée of Peregrinus Tyss) and in her manner of bearing herself to the heroine Dörtje
Elverdink. Schreckenfeld plays the same role in "Blaženstvo bezumija"
as does Hoffmann's Leuwenhoek, and the similarity of the "evenings"
they hold is striking. Both Pepusch and Antiox come to the entertainment unwillingly and sit at the side, paying little attention until the girl
appears to perform. Each has the strange feeling that he has known her
somewhere before, and in both cases the couples come slowly to the
realization that they existed together before in some mythological life.
However, the two magical worlds are not the same, for Hoffmann's depends much more on nature than does Polevoj's. And the idea of the
divided soul which seeks reuniting is not from Hoffmann, but, as
Rodzevič convincingly argues, from Plato. Hoffmann's "Meister Floh"
ends happily — with the marriage of Dörtje Elverdink and George Pepusch
in the magical realm, whereas Polevoj's story is a tragedy, because we are
definitely given to believe that, as the title already suggests, the couple's
bliss resulted only from madness, and Antiox's death is not a triumphant
one.

The figure of Schreckenfeld, though parallel to Hoffmann's Leuwenhoek, does not really resemble him in details. He starts out as a demonic
personage and ends up as a very human and pitiful being. Rodzevič suggests that he owes something to Hoffmann's diabolical agents (such as
Coppelius of "Der Sandmann"), and this may well be true, although there
is no model in Hoffmann for the transition which takes place in his role.

Furthermore, he is not successfully drawn, for Polevoj merely tells us that he *seems* diabolical, instead of letting him create that effect himself.

In tone "Blaženstvo bezumija" is quite unlike "Meister Floh"; it is serious throughout, while Hoffmann's story is light and often ironic. Rodzevič found a fundamental difference between them when he pointed out that Polevoj's story makes much less use of the bond with nature. We might add that the "other world" in "Blaženstvo bezumija" owes a debt to the broader romantic tradition and does not derive exclusively from Hoffmann (consider the hints of Goethe's *Wilhelm Meister*). One cannot resist a comparison of Polevoj's tale with Pogorel'skij's "Pagubnye posledstvija neobuzdannogo voobraženija," for the moral is very similar. In fact, at one point Leonid says of Antiox:

> Let his example be a lesson to us not to fly up too high on our wax wings. It is better to slumber on the edge of a pool than to drown – even in the ocean.

The final question, "Were not Antiox's madness and Adel'gejda's death bliss?" contrasts significantly with the closing words of "Der goldne Topf": "Ist denn überhaupt des Anselmus Seligkeit etwas anderes als das Leben in der Poesie, der sich der heilige Einklang aller Wesen als tiefstes Geheimnis der Natur offenbaret?"


3


"Živopisec" (vol. 2 to *Mečty i žizn'*) is also told by a narrator who was a friend of the young hero, much as in "Blaženstvo bezumija" and in Pogorel'skij's "Pagubnye posledstvija." Mamaev, about to leave for Petersburg, is asked by a friend to look up his son Arkadij, who is living in the capital as a painter. (This obligation is once more reminiscent of

Pogorel'skij.) Mamaev begins to conjure up in advance the image of the ideal artist, drawing on romantic writers. But his first impression of Arkadij is disappointing, for he seems to be an average young man.

> Why did I get the idea to look for Byronism or Hoffmannism in Arkadij's appearance? Must the artist and the poet really be distinguished from other people by a half-mad appearance or strangeness of dress? Our time seems to be one lacking strong passions within and sharp differences on the outside.

All the same, on leaving Arkadij Mamaev says, " . . . It seemed to me as though I had started to read Hoffmann's *Tomcat Murr.*" On getting to know Arkadij better, Mamaev grows to respect him, despite the fact that he is not the ideal artist.

> In his dress there was no Byronic refinement and nothing Oriental; he had neither Schiller's long locks nor a Hoffmannesque wildness.

Mamaev tells Arkadij that he ought to devote himself to higher art, but the young hero replies that he is a dreamer to say so! (This is certainly a switch from Pogorel'skij and from Polevoj's own "Blaženstvo bezumija," where the narrator accuses the *hero* of being a dreamer.) Arkadij says that he has torn up all his serious drawings and now devotes himself to painting cheap portraits. (This theme connects the story with Gogol''s "Portret"; see Chapter VII.) Mamaev is something of a woman-hater and guesses that the hero's troubles all stem from a female. Arkadij tells him that he has found his ideal in a certain Verin'ka. It develops, however, that she is a very ordinary girl. In the climax of the story she, despite her affection for Arkadij, marries a rich *činovnik.* The hero is very much hurt by this and goes away to Italy, where he becomes a well-known artist but dies soon afterward.

The plot of "Živopisec" has no extensive parallel in Hoffmann, as that of "Blaženstvo bezumija" does. But Polevoj made use here of the general conception of the artist and his sufferings from "Die Jesuiterkirche," "Artushof" and possibly *Kater Murr* and "Kreisleriana." Rodzevič aptly stated that the borrowing centers around two themes: 1) the artist's uncertainty of himself and 2) his disillusionment in love. The artist's doubt of his own talent is common among Hoffmann's heroes, including Johannes Kreisler. Rodzevič juxtaposed passages from "Živopisec" and "Die Jesuiterkirche" to show that Arkadij and Berthold both are quoted as fearing they were mistaken in choosing painting as a profession.

The love theme is even more reminiscent of Hoffmann. It is of course typical of his heroes – not only artists – to conceive of their ideal as embodied in a woman; and more than once their expectations are disappointed. Berthold marries his ideal but finds he cannot live with her. More to the point is the case of Traugott, protaganist of "Der Artushof," whose beloved is a certain Felizitas. Losing her for a time, he seeks her all through Italy, only to find on returning that she had never left Danzig and had married the *Hof- und Kriminalrat* Mathesius. Traugott's ideal turned out to be a rather ordinary girl after all, as did Arkadij's. Both Hoffmann and Polevoj accompanied their stories with attacks on the philistine environments of the artists, although, as Rodzevič points out, in Polevoj's case criticism of milieu is to be found more in the tone of the piece than in details. The Russian's story omits fantastic episodes (which enhance "Der Artushof") and makes less use of irony. It is characteristic that Polevoj's hero dies broken-hearted in Italy, while Hoffmann's recovers from his disillusionment.

Polevoj's story "Èmma" bears similarities to "Živopisec," but the chief character is a woman, who, moreover, is not an artist. Èmma is endowed, nevertheless, with an extraordinarily sensitive soul akin to that of the artist. Daughter of a poor teacher, she lives nextdoor to the family of Prince S., which includes an insane son. It is accidently dis-

covered that Èmma has a strange power over the boy, a sort of hypnotic
influence. She is invited to live with the family in an effort to help effect his cure. But when he recovers from the insanity, it turns out that
he is a mediocre kind of person. Èmma is alone, with no one to understand her. She dies from consumption, and the young prince is killed in
battle, so that they end up buried next to one another.

It is clear that this is all a development from "Živopisec." Again we
have the sensitive soul in love with an individual who is unworthy. The
tragic ending is already familiar from Polevoj's other stories. If we did
not know the bridge which "Živopisec" forms between this novella and
Hoffmann, we should probably not be inclined to see anything Hoffmannesque about it. Rodzevič saw something of Hoffmann's "ideal woman" in Èmma, and he compared Polevoj's doctor to Peter Schönfeld (Die
Elixiere des Teufels) and pointed to Hoffmann's use of hypnotism. However, these parallels are rather vague, and the story overall is unlike the
German, whose heroines are rarely such active figures. [55]

In the novel Abbaddonna (1834) Nikolaj Polevoj developed further
the conception of the artist and his plight. The hero Wilhelm Reichenbach (the story takes place in Germany) is a poor young writer who
reaches local fame with the staging of one of his plays. He is in love with
the simple Henrietta but slowly becomes involved with the courtesan Eleo-
nora. Traces of Hoffmann in the novel are few and dubious, and the principal model appears to have been Schiller's play Kabale und Liebe, together
with elements taken from George Sand, Goethe, Nodier, Dumas, Klopstock
and others. Kozmin and Rodzevič thought to see prototypes in Hoffmann
for the figures of the two heroines, but the comparisons they offer ("Meister Floh" and "Der Sandmann") are too superficial. A critic of the Literaturnaja gazeta (1841, no. 28) said that the description of the prince's court
is reminiscent of Kater Murr, to which Rodzevič adds Die Elixiere des Teufels as a further parallel. But the similarity seems to be limited to the fact
that the nobleman in each case likes to consider himself a patron of the arts.

It is true that Reichenbach and Medardus *(Die Elixiere des Teufels)* both dislike the miniature copies of ancient art which they see at the courts.

Curiously, Rodzevič does not mention the fact that Hoffmann's name appears more than once in the text of *Abbaddonna.* In part one there is the observation that "Hoffmann's fantasies were created in a dirty wineshop." Later a certain Weiße describes to Wilhelm an almanac he is planning to print with unpublished material by great writers. The contents turn out to be unliterary jottings by famous people, including "a bar tab of Hoffmann's for five bottles of wine"! Polevoj (in Weiße's name) groups Hoffmann, Goethe, Schiller and Jean Paul, in that order, as "imena pregromkie." Jean Paul and Hoffmann are mentioned with admiration also in the last volume of the novel.


4


In summary, at the time of Hoffmann's first discovery in Russia, one of his important admirers was Nikolaj Alekseevič Polevoj, who fostered his cause in the magazine *Moskovskij telegraf* and adopted some of his ideas in original fiction stories. The title of Polevoj's collection *Mečty i žizn'* is very revealing, because it shows Hoffmann's influence and at the same time illustrates Polevoj's tendency to keep fantasy and reality separate. The story "Blaženstvo bezumija" is further proof of this. The plot is almost wholly adapted from Hoffmann's "Meister Floh" (with additional ideas from Plato and perhaps Goethe and the romantic poets), but its mythological world exists only in the minds of the "mad" protaganists, who end tragically. The moral is similar to that of Pogorel'skij's "Pagubnye posledstvija."

In "Živopisec" Polevoj employed the theme of the artist's sufferings which Hoffmann had propagated, although the details of the plot show much more freedom from the German than in the preceding story.

"Èmma" is a variant of this theme, only with a woman the center of interest, and any prototype in Hoffmann can be traced only through the intermediary of "Živopisec." The novel *Abbaddonna* also treats the fate of the artist, but in the more expansive story less emphasis is given to his internal sufferings than to plot complications. If we feel the presence of Hoffmann at all, it is because we are aware that he originally contributed to Polevoj's interest in artists. The other stories of this period, "Rasskazy russkogo soldata" (Tales of a Russian Soldier) and "Mešok s zolotom" (The Bag of Gold) represent a change to new ideas.

While the reading of Hoffmann's works was obviously a deep-felt experience for Nikolaj Polevoj, it is clear that he adopted for his own works a limited number of themes and soon put aside the German as a literary model.

# VI

## Mel'gunov

1

A little-known but fascinating Russian literary figure of the second quarter of the nineteenth century was Nikolaj Aleksandrovič Mel'gunov (1804 – 1867). Journalist, music critic, fictionist and dilettante composer, his life and career spanned key periods in Russian literature, and he was an acquaintance and associate of many of the major figures of his time. A. I. Kirpičnikov wrote the most extensive article on Mel'gunov, [56] characterizing him as a "mediator" who, despite his long years of service to literature, left no name for himself "because he too carefully avoided sharp words and extremes." Mel'gunov was a friend of Belinskij, Granovskij and Gercen and tried to act as an intermediary between Slavophils and Westernizers. In the 1830's he stood in the middle between the worshippers and detractors of Puškin. Somewhat later he was a go-between for the German and Russian cultures. And finally in his declining years he tried to mediate between the conservatives and the radical youth. He seems to have been a typical Russian intellectual nobleman in the 1840's, whose life, Kirpičnikov remarks, forms a valuable commentary to the novels and stories of Turgenev and evidence that Dostoevskij was not far off in his painting of Versilov as a noble *intelligent.*

Mel'gunov was born in the provinces in 1804, son of a well-to-do noble family. He did not attend a university but was enrolled for a time in a Petersburg boarding school. In the capital he formed a long-standing friendship with the composer Glinka, whose esthetic ideals he at times propagandized. From about ages sixteen to nineteen he travelled leisurely in Western Europe, becoming a cosmopolitan gentleman. On returning, he settled near Moscow, passed examinations for government service, be-

came an *aktuarius* and started working in 1825. He belonged thus to the
"archive youth" which produced the idealist-oriented Ljubomudry. He
knew and worked with Venevitinov, Ševyrev, Xomjakov and others. In
1826 Mel'gunov, well acquainted with German, collaborated with Ševyrev and Titov on a translation of Tieck's *On Art and Artists (Herzensergießungen eines kunstliebenden Klosterbruders,* composed with
Wackenroder).

Mel'gunov started publishing fiction works in the early 1830's. The
most successful was undoubtedly the story "Da, ili net?" (Yes or No?)
which helped give him a place in the more progressive group. His conversations with König in Germany during the winter of 1836–37 led to
the latter's book on Russian literature (not allowed in Russian translation until 1862). The strong statements in it against Bulgarin, Greč et
al. spurred a polemical battle with their camp which evidently had as a
result Mel'gunov's partial retirement from the literary world. He married a German girl, travelled much abroad and finally settled down in
Moscow in 1846. In his last years he was beset with financial troubles.
He wrote numerous articles in this final period, mostly on philosophical
matters. His death came in Moscow on February 4, 1867.

There are abundant facts to demonstrate Melgunov's knowledge of
the German language and acquaintance with contemporary German literature. He travelled and lived in Germany for considerable periods at
different times in his life; we have his own published words to show
his high estimation of German literature, and we know that he helped
translate the book by Tieck and Wackenroder. Unfortunately, we have
no express testimony to his acquaintance with the works of E.T.A. Hoffmann, but it would be inconceivable that he be wholly unacquainted
with them. It is believed that most of Mel'gunov's papers have perished,
although a few of his unpublished letters are extant.

2

Mel'gunov's two major attempts at belles-lettres were the collections
*Rasskazy o bylom i nebyvalom* (1834) [57] and "Putevye očerki"
(1836).[58] One of the stories from the first collection, "Kto že on?"
was first printed in the *Teleskop* in 1831, [59] and a chapter from another, "Da, ili net?" appeared in advance in the *Teleskop* of 1834. [60]
All are marked to show they were written before 1834.

*Rasskazy o bylom i nebyvalom* (Stories of the True and the Imaginary)
has a very interesting preface containing a sort of literary credo. The
author starts out with the conventional statement that the stories in the
collection were not written for print; that friends persuaded him to publish them. Then he suddenly proclaims that this is not true; on the
contrary, he worked hard on the stories and hopes to build a reputation
with them. Finally, he says that neither extreme is true.

> Moderation is needed in everything – in modesty as in frankness.
> . . . And in art as well. Neither naked truth nor naked invention.
> Truth is bashful and wears a veil; but that veil should not conceal,
> but merely screen her severe forms. The task of art is to fuse fan-
> tasy with real life.
>
> Happy is an author, if in his stories people listen with delight
> to actual happenings as to a fable and believe the imaginary as a
> true story.

The credo "The task of art is to fuse fantasy with real life" (Zadača
iskusstva – slit' fantaziju s dejstvitel'noj žizn'ju) tends to put Mel'gunov
in the camp of the German fantasists such as Tieck and Hoffmann, the
latter especially being the master of the blending of fantasy and reality.
We shall see, however, whether Mel'gunov, with his constant desire for
moderation, actually practiced what he preached in his preface.

The book is divided into two parts, of which the first contains "Zimnij

večer" (1830), "Kto že on?" (1831), "Proročeskij son" (1833) and
"Ljubov'-vospitatel'" (1833). Part two is composed of the longer story
"Da, ili net?" In "Zimnij večer" (A Winter Evening) an old man tells
a story to a gathering on a Russian estate. A certain count who loved
his cousin Vera in youth returns from the army to find her cold and
worldly. She marries an important person, and the count weds a beautiful woman he does not love. His wife dies not long after from consumption, warning him not to be unfaithful, or else "I will have revenge even after death." He later meets the widowed Vera, and they
decide to marry. However, she becomes strangely ill, evidently dies,
and is buried. The count awakens from a dream shouting, "She is not
dead!" On opening her grave they find the body in a horribly contort-
ed position which indicates she was buried alive and later awoke only
to suffocate. There is nothing particularly original in all this; the plot
fits into the conventional pattern of horror stories. However, it is interesting that Mel'gunov did not leave the story in this form but added
an epilogue. After hearing the old man's tale, the company discusses
the subject of being buried alive. Another old man offers to tell the
story in a different way and explains that a certain monk who tried to
cure Vera from her illness with healing prayers was actually a disappointed suitor, who, his latest attempts to win her having failed, afterwards spread the vicious rumor that she had been buried alive. A rec-
ognition scene follows when the second old man reveals himself to be
the count of the story and his old wife to be Vera.

Of the greatest interest to us in the literary production of N. A.
Mel'gunov is his story "Kto že on?" (But Who Is He?) which was first
published in 1831 and included in *Rasskazy o bylom i nebyvalom*. It
bears an English epigraph taken from *Hamlet:* "Is not this something
more than fantasy? What think you of it?" and a dedication to X – v
(spelled out in 1834 as A. S. Xomjakov). It is necessary to recount the
plot in some detail. The speaker in the first-person account says that

his best friend died nearly a year ago, but he imagined that he saw the deceased once in a bank and again in a theater. A strange man wearing violet-tinted glasses looks like the dead friend when he removes the glasses. Glafira Lindina was secretly in love with the dead friend and is still sad over his death. She swore never to marry anyone else. Her father meanwhile, unaware of her sorrow, is preparing to put on an amateur performance of Griboedov's play *Gore ot uma* (Woe from Wit) in his home. Lindin will play Famusov.

The narrator and the Lindin family attend an auction of the belongings of a deceased nobleman, Count X. One item offered for sale is a ring bearing a likeness similar to that of the deceased fiancé of Glafira. She wants to have it, but a stranger buys it at a high price. An old friend of Lindin's now appears to play the role of Čackij in the play. He is introduced as Vašiadan, and the speaker recognizes him as the stranger in violet glasses he had seen at the theater. Lindin cannot seem to memorize Famusov's lines, and Vašiadan ends up playing both Čackij and Famusov during the rehearsal. Later, at the dress rehearsal, Vašiadan suddenly removes his glasses at a crucial moment, and Glafira, acting the role of Sofija, faints. On the following day Vašiadan arrives again at Lindin's house, puts all in a spell by removing his glasses and abducts Glafira. She is missing without a trace nearly a full year. Then one day the narrator is strolling in the woods far from Moscow and *happens* upon Glafira. She tells him how she had been brought to the fantastic castle of Vašiadan, how he finally convinced her that he really was her dead lover and how she lived with him for a year. At the end of that time demons came and carried off Vašiadan, and she escaped. Hearing from the speaker that her bereaved parents have passed away, she announces that she will do likewise and promptly proceeds to keep her word. She was abducted, says the narrator, exactly one year from her fiancé's death at the exact same hour, and she died at that hour two years from his death.

To this unlikely tale Mel'gunov added a "P. S. for the Few" in which
he puts the question as to the identity of Vašiadan and also asks, "Do
you believe in the *evil eye*, or, in other words, do you believe in the
magnetic power of gazes?" After toying with these matters for a short
space he ends by telling the reader, "Guess for yourself!" The story is
quite unsatisfactory. The "magnetic" device is too crude, as is the ending of the story, which reads like a parody. Mel'gunov lumped together
too many elements without integrating them. For example, the ring sold
at auction, hinted to be magic, is virtually forgotten and serves no further function in the tale. There are quite extraneous passages, and in
particular a moralizing section about the Count X. whose possessions
were auctioned off. It is an attack on men of his sort who are said to
waste their time and money buying forged art objects in Italy. As some
literary historian has remarked, Russian writers in this period could not
resist temptations to criticize aspects of contemporary society. In short,
"Kto že on?" is a hodge-podge. Kirpičnikov was certainly right in com-
menting that Mel'gunov did not successfully blend fantasy and truth in
this tale.

There can be no doubt that the story owes much to the German fantastic tradition. Tieck, so well known by Mel'gunov, is suggested by
Vašiadan's castle (cf. "Das Zauberschloß"). But the central situation may
be traced to E. T. A. Hoffmann. Vašiadan is like a whole line of satanic
villains in Hoffmann, especially those who employ hypnotism. The se-
duction of a girl by "animal magnetism" is the subject of "Der Magnetiseur" and "Der unheimliche Gast," both of which we discussed in connection with Pogorel'skij (see Chapter II). And there is a direct parallel
here with the latter story, for Vašiadan appears on the scene as an old
friend of the father, just as Count S. makes his entrance as a friend of
Angelika's father. Her true love, Moritz, is not dead as is Glafira's, but
part of the count's plot is to convince her that Moritz has actually died
in battle. He uses "animal magnetism," as does Vašiadan, and it is his

gaze which exercises the fatal influence. Key coincidences of time play
a role in "Der unheimliche Gast" (and elsewhere in Hoffmann), as they
do in "Kto že on?" Also, the violet glasses remind one of the various
"optical" objects common in Hoffmann (e.g., in "Der Sandmann"). It
is interesting that "Der unheimliche Gast" and "Der Sandmann" were
both recommended in articles appearing in Russian magazines in
1829–31 and were both translated into Russian in 1830 and 1831, the
very time when Mel'gunov was evidently working on his story. The device of making Glafira believe the villain is her actual fiancé is also not
without parallel in Hoffmann. In "Klein Zaches" the girl Candida is simi-
larly deceived:

> Nun erzählte sie, alles, alles um sich her vergessend, wie ein böser
> abscheulicher Traum sie verstrickt, wie es ihr vorgekommen als
> habe sich ein häßlicher Unhold an ihr Herz gelegt, dem sie ihre
> Liebe schenken müssen, weil sie nicht anders gekonnt. Der Unhold
> habe sich zu verstellen gewußt, daß er ausgesehen habe wie Bal-
> thasar; und wenn sie recht lebhaft an Balthasar gedacht, habe sie
> zwar gewußt, daß der Unhold nicht Balthasar, aber dann sei es ihr
> wieder auf unbegreifliche Weise gewesen, als müsse sie den Unhold
> lieben, eben um Balthasars willen.

Thus the facts strongly suggest that "Kto že on?" resulted partly from
Mel'gunov's reading of Hoffmann. This argument will gain added per-
suasiveness as we see that he elsewhere made use of other motifs from
the same "Unheimlicher Gast."

The third story of *Rasskazy o bylom i nebyvalom,* "Proročeskij son"
(A Prophetic Dream), is a harmless tale. The heroine had a dream that
she would die before a certain date. She actually takes to bed with a
strange sickness and is sinking fast. But in a surprise ending she recovers
and does not die at all. "The prophetic dream was not fulfilled." Here
Mel'gunov is making fun of literary conventions. "Ljubov'-vospitatel'"

(Love Is a Teacher), written in a more expansive style, is a study in the psychology of love. The story "Da, ili net?" relates a sensational trial in Paris. Neither applies to the particular literary tradition we are tracing.

*Rasskazy o bylom i nebyvalom* clearly did not fulfill Mel'gunov's high goal of fusing fantasy and reality. A reviewer in the *Moskovskij telegraf* (1834, č. 56, pp. 149—51) took issue with this very definition of the purpose of art. "We are not entirely in agreement with this. The task of art is creativeness, and for that it is all the same where the subject is taken from. . . ." He praised Mel'gunov as an "educated" author but added that something was missing in his works, namely that very creativeness which is necessary to art. One does not care to read Mel'gunov a second time, he concluded. The reviewer in *Molva* (10, no. 12, pp. 182—85 and 221—22) had good words for "Da, ili net?" but wished Mel'gunov had avoided the mystification of "Kto že on?" and stuck to simple stories. A letter in *Molva,* signed by "F.," defended the book and singled out memorable scenes, especially from "Da, ili net?" In *Biblioteka dlja čtenija* (vol. 3, otd. 6, pp. 5—6) Baron Brambeus (Senkovskij) in a forcedly witty review proclaimed Mel'gunov's stories the first enjoyable ones in Russian he had seen in a long time. He called the author "un joli conteur."

3

Mel'gunov was busy in the early thirties with other writing, some of which got published only much later. In 1844 the magazine *Moskvitjanin* (The Muscovite) printed his "Živaja i mertvaja voda" (The Waters of Life and Death), a love story set in a German *Kurort* and actually dated 1835; also a fragment of a historical novel "T'ma i svet" (Darkness and Light) dated 1833. [61] In 1845 *Moskvitjanin* published "Svidetel'" (The Witness), the opening of an unfinished novel on Russian provincial life dated 1834. [62]

These *Moskvitjanin* works appeared at a time when Mel'gunov's recent battle with Greč and company led him to use the pseudonym "N. Livenskij." He continued to be interested in music, as witness articles such as "Muzykal'naja letopis'" (Music Chronicle) in the *Moskovskij nabljudatel'* (1835, č. 1, pp. 144–69), which he helped to found.

Then came the "Putevye očerki" (Travel Sketches) in the *Nabljudatel'*, 1836. The piece is signed "N. Mel'gunov, Berlin, June, 1836." Kirpičnikov suggests that the form of the frame story is taken from Hoffmann's *Serapionsbrüder*, but that is unprovable. In Mel'gunov the passengers of a becalmed ship pass the time in conversation, and a lady suggests that the men each tell an interesting episode from their lives. This is a chance group who recount stories with no regard for esthetic theories, bonds of friendship, etc. Neither are the stories read from manuscript, as in Hoffmann.

The first man relates how he was once captured and was about to be put to death by Tunisian pirates, but that turns out to have been only a nightmare. The second story is one of faithful love. Only the third and last tale is of interest. The narrative begins with an old man found dead in a house near Petersburg. To explain this, a time-shift is made. The speaker was once friends with a certain Frenchman in Paris. Later, avenging his own seduced fiancée, he finds at the duel that the villain was his old friend. He leaves the Frenchman for dead after the duel. Years afterward in Naples he imagines that he sees his fiancée and the Frenchman in a window. Moreover, in the room with them is a young man who turns out to be the narrator's *double* (the word *dvojnik* is used three times). He wants to help the double and the girl in the struggle which he witnesses, and he jumps into the window, only to be captured by armed men and abandoned outside Naples. The narrator continues, "Just imagine that the old man who died near Petersburg was none other than . . . ," when shore is sighted and the storytelling comes to an end.

Thus the rather clumsy tale remains without an explanation. The first
part has a parallel once more in "Der unheimliche Gast" of Hoffmann.
There Bogislav relates that a number of years ago in *Naples* Count S. robbed
him of his true love. He stabbed the count, but not fatally, and the latter
recovered enough to pursue the girl again. The window scene in the second
part of the story is also very Hoffmannesque. Consider, for example, the
moment in "Meister Floh" when George Pepusch suddenly espies his lost
love and a mysterious man in a window (cf. Gogol' 's imitation of this
scene, Chapter VII). And the presence of doubles at the rescue of a
heroine is described in "Die Doppeltgänger." There Deodatus Schwendy,
who has just caught sight of his double George Haberland, is prevented
by armed violence from following (namely, he is wounded by a shot).
It is true that in "Die Doppeltgänger" he is not inclined to help the
double, but the similarity is clear nonetheless.

One of the *Moskvitjanin* pieces of 1844 (no. 3, pp. 45–69) was "Siste-
matik," a charming story about a vegetarian, dated 1836. In 1839 Mel'-
gunov printed articles on the Germans Schelling and Alexander von Hum-
boldt in *Otečestvennye zapiski* (nos. 3 and 6). And the *Literaturnye
pribavlenija* of 1839 carried a series of short pieces by him entitled col-
lectively "Žurnal'nye vyderžki" (Journal Extracts). [63] In one of them
he quotes from a German article and then gives his own high evaluation
of contemporary German literature:

> The inadequacies — the dark side of German literature — be-
> long to the times; they are repeated more or less in all liter-
> atures, and consequently in ours; but merits belong to it
> [ German literature ] alone, and God grant that Russian liter-
> ature might count in an entire decade as many substantial,
> learned and profound works as come out in Germany in the
> course of a single year! . . . Our writers are unoriginal even
> in their inadequacies, so that their ideas are often like little wood-
> cuts ordered from abroad; whatever ones are sent people are

satisfied with. And why? Because we do not have our own artists.

The last comments might serve as criticism of Mel'gunov's own attempts at fiction.

His last work of real interest to us was published in *Odesskij al'manax* (Odessa Almanac) for 1840 (pp. 204—37) under the title "Žizn' est' son" (Life Is a Dream). It opens with a lively description of a resort near Moscow. Mel'gunov was at his best in just such a subject, which allows him to exercise considerable charm and wit, the mark of a cultured conversationalist. His portrayal of the society at the mineral springs contains some fine irony. The narrator says that he often noticed a certain sick girl at the resort and became curious about her. Much later, after her death, he had access to letters and a diary which revealed her story. The heroine tells in the letters that she had been upset by a series of dreams. She dreamed that she met *him* — her ideal — at a dance. He went away to war and was wounded. Meanwhile, the girl's parents tried to marry her off to an unattractive suitor, but she went to serve as a nurse and cared for *him.* The wicked suitor cast a spell over her and showed her a vision of *him* marrying another girl. This naturally called forth her jealousy. The girl, who, according to her doctor, had been psychologically ill, now became physically sick because of the dreams and, despite the Moscow waters, died.

The story is quite readable and surely the most successful of those in which Mel'gunov attempted to blend fantasy and reality. It is well motivated throughout; the dreams are very well constructed, that is, scenes and images shift much as in actual dreams. In a sense, of course, there is no real fantasy, because the unreal elements are all rationalized as parts of the heroine's dreams. Life is a dream only for the girl, not for the reader. Kirpičnikov belittles this story, but unjustly. By keeping the text short and simple Mel'gunov was able to maintain control and integrate

the whole. The very title "Life Is a Dream," even if derived from Cal-
derón, points to a connection with the German fantastic conception.
Hoffmann would approve of a theme in which the heroine's dreams
become more real to her than life and finally destroy her. There is no
complete parallel in his works, but we are reminded still again of "Der
unheimliche Gast," in which the hero Moritz goes away to war leaving
his sweetheart Angelika to an unloved suitor forced on her by her
parents. This suitor has her in a spell, as does the suitor of "Žizn' est'
son," and he tries to win her by convincing her that Moritz has died
in the war. Angelika also becomes seriously ill.


                                    4


These, then, are the relevant works of a man Kirpičnikov called interesting not so much for what he accomplished as for what he undertook
to accomplish. N. A. Mel'gunov's literary production has very little
inherent value, but it is interesting as a symptom of some of the forces
working on Russian prose writers of his generation. That one of the
influences on him was E. T. A. Hoffmann, as P. N. Sakulin suggested,[64]
is evident from borrowings to be found in certain of Mel'gunov's works.
One story by Hoffmann, "Der unheimliche Gast," was a particular source
of motifs for him. Needless to say, Hoffmann's influence penetrated
very little below the surface.

# VII

## Gogol'

### 1

In the 1830's the vogue of E. T. A. Hoffmann in Russia touched two major writers — Aleksandr Puškin and Nikolaj Gogol'. We have noted that Puškin was affected only slightly. The case of Gogol' is somewhat different. It has been given attention by a series of distinguished scholars, and we are fortunate to have a responsible study which embodies the best of their results, M. Gorlin's book *N. V. Gogol und E. Th. A. Hoffmann.* [65] It is both concise and thorough, and Gorlin impresses the reader with the soundness of most of his judgments. We shall not attempt to reproduce all the details which can be found in his work but to present the main information and add further observations.

In earlier chapters we have already recognized as a fact that well-read Russians in the 1830's could hardly fail to know at least part of Hoffmann's works. Although his knowledge of German was shallow, Gogol' read French fluently, and the translations of Loève-Veimars were without doubt available to him. He was living in Petersburg during most of this decade and frequented the literary circles in which we know Hoffmann was a fashionable topic of discussion. The German is specifically referred to in the story "Nevskij prospekt" (completed 1834) and in a letter written by Gogol' to Balabina, November 7, 1838 (as quoted by Gorlin):

> Of course I cannot deny that there are moments when one would like to fly on the fantastic cape of a German student out of an environment of tobacco smoke and German cooking to the moon, as I believe you put it. But I doubt very much whether this

Germany is now the way we imagine it. Perhaps it appears so
to us only in Hoffmann's tales?

Some writers have thought to see an influence of E. T. A. Hoffmann
in Gogol' 's works as early as the *Večera na xutore bliz Dikan'ki* (Evenings on a Farm Near Dikan'ka). Fantasy plays a very large role there,
yet, as Gorlin contends, it is not Hoffmann's brand. And Gogol' 's romantic Ukrainian tales contain two things which are alien to Hoffmann
– the folk quality *(Volkstümlichkeit)* and religiosity. They share with
the German's manner the polarization of a concrete world with a supernatural one, but their types of the supernatural are quite different. Attempts at tracing individual motifs to Hoffmann also remain unconvincing. The villain of "Strašnaja mest' " (A Terrible Vengeance) has been
compared to Ignaz Denner, but Gorlin shows that the parallel is superficial and superseded by another source. Whereas it is not doubted that
*Večera* depended to a degree on the German school (reflections of Tieck
evidently may be demonstrated), it cannot be proved that the book
traces in spirit or in any details to E. T. A. Hoffmann.

Gorlin makes much of a certain fragment which Gogol' seems to
have written in 1832 or 1833 as a sketch for a story. Some editors
separate the brief fragment "Strašnaja ruka" (The Terrible Hand), which
title Gorlin cites, from the longer piece beginning "Fonar' umiral . . ."
(The lamp was dying out). The former seems to be a variant of the
opening of the latter, and both appear to be early studies for the story
"Nevskij prospekt." In "Fonar' umiral" a young student, full of romantic longing, is wandering about the streets of Vasil'evskij Island at night,
when suddenly he spies a very brightly lighted window. Looking in, he
is fairly blinded by the sight of a most beautiful woman standing in the
middle of the room. Gradually he also becomes aware of a man beside
her – a grotesque figure dressed in black. Gorlin is quick to observe
that this entire scene is very Hoffmannesque. We have a young hero
possessed by vague longing *(Sehnsucht),* a deserted street, the vision of

a beautiful woman who at once inspires love and, finally, a mysterious male figure associated with her. Not only is the atmosphere Hoffmann-esque, but there is in fact a complete parallel in "Meister Floh," where George Pepusch runs through the streets at night and suddenly catches sight of a brilliantly lighted window. When he looks in, he sees his beloved Dörtje Elverdink, who has been missing. Near her is a strange-looking man. There can be little doubt that Hoffmann was the model for this sketch. We shall see, however, how the material eventually became transformed in "Nevskij prospekt." The fragment itself was first published after the author's death.

## 2

Ševyrev was probably the first to say that Gogol''s *Arabeski,* in contrast to *Večera na xutore bliz Dikan'ki,* represented a greater concession to the Germans. Of the earlier collection he wrote:

> Mr. Gogol' dissuaded me from the idea that humor is the exclusive possession of the English and Germans, of Jean Paul and Hoffmann. He imparted humor to our short story, taking it, as it seems, from Ukrainian tales. . . . It is a humor without that British peevishness which so sharply distinguishes Fielding, and without the German pedantry which is so striking in Jean Paul and Hoffmann.

Then he sees a change in the new collection:

> But one cannot but notice that in the new stories we read in *Arabesques* that Ukrainian humor did not stand its ground against Western temptations and in its fantastic creations surrendered to the influence of Hoffmann and Tieck — and to me this is a pity. [66]

Ševyrev perhaps overestimated the originality of *Večera*, but he was correct that the German influence was augmented in *Arabeski* (1835), which included among its stories "Portret," "Nevskij prospekt" and "Zapiski sumasšedšego."

It should not be necessary to more than outline the plot of the well-known "Portret" (The Portrait). The artist Čertkov acquires a mysterious portrait of a man, whose terrible life-like eyes have a great effect on him. He imagines the portrait to come alive, and under its strange influence he gives up his serious art and his studies, to become a bad but fashionable portrait painter. Realizing his mistake too late in life, he goes mad and dies. The second part of the story reveals how the portrait came to be painted. A young artist did a likeness of the hateful usurer Petromixali, whose satanic spirit became preserved in the portrait after death. The painter was plagued with unhappiness for his inadvertent sin and retired to a monastery.

It has been shown that the motif of the evil portrait itself derives from an English source (Maturin) and that the physical description of Petromixali was suggested by a real person in Petersburg (see Gorlin). However, the overall theme and the atmosphere of the story are distinctly Hoffmannesque. Belinskij noticed this, and remarked in *Molva*, ". . . Mr. Gogol' got the idea to write a fantastic story *à la* Hoffmann ("The Portrait"), and this story is absolutely worthless *(rešitel'no nikuda ne goditsja)*." [67] As is well known, the original "Portret" of 1835 underwent a considerable revision by Gogol' for republishing in 1842. In the process, the supernatural was reduced in importance, and thereby the Hoffmannesque details to a large extent were eliminated. The portrait no longer appeared mysteriously in Čertkosv's apartment but was brought there by him; its coming to life at night was more clearly a dream of Čertkov's; Petromixali was not explicitly satanic; etc.

The figure of the usurer, especially in the earlier version, cannot fail to remind one of the evil old men in several of Hoffmann's works. Gorlin refers, on the other hand, to Petromixali's "static" quality in contrast to the dynamism of Hoffmann's figures, and he believes that this feature derives from Odoevskij's villain Segeliel' of the story "Improvizator" (see Chapter VIII). If that is true, then Petromixali has only a vague and indirect connection with Hoffmann. But it seems to us that we have too little proof of a tie-up with Odoevskij and it is possible to view both Segeliel' and Petromixali as variations of the Mephistopheles theme which was frequent in current popular literature. This is clearer in the case of Gogol''s usurer, who exacts some terrible secret price for the loans he makes to desperate people.

We wish to emphasize more than Gorlin does the parallel between "Portret" and Hoffmann's *Die Elixiere des Teufels.* The latter is a full novel, and hence a more complex work than Gogol''s story, but it bears a similarity to it in tone, general construction and a number of details. The core of the first half of "Portret" is the penetration of a diabolical agent into the life of the painter and his abandonment of serious art. The first Francesko of Hoffmann's book ("Das Pergamentblatt des alten Malers"), reviving with his friends an orgiastic heathen cult, also forsakes good standards of art in order to paint in a cheaper manner. Like Čertkov, Francesko maligns the masters, and especially his teacher Michelangelo (Čertkov speaks negatively of Raphael and Michelangelo). It is true that cause and effect are different in these sections of Gogol' and Hoffmann, for in *Die Elixiere des Teufels* the hero's sinful conduct invokes the evil agent ("Frau Venus"), while in "Portret" the evil painting first appears and draws Čertkov onto the wrong path. Nevertheless, the similarity of themes is unmistakable.

The second part of "Portret" is even closer to *Die Elixiere des Teufels.* In terms of structure, it repeats the pattern of the novel by using an account of events preceding the main plot by a number of years in order to resolve the mysteries. In Hoffmann several generations of one

family are involved; in Gogol' the period of time is much shorter, and
the protaganists of the two parts are not related. However, in each case
a chain of evil events in the lives of the characters is traced to the "sin"
of painting the portrait of a diabolical person. Francesko painted the
face of Venus on his picture of St. Rosalia; Gogol' 's painter completed
a likeness of Petromixali, who is revealed to be Antichrist, or a part
thereof. It is true that only Francesko's guilty act was willful, but in
both cases the sin must be borne by a series of people until it is expiated at the end of the narrative. Moreover, the two painters experience a
very similar feeling as their portraits near completion. Francesko suddenly notices the life-like eyes of the Venus face and, as though struck by
lightning, falls to the floor. He cannot bear to look at the picture again
until he has drunk more wine. In the first version of "Portret" the painter suddenly becomes aware of the vivid eyes of the likeness and,
frightened, drops his palette and makes for the door. Only the grasp of
the dying Petromixali prevents him from running away instantly.

   Despite the fact that the motif of the evil portrait which comes alive
definitely seems to trace to Maturin, there is no reason why ideas from
Hoffmann cannot have supplemented the notion in Gogol' 's mind. There
is more than one interesting painting in *Die Elixiere des Teufels,* and no
one, including Gorlin, seems to have paid attention to the portrait of
Francesko (great-grandson of Francesko the painter) which the innocent
Aurelie describes in her letter to the abbess. It is true that this painting
produced a pleasant effect on her as a little girl and that it is not actually said to come alive. However, the circumstances of its introduction into the story are suggestive. The brother Hermogen tells Aurelie that
their mother often goes into the "Blaues Kabinett" and "talks with the
Devil." Aurelie later accidentally witnesses how her mother causes the
mysterious portrait to appear on the wall and calls, "Francesko, Francesko!" When, after the mother's death, the concealed picture is discovered
by workmen, Aurelie's father is gripped with horror and orders it re-

moved. There is nothing truly fantastic about this portrait; it acquires
its supernatural aura because we see it through the eyes of the child.
Aurelie mentions specifically the portrait's "lebendig strahlende Augen,"
from which she cannot turn away. It appears that only in this Hoffmann passage (not in Maturin or Irving) do we have the implication
that the personage of a portrait *is* the Devil.

The sin committed in painting the picture is finally expiated in
both the German and the Russian works by purification in a monastery.
In Gogol' 's case it is the original sinner who does this; in Hoffmann's
it is his descendant Medardus. Furthermore, as Gorlin does point out,
both the first Francesko and Gogol' 's painter find a measure of blessing when they paint the Virgin and thereby redirect their art to their
salvation.

The resemblance of "Portret" to Hoffmann in both tone and content is too great not to convince one of an influence. It does not suc-
ceed, as Hoffmann's works do, and the reason is that Gogol' was not
willing to embrace his model's artistic faith as a whole. Gorlin states
very aptly that the Russian writer merely juxtaposed reality and fantasy,
while the German intertwined them *(Nebeneinander* vs. *Ineinander).*
Gogol' evidently was aware that "Portret" fell short of perfection, and
his revision of 1842 — probably inspired in part by Belinskij's criticism
of the original version — represented a rejection of Hoffmannesque
fantasy.


3


"Nevskij prospekt" (1834), as is well known, contains the adventures of
two men, Piskarev and Pirogov, each of whom follows an attractive
woman on Nevskij Prospekt. Piskarev is an artist, a modest, sensitive
young man with a considerable capacity for romantic emotion. In short,

he is the type of the protaganist in Gogol''s fragment "Fonar' umiral"
— and the young dreamers of Hoffmann's works, as for example the
student Anselmus of "Der goldne Topf." He even hesitates to follow
the beautiful woman he has seen, though she is his ideal and seems to
have fallen from heaven; but he decides he will at least see where she
lives. In the famous climax it turns out that the woman is a prostitute.
Piskarev's world is destroyed by the discovery, and he commits suicide.

It has been demonstrated that the central idea of the Piskarev story
— the attractive girl who turns out to be a prostitute — probably derives from Jules Janin (see Gorlin). Nevertheless, the search of the young
dreamer for an ideal in a woman is typical of Hoffmann, and certain
details of the story are common with the more obviously Hoffmannesque fragment "Fonar' umiral." Hoffmann's stories with this theme do
not ordinarily end tragically (there are exceptions, such as "Die Jesuiterkirche in G.," "Der Artushof"). The degree of the disillusionment is
such that we sense Gogol' is saying to Hoffmann and the entire German
school that the romantic dream is a vain and even dangerous self-deception.

Gogol' adds to this impression with the comic counterpart to Piskarev's tragedy in the second half of "Nevskij prospekt" — the story of
Pirogov. The blond woman Pirogov follows turns out to be the wife of
the German craftsman Schiller, who is at that moment drinking beer
with his friend Hoffmann. "Before him stood Schiller, not the Schiller
who wrote *William Tell* and the *History of the Thirty-Years War,* but
the well-known Schiller who was a tinsmith in Meščanskij Street. Beside
Schiller stood Hoffmann — not the writer Hoffmann, but a rather good
cobbler from Oficerskij Street, a great friend of Schiller's." Gogol'
amuses himself with a description of the drunken Germans, but there
is nothing of an individual caricature in his Hoffmann; he is merely
making fun of Germans in general. Pirogov, pursuing the blond wife on
another occasion, receives a thorough beating from Schiller and his

friends, who are once more drunk. The story ends with the famous remark: "Vsë obman, vsë mečta, vsë ne to, čem kažetsja! . . . On lžet vo
vsjakoe vremja, ètot Nevskij prospekt. . . ." (Everything is deception,
everything is a dream, everything is other than it seems! That Nevskij
Prospekt lies at all times.) Gogol' is telling us that the romantic vision
is no match for cold reality; and he is parodying a convention of fantastic literature by having the ideal yield place to that reality instead of
vice versa. The idealist Piskarev perishes, but the unimaginative sensual-
ist Pirogov eats a *pirog* (a kind of small pie) or two and soon forgets
his misfortune.

Gogol' 's tale "Zapiski sumasšedšego (Notes of a Madman; written
1833–34) seems to trace to an earlier plan to write a "Zapiski
sumasšedšego muzykanta," the hero having been changed from a musician to a minor clerk. The idea attracts our attention because of Hoffmann's treatment of mad musicians, especially Johannes Kreisler. How
much of such a theme remained in "Zapiski sumasšedšego"? Gorlin's
discussion of this story is the weakest section of his book. He builds
too much of a hypothetical structure on the suppositions that Popriščin was originally to be a musician and that all crazy musicians in literature owe their existence to Hoffmann. He theorizes that Gogol',
having explored the first resolution of the artist's vain love in "Nevskij
prospekt" (i.e., suicide), intended to describe the second possibility –
insanity; and that in this he may have been influenced by Odoevskij
(who planned a cycle "Dom sumasšedšix") and Polevoj. [68] But here
Gorlin goes too far into the realm of conjecture, because there is hardly
a trace of the artist in Popriščin, and his attraction to the director's
daughter is neither like the artist's ideal love, nor is it even central to
the story.

The part of "Zapiski sumasšedšego" which is of definite interest to
us is the letters written by the dogs. There is no doubt, as many readers
have remarked, that they bear a resemblance in tone and content to

passages from Hoffmann's *Kater Murr.* They have the same blend of human thoughts with purely animal reactions; there is a parallel of Medži's span of experience to that of the cat Murr, for both have (at least at first) wandered no farther into the world than the limits of the household. Also, the dog expresses, with very similar words, the same feeling as Murr about the coming of spring. Moreover, there are like scenes in which the animal overhears a conversation of the master (mistress). Although the ultimate common source in Cervantes is undeniable, [69] the greater similarity of *Kater Murr* shows it to be Gogol''s immediate inspiration for the dogs.

The last story [70] which concerns us is "Nos" (The Nose), begun by Gogol' in 1833 but finished only in 1835 or 1836. It employs all the devices of literary fantasy without serious purpose. Here the interference of unnatural elements in everyday life has nothing of the supernatural about it, for there is no feeling of the powers which are at work; the author simply gives no explanation of how Major Kovalev's nose came to be in a loaf of bread and how it later went about the city masquerading as a state councillor. Gorlin comments that the composition of "Nos" is reminiscent of Hoffmann but does not make any specific comparisons. We may point out that in tone and in the type of mystifications used it is closest to "Die Brautwahl." The hero of that Hoffmann story is also a minor official who is persecuted by strange events. As in "Nos," much insistence is made on social rank. And, incidentally, Tusmann is also for a time deprived of part of his body. In the third chapter he tells how at a crucial moment someone came running down the street, stole his legs out from under him and raced off with them. Tusmann cried for the police to stop the thief, but to no avail. In a few minutes the man went by again and threw Tusmann's legs back in his face. Shortly afterward the hero believed he saw his own double at his door. (Of course there is no direct connection between the double and the legs.)

"Nos" may be seen in part as parody of a favorite theme of Hoffmann's, though not of any particular tale. Instead of losing something as symbolic as his shadow or mirror image ("Abenteuer der Silvester-Nacht"). Gogol''s hero is comically separated from his nose. The transformation of this indispensible appurtenance into the *statskij sovetnik* reduces the concept of the double to an absurdity. Gogol' crossed a new threshold of fantasy here, because so ridiculous is the idea of the disguised nose that it is impossible even to conjure up a picture of it. We are asked to accept that it is at one time recognizable as a state councillor and as Kovalev's nose — an intentionally irresoluble paradox.

4

Nikolaj Gogol' was one of very few Russian writers of his period whose poetic vision actually seems to have been affected for a time by contact with E. T. A. Hoffmann. While others felt an attraction to the German's works and borrowed certain devices and motifs, a whole stage of Gogol''s development seems to have been influenced by him. After the more original atmosphere of *Večera na xutore bliz Dikan'ki,* he showed awakened interest in Hoffmann in the unpublished fragment "Fonar' umiral" and employed Hoffmannesque tone and subject in "Portret." Later he began to incline away from the German's manner. The revision of "Portret" erased the most conspicuous fantastic features. In "Nevskij prospekt" he exposed the tragic self-deception of a romantic hero, and incidentally made fun of the Germans. "Zapiski sumasšedšego" used only selected motifs from Hoffmann, and the tale "Nos" represented a final rejection of fantasy for serious purposes. As Gorlin put it, the moral of the latter, if one can speak of a moral, is that fantasy can "play with everyday life but not transfigure it."

Gorlin believed that Gogol' came closer to Hoffmann than did any other Russian author, before his abandonment of the German's "ästhe-

tischer Erlösungsweg." This is probably true if one includes only *major*
writers. In any case, it is clear that the reading of Hoffmann was something more than a superficial experience for Gogol'.

# VIII

## Vladimir Odoevskij

### 1

Many have thought to see in Prince Vladimir Fedorovič Odoevskij (1803 – 1869) the most obvious and thoroughgoing Russian disciple of E. T. A. Hoffmann. Both his contemporaries and later readers have made the comparison. A. I. Del'vig noted in his memoirs that Odoevskij was among those attending the literary evenings of A. A. Del'vig, adding that the prince "was writing at that time stories in the manner of Hoffmann." [71] And Jurij Arnol'd said of him:

> . . . In literature he imitated the forms and fantastic plots of the German novelist E. Amadeus Hoffmann, and in music [ he imitated] Bach and Mendelssohn. The former, i.e., Hoffmann, Odoevskij came to love so much that in imitation of him he too acquired as a favorite a big black tomcat, named by him, like Hoffmann's cat, "Katter Murr" [ sic ], which, all the while Odoevskij worked, lay on his lap or sat on the table in front of him. More than once, arriving at the prince's before dinner, I found him fussing over his "cat Murr." They told me that because of this imitation of the writer Hoffmann, as well as for the fact that he constantly treated himself with Hoffmann ether, [72] Puškin is supposed to have nicknamed Odoevskij "Hoffmann Drops" *(Gofmanskaja kaplja).* [73]

In the same anecdote of Wilhelm Lenz which we quoted in Chapter IV we learn that a discussion of Hoffmann led Puškin's thoughts to Odoevskij:

> "Odoevskij is also writing fantastic pieces," said Puškin with inimi-

table sarcasm in his tone. I objected quite innocently, "Sa pensée
malheureusement n'a pas de sexe," and Puškin unexpectedly showed me the whole row of his fine teeth — such was his manner of
smiling. [74]

A. Veselovskij stated that Hoffmann found a "masterful follower" in
Prince Vladimir Odoevskij, as evidenced by the latter's books *Pestrye
skazki* and *Russkie noči.* [75] And Žirmunskij has said that Odoevskij's
romantic stories were oriented to the "two worlds" ("dvoemirie") of
Hoffmann, combined with an idealistic cult of art and the artist in the
spirit of Wackenroder and Tieck's *Herzensergießungen.* [76] A major
dissenter from this chorus of views was the best-known expert on Odoevskij, P. N. Sakulin. In his lengthy study, published 1913, Sakulin mini-
mized foreign influences and tried to establish the originality of his subject's genius. [77] D. Filosofov contradicted Sakulin's conclusion, saying
that one must seek the similarity with Hoffmann not in details but in
the spirit of his works. Odoevskij, Filosofov claimed, was one of Hoffmann's "musical men." [78]

And then we have the testimony of the man himself. Odoevskij was
preparing in his last years a second edition of his collected works (the
first appeared 1844), which, however, never was realized. His notes for
the proposed collection were preserved in manuscript and were consulted for the 1913 edition of *Russkie noči.* One of the variants of a preface, "Zamečanie k Russkim nočam" (A Note on *Russian Nights*), was
added to the text. In it Odoevskij remarks that many people had either
praised or criticized him for a supposed attempt at imitating Hoffmann.
He answers that the charge does not trouble him, because no writer has
ever failed to echo some of other people's ideas; the history of thought
is a connected whole, each idea having its natural predecessors. If a
writer, he protests, had to avoid other people's thoughts, he would have
to give up feeling — and hence living.

Naturally I am not in the least insulted when people compare me
with Hoffmann, and, on the contrary, I take the comparison as a
compliment, for Hoffmann will always remain *in his own way* a
genius of a man, like Cervantes, like Sterne. And there is no ex-
aggeration in my words if the word genius is synonymous with in-
ventiveness, for Hoffmann invented a special type of the fantastic
*(čudesnoe).* . . . [79)]

Odoevskij goes on with praise for Hoffmann's craftsmanship but then
says, "At the same time, I did not imitate Hoffmann." Acknowledging
the parallel between the form of *Russkie noči* and that of *Die Sera-*
*pionsbrüder,* he claims that an influence is impossible because the germ
of *Russkie noči* was in his mind as early as the 1820's, when he had
seen no Hoffmann other than the one story "Das Majorat." Odoevskij's
denial of Hoffmann's influence must, of course, not be overlooked. But
an examination of his words shows that he specifically answered only
one limited, and by far not the most important, parallel. The passage
from "Zamečanie k Russkim nočam," though written late in his life, is
very revealing in general as regards Odoevskij's views of Hoffmann, and
we shall return to it later.


2


Vladimir Odoevskij was a highly erudite man; the breadth of his reading
was enormous, and there can be no doubt that in the 1830's, when he
himself was writing fiction, he was acquainted with the works of E. T.
A. Hoffmann. The evidence to that effect was not even doubted by the
skeptical Sakulin. Furthermore, Odoevskij was an accomplished linguist,
and it is likely that he read at least part of Hoffmann in the original.
Indeed, if we accept the testimony of Jurij Arnol'd's memoirs, it was
Prince Odoevskij who did the translations of "Nußknacker" and

"Fremdes Kind" which appeared in 1840 as *Podarok na Novyj god* (T52).[80]

Aside from the section in "Zamečanie k Russkim nočam," Hoffmann is directly referred to only a few times in Odoevskij's published writings. He used a quotation from "Rat Krespel" as an epigraph to "Poslednij kvartet Betxovena" (see below). In the story "Sebastijan Bax" we encounter the phrase "gofmanovskie povesti vizantijskix letopiscev" (Hoffmannian tales of Byzantine chroniclers). This is explained by the fact that in Odoevskij's day the early chronicles were considered forged, and Odoevskij was using them as a synonym for wild invention. It certainly was not a compliment to Hoffmann.

In his articles on music Odoevskij mentioned Hoffmann in connection with performances of Mozart's opera *Don Giovanni.* Discussing a production of 1833 (*Severnaja pčela* [The Northern Bee], October 28), he said:

> Donna Anna's acting reminded us of the description of this opera by the inimitable Hoffmann, which we advise all those playing in *Don Giovanni* to reread more often. . . .

Unfortunately, he does not give details of the interpretation which would allow us to compare it with that in Hoffmann's "Don Juan." It is interesting that eight years earlier *(Moskovskij telegraf,* 1825) Odoevskij presented a much more superficial view of this opera, claiming that it lacked unity. The fact that by 1833 he considered it, as Hoffmann did, the supreme opera of course may be due to his musical maturing rather than to any lesson learned from the German. In 1859 or 1860 Odoevskij evidently wrote a review of another *Don Giovanni* production. It was not published and survived only in a manuscript written in another person's hand with corrections by Odoevskij. It was first printed in 1955. At the time of this performance, he says he had heard *Don Giovanni* perhaps fifty times in numerous European theaters but the present Donna Anna was the best he had seen.

If I am not mistaken, Hoffmann was the first to express the opinion that Donna Anna would never marry Ottavio, because she *loves* Don Giovanni and cannot love anyone else.

Donna Anna is certainly upset, he continues, because of the attempted rape and the murder of her father, but also because Giovanni has hurt her pride by regarding her as a woman like all others — and because she is jealous.

> From the time of Hoffmann few singers have interpreted the role of Donna Anna in this way, for they have sought the meaning in the text rather than in the music. [81)]

3

There are two fiction stories by Vladimir Odoevskij which, if read in isolation from the remainder of his works, would give the impression of a true continuation of E. T. A. Hoffmann. They are "Opere del Cavaliere Giambatista Piranesi" and "Sil'fida." Curiously, both are connected with the name of Aleksandr Puškin, for the first was printed in *Severnye cvety*, 1832 (issued on Puškin's initiative in memory of Del'vig), and the second in Puškin's *Sovremennik* (The Contemporary), 1837 (with censor's approval of November 11, 1836).

"Opere del Cavaliere Giambatista Piranesi" opens in Russia, but the scene soon changes to Naples. Apart from the Italian setting, we are immediately struck by a similarity to Hoffmann in the device of introducing the narrative with a picture. The Russian speaker refers to a drawing of a bookstall in Naples, in front of which a young man is standing. He says the young man was no one but himself, and proceeds to recount a strange incident which occurred there. (Cf. especially "Die Fermate" of

Hoffmann for a story derived from a picture.) Standing beside him at the bookstall the Russian spies a strange old man *(čudak, original)* and strikes up a conversation with him. This odd individual claims that he is the famous architect Giovanni Battista Piranesi, despite the fact that the latter died in 1778. He informs the young Russian that that is a lie; he did not die at all. He adds that he is in need of money — because he wants to build a triumphal arch connecting Mt. Aetna with Mt. Vesuvius! Drawn aside, this "Piranesi" tells his life story. He was never able to get adequate support for his grandiose architectural schemes and still travels about hoping to collect funds for them. His fantastic plans have long since become a strange obsession.

> "I learned now from bitter experience that in every work pro-
> ceeding from the mind of the artist there is born a tormenting
> spirit; every building, every picture, every stroke by chance put
> on canvas or paper serves as dwelling for such a spirit. These
> spirits are of an evil quality; they like to live, like to multiply
> and to torment their creator for their close dwelling-place. . . ."

On his deathbed, says Piranesi (did he or did he not die?), visions of palaces, castles, houses, columns, etc., surrounded him and have pursued him ever since. Jealousy overcomes him when he sees the works of his more famous colleagues. Everywhere he hopes for destruction, rejoices at earthquakes and other natural disasters, thinking that his creations can replace the wrecked buildings. With the statement that just now he needs money to remove Mont Blanc, because it obscures the view of one of his castles, the strange old man runs off.

Piranesi is an obvious offspring of Hoffmann's mad artists. He resembles the German's Ritter Gluck in certain features — the chance meetings with the strange men are equally unexpected and mysterious, and both of them claim to be famous men who in fact died a number of years earlier. (Hoffmann brought illustrious people back to life in other stories as well.) In each story there is some doubt as to the intended interpretation of the men. Are they really ghosts, or are they madmen who believe they are famous personages? Hoffmann's Gluck, however, is the greater puzzle, because he has genuine talent and plays the scores of operas from memory, even improving on them. Odoevskij's Piranesi shows no particular genius, and his schemes are so wild that we are much readier to see him as insane.

In the spirits which haunt Piranesi one cannot fail to see a parallel with Hoffmann's Johannes Kreisler. On a number of occasions we read that Kreisler was tormented by musical notes and harmonies, although they are by no means all inimical to him. As an example, compare "Brief des Kapellmeisters Kreisler an den Baron Wallborn," where he tells that he is bothered by sevenths, which are nevertheless vanquished by friendly thirds. Music is for Kreisler an organic and omnipresent thing that is perceived by more senses than just hearing. Piranesi is a martyr to art and doomed to roam the earth like the Wandering Jew (to whom he in fact refers). In his madness he does not display naked genius, as does Kreisler. His wild designs connect him with another abnormal group in Hoffmann — that exemplified by the Baron von B. and, to a lesser extent, Krespel. In the anecdote preceding the tale of Baron von B. there is told of a certain Baron von R. who travels about seeking beautiful views and having trees and other obstacles removed to uncover vistas. He is in this respect a close relation of Odoevskij's Piranesi who wants to dispose of Mont Blanc for the sake of a view.

Odoevskij's story "Sil'fida" (The Sylph) bears the subtitle "Iz zapisok blagorazumnogo čeloveka" (From the Notes of a Rational Man). The rational narrator in question receives a series of letters from his friend Mixajlo Platonovič, who has gone to the country to take possession of the estate recently inherited from his uncle. Mixajlo Platonovič is simpler and less rational, and when he discovers books on black magic among his uncle's belongings he slowly becomes engrossed in them to the ex-

clusion of all else. He is visited by a beautiful sylph, which entreats him
to forget his fiancée, the simple and faithful Katja. A plea from the latter's father brings the narrator to the country, and the efforts of the
friends result in Mixajlo Platonovič's reluctant "cure" and subsequent
wedding with Katja. While she ably manages the affairs of the estate, he
subsides into the dull mediocrity of a country squire, goes hunting, in-
dulges too much in drink and chases the chambermaids. The letter form
of the story is varied at the end with direct narration and excerpts from
the hero's diary.

We have before us what Pogorel'skij and others could not, or more
likely did not wish to, produce: the "other world," the poetic world, of
the romantics put into a Russian setting. Not even Polevoj in his "Blaženstvo bezumija" approached it so closely. In a certain sense, "Sil'fida"
is the most Hoffmannesque of all Russian stories of the period, for in
spirit it approximates Hoffmann's poetic vision, as it is seen in "Der
goldne Topf" and carried to its ultimate conclusion in "Meister Floh"
and "Prinzessin Brambilla." In "Sil'fida" *pošlost'* is opposed to the magic realm to which only the initiated can attain. Katja is a cousin of Veronika ("Der goldne Topf"), symbolizing as she does forces trying to
draw the hero into humdrum mediocrity, whereas the sylph (Hoffmann
also wrote of elementary spirits), like Anselmus' Serpentina, entices him
with poetry and eroticism. But at the same time there are important
differences between Hoffmann's conception and that given life by Odoevskij in "Sil'fida." And here we come to the fundamental contrast between the two men − one we shall have to insist upon. Hoffmann was
almost entirely a poet, an artist; Odoevskij was first and foremost a
thinker, a philosopher. While Hoffmann views the "poetic world" as
preeminent in its own right and deserving of defense against the philis-
tines, Odoevskij evidently sees his magic realm as an escape from inhu-
manity. Moreover, the respective "other worlds" are not conceived alike.
Hoffmann's is inextricably bound up with nature. The theme of "Meister

Floh," for example, is the gradual rediscovery by certain characters of
their mythical origin and earlier life in nature (specifically, as vegetation). Odoevskij's fantastic realm is that of thought; nature has no part
in it and in fact is said to be inimical to it. He refers to "dead nature"
and to "the triumph of human thought," which seems to be the true
path to immortality. The other world is for Hoffmann a place where
elementary spirits and vegetation are transformed into men and vice
versa; but for Odoevskij it is where time is not separated from time, nor
"space from space," nor "desire from hope," nor "idea from its fulfill-
ment." Able to conjure up other times and places, Mixajlo Platonovič
is transported, for example, to ancient Rome. In this world all the sor-
rows of the earth which Odoevskij so often pondered, "the curses of
men, . . . the sobbing of mothers, . . . the murmur of everyday need,
. . . the derision of evil men, . . . the poet's sufferings . . . everything
merges in sweet harmony. . . ."

   Finally, we cannot overlook the fact that, while Hoffmann's heroes
actually attain the magic world and receive immortality, Mixajlo Platonovič is called back from it by "rational" men. This reflects a certain pes-
simistic strain which runs all through Odoevskij's works. And, although
in the case of "Sil'fida" the author's sympathies are clearly on the side
of "poetry," it does not follow that he believed in, or wanted us to
believe in, the world of the sylph. He was much too rational for that
himself and made it quite easy to explain away the hero's visions as
the delusions of a sick man. In fact, he might well have borrowed a
name for his story from Nikolaj Polevoj, because "the bliss of madness" would best describe Mixajlo's state as evidently conceived by
the author.

4

No other works of Vladimir Odoevskij are as reminiscent of Hoffmann
as are "Piranesi" and "Sil'fida." But there are stories with limited features of similarity, and we shall need to know also how his remaining
nonrealistic pieces compare with those we have discussed. "Imbroglio"
(1835) is a rather good adventure story set in Naples and Venice. While
the plot recalls nothing in Hoffmann, two of the figures do. A certain
mysterious countess who keeps entering the young hero's life is the
embodiment of an elusive ideal of beauty not unknown to the German.
And developments of the story are somewhat aided by Ambrosio Benevolo, a dishonest but harmless old fellow. Within bounds, he bears a
resemblance to the Peter Schönfeld (or Pietro Belcampo) of *Die Elixiere
des Teufels,* and the relationship of Benevolo to the countess is rather
like that of Krespel to Angela before and just after their marriage. (Odoevskij's countess and Hoffmann's Angela are both opera singers.)

Odoevskij's stories about Bach and Beethoven, where we might hope
to test his reception of Hoffmann's writings on music and composers,
are overall quite unlike the German's approach. "Sebastijan Bax" and
"Poslednij kvartet Betxovena" (Beethoven's Last Quartet) are both written in an anecdotal manner. Bach's entire life is recounted on the basis
of current traditions; in the case of Beethoven, only one or two fictional
scenes, set at the end of his life, are drawn. The narrator of the biography of Bach is a somewhat eccentric student of art who travels a lot
and collects manuscripts of composers. He believes that their music
reveals something of their lives and that certain musical themes may be
associated with specific feelings. This is very much a Hoffmannesque
reaction to music (cf. "Kreislers musikalisch-poetischer Klub"), as is the
insistence on calling musical notes "hieroglyphics." But the burden of the
text is the story of Bach's life, in which the theme is that art completely
removed the great genius from life. "Poslednij kvartet Betxovena" has

an epigraph taken from Hoffmann's "Rat Krespel," but Odoevskij's conception of Beethoven has little or nothing to do with the mad violinmaker. Beethoven is painted as a pitifully poor, confused and unappreciated old man. Musicians playing his latest works no longer understand him and criticize him for becoming a "mere contrapuntist." A feature reminiscent of Hoffmann is Beethoven's remark, "From the days of my youth I saw the gulf separating idea from its expression." Also, like Hoffmann, Odoevskij sets up a triumvirate of great composers consisting of Mozart, Haydn and Beethoven. However, it is entirely possible that he arrived at these thoughts independently of Hoffmann. When Odoevskij treated the plight of the artist in "Živopisec" (The Painter), there was no echo of Hoffmann. We are not even certain whether the hero has any real talent. Danilo Petrovič is a desperately poor and pitiful figure who comes to a tragic end, and the pathos of his condition is worthy of Dostoevskij.

Vladimir Odoevskij used fantasy in many of his stories where we find no trace of Hoffmann. His "Improvizator" (The Improviser) contains the figure of the Mephistophelian Segeliel', who bestows on the hero the power of total knowledge – which turns out to be a curse rather than a blessing. Segeliel' 's resemblance to satanic characters in Hoffmann is superficial. (It is true that the description of his estate – especially the park – is very much like that of Prosper Alpanus' in "Klein Zaches.") The story "Prividenie" (An Apparition; 1838), put into the mouth of the fictional storyteller Irinej Modestovič, is rather like a debunking of ghost stories, for the climax is precipitated by very live human beings dressed up as spirits, and the narrator at the end as much as admits the supposed workings of fate were an invention.

Odoevskij composed children's fantasies, such as the delightful "Igoša" (which, Belinskij's statement notwithstanding, [82]) has no apparent connection with Hoffmann's tales for children), and also many skazki (fairy tales) with allegorical meaning for grown-ups. The goal of the latter is

usually criticism of contemporary society. For example, the collection
*Pestrye skazki* (Variegated Tales; 1833) opens with "Retorta," in which
the speaker, attending a ball, suddenly discovers that the house with all
its occupants has been put in a retort by a young devil and is being
heated over a flame. "Žizn' i poxoždenija odnogo iz zdešnix obyvatelej
v stekljannoj banke" (Life and Adventures of a Local Inhabitant in a
Glass Jar) is *ostranenie* in the extreme. The adventures of a young
spider, including his capture as an entomological specimen, are described. In a certain sense, some of the *skazki* show a greater capacity
for fantasy than even Hoffmann possessed. In the brief piece "Prosto
skazka" (Simply a Tale) various items of furniture and wearing apparel
become animated in an allegory of human life.

Among the most interesting of Odoevskij's *skazki* is "Skazka o tom,
kak opasno devuškam xodit' tolpoju po Nevskomu prospektu" (Tale
About the Danger of Girls' Walking in a Group Down Nevskij Prospekt).
A young Russian maiden is left behind by mistake in a foreign shop
and is turned into a doll *(zamorskaja kukla)* by the proprietor. Despite
this fact, she is soon married and starts a very narrow and empty life.
As a sequel Odoevskij composed "Ta že skazka, tol'ko na izvorot" (The
Same Tale, Only in Reverse), containing "Derevjannyj gost'" (The
Wooden Guest), which depicts a typical husband as wooden and equally
useless. The attack on contemporary society here is very sharp, especially with regard to the fashion of adopting everything foreign. The device
of the doll reminds us of the passage in "Der Sandmann" to which we
referred in connection with Pogorel'skij (see Chapter II), but Odoevskij
seems to reveal the source of the idea when he uses a quote from
Goethe's *Werther* as an epilogue to *Pestrye skazki:*

> . . . And all the time it seems to me that I am standing before a
> box of dolls. I watch how little men and little horses move in
> front of me, and I often ask myself if it isn't an optical illusion.
> I play with them, or it would be better to say they play with me

as with a doll. Sometimes, forgetting myself, I grasp my neighbor by his wooden hand, and then I come to with horror. . . ."

"Skazka o tom, po kakomu slučaju kolležskomu sovetniku Ivanu Bogdanoviču Otnošen'ju ne udalosja v Svetloe voskresen'e pozdravit' svoix načal'nikov s prazdnikom" (Tale About How It Happened that the Collegiate Councillor Ivan Bogdanovič Otnošen'e Was Unable to Greet His Superiors on Easter Sunday) recounts how the clerk and his colleagues played *boston* endlessly, or rather until the cards came alive and replaced the men at the playing table. It is an enjoyable tale, and the transition to fantasy at the end is adequately prepared. One detects a certain affinity here with Gogol'.

Not all of Odoevskij's nonrealistic works are humorous or innocuous. Some, such as "Bal" (The Ball) and "Nasmeška mertveca" (A Corpse's Mockery) are dark and even terrifying. In "Bal" the observer imagines that he sees skeletons in a dance of death, and the second tale is the nightmare of a dead man's revenge.


5


It is time to return to the question of *Russkie noči* (Russian Nights) and Odoevskij's general attitude toward the fantastic and E. T. A. Hoffmann. Let it be said immediately that Odoevskij's denial of Hoffmann's influence on *Russkie noči* does not apply to the interpolated stories, for most of them were evidently written in the 1830's. He was referring only to the phenomenon of the frame, and he makes that clear in the remainder of the "Zamečanie." Odoevskij claims that the idea for this format had its origin in his mind before he read *Die Serapionsbrüder*. What are the points of similarity with that book? In each case a group of sensitive young men gather on a series of evenings to discuss profound questions and hear the reading of original fiction stories from manuscripts. The fact that the stories are *read* is important, because in typical frame stories they are merely recited. This similarity links *Russkie noči,* as it did Pogorel'skij's *Dvojnik,* to *Die Serapionsbrüder.* Moreover, Odoevskij's frame resembles Hoffmann's more than does Pogorel'skij's due to the nature of the gathering. At the same time, there are significant differences in Odoevskij's and Hoffmann's frames. In the Russian instance the manuscripts are not the work of those present, but of an earlier group of young men, and they are all read by one person. Furthermore, the dialogue in Odoevskij is not equally shared by the friends; rather, a great part of the text consists of lectures by the intellectually superior Faust. And, most importantly, the youths in *Russkie noči* talk principally about philosophy, while the Serapion Brothers' orientation is primarily to art. Odoevskij's heroes are hardly interested in the artistic quality of the manuscripts they hear, but in the idea-content, while Hoffmann's may discuss both. The notion of a frame story may have been vaguely in Odoevskij's mind early, but it is entirely possible that it matured after a reading of *Die Serapionsbrüder.* In any case, he used the form to express his own interests. [83)]

Also in "Zamečanie k Russkim nočam" the author left us a very revealing statement about Hoffmann's works:

> . . . His miraculous always has two sides — one is purely fantastic; the other realistic. Thus the proud nineteenth-century reader is not at all asked to believe unconditionally in the miraculous happening told to him. In the conditions of the story there is exhibited everything by which the happening itself may be explained quite simply, and in this way you can have your cake and eat it too. Man's natural inclination to the wondrous is satisfied, and at the same time the inquisitive spirit of analysis is not offended. Reconciling these two opposing elements was the work of true talent.

There can be no doubt that in this characterization of Hoffmann Odoevskij is mistaken. While in many instances the German fantasist allowed the possibility of natural explanations, there are at least as many
cases where no amount of "analysis" will wipe away the fantasy. Even
apart from the true *Märchen*, there are unexplainable motifs and scenes
in otherwise quite realistic works. The ghost of Daniel in "Das Majorat"
serves as an excellent example. Furthermore, ambiguously fantastic
elements were often used by Hoffmann as a transitional stage between
reality and true fantasy. One of the secrets to the masterful construction of "Der goldne Topf" is that the first miraculous events can be rationalized (as dreams or the effects of wine), whereas later happenings
cannot; and the reader is never quite sure just when the new threshold
was passed. Hoffmann's accomplishment was greater than that with
which Odoevskij credited him, for he makes us *believe* in spite of ourselves. It is precisely into the realm of true fantasy that the imitators of
Hoffmann often refused to follow him; and Vladimir Odoevskij was one
of them. Although his generalization cannot be rightly applied to Hoffmann's output, it does describe his own. The key words are "fantastic"
and "analysis." Odoevskij possessed an uncommon talent for fantasy,
and the number of his stories containing nonrealistic motifs is remarkable. But this trait was at odds with his philosophical outlook, and one
sees in his writings a strange polarization between the rational and the
irrational. It is as though Odoevskij was never able to accept the bridge
between ideal and natural worlds which the German idealists offered.
His application of "analysis" is of course especially noticeable in *Russkie
noči*. In "Pis'ma k grafine E. P. R...j o prividenijax, suervernyx straxax,
obmanax čuvstv, magii, kabalistike, alximii i drugix tainstvennyx naukax"
(Letters to Countess E. P. R. Concerning Apparitions, Superstitious
Fears, Deceptions of the Senses, Magic, Cabalistics, Alchemy and Other
Occult Sciences) Odoevskij says, revealingly, that he is interested in
supposedly supernatural phenomena both for their "poetic side" and
for the possibility of seeking explanations for them on natural grounds.

Their sources, he tells us, are in ourselves, for they result from deceptions of the senses: illusions, hallucinations, etc. He examines several cases and shows in detail how they may be explained away.

The article "O vražde k prosveščeniju, zamečaemoj v novejšej literature" (On the Hostility Towards Enlightenment Noted in Recent Literature; dated 1836) speaks out against the anti-enlightenment trend in European, and more recently in Russian, literature. Odoevskij says that Russian writers tend to imitate all developments in Western literature, one of which has been the "fantastic" style.

> The fantastic genre, which too had a vogue in Europe and which, perhaps more than all other genres, must change according to national character — for it ought to combine national beliefs with the innocent dreams of childhood — this genre was wholly taken over in our writings and attained the state of genuinely insane ravings *(bred),* with the difference that these ravings are coldly transferred from a foreign book.

Everyone with or without talent, says Odoevskij, rushed to imitate the new satirical, historical and fantastic genres. The critics and the readers who tolerated this are at fault.

When Odoevskij himself used fantasy in his fiction stories, it was always either rationalizable or obviously allegorical. The nightmare worlds of "Nasmeška mertveca" and "Živoj mertvec" (The Live Corpse) turn out to be precisely that — bad dreams; the nonrealistic motifs of "Piranesi" can be explained as the delusions of a madman. In the *skazki* they are merely a vehicle for the moral.

6

It must be clear by now why a number of people have called Vladimir Odoevskij "the Russian Hoffmann" or "Hoffmann II," and why at the same time it was possible for a reputable scholar like Sakulin to deny any true influence of the German on him. On the artistic side they had a great deal in common. Odoevskij used fantasy extensively and at times approached close to the "two worlds" concept of Hoffmann. The Russian's deep interest in music and his frequent use of it as a significant motif are reminiscent of the German writer. Furthermore, one can point to stories which embody ideas and details borrowed from him. On the intellectual plane, however, Odoevskij was rather unlike his counterpart. An amateur philosopher and scientist with broad interests, he remained a rationalist and in his mature years did not accept the idealists' poetic vision. Most of his nonrealistic stories can be explained on natural grounds or are overtly didactic. He wrote articles against superstitions and against the fantastic school in literature.

We might be inclined to say that Odoevskij's reception of German romanticism was like that of Pogorel'skij, except that he was a greater and much more complex figure than the author of *Dvojnik*. Indeed, Odoevskij was many-sided and original enough that it is difficult to judge how much of his resemblance to E. T. A. Hoffmann was the result of influence and how much was coincidental affinity.

# IX

## Hoffmann Reappraised, 1836 — 1840

### 1

Russian readers and critics in the first half of the 1830's found E. T. A. Hoffmann an exciting novelty, an eccentric writer who employed a different and inimitable kind of fantasy. Few indeed were the people who saw beyond the surface and understood Hoffmann's unified world-view or the problematics of his works. When, in the second half of the decade, after a slight lull attention was once more focused on him, the attitude both in publishing and criticism was more serious and responsible. The period was opened in 1836 by Bessomykin's translation of the complete *Serapionsbrüder* and by Aleksandr Gercen's original article on Hoffmann in the *Teleskop*, and it ended brilliantly with Ketčer's translation of *Kater Murr*, finally published in 1840. In the first of these years Hoffmann's greatest supporter turned out to be Nikolaj Nadeždin, and in the last the magazine *Moskovskij nabljudatel'*. A veritable cult of Hoffmann grew up among contributors to the *Nabljudatel'*, of whom the principal were Belinskij and Botkin. Their friend Ketčer was induced to supply more new translations. In general the quality of selections from Hoffmann works was improved in this period, and particular interest was shown in the music stories ("Don Juan," "Kreisleriana," *Kater Murr*). In this once again the Russians followed the steps of the French, for in France too it was the music theme which became predominant in 1834 to 1836 after the first Hoffmann vogue.

In January, 1836, an issue of *Molva* (no. 4), supplement to Nadeždin's *Teleskop,* carried Belinskij's review of the story "Othello" by Wilhelm Hauff, which had been translated into Russian. In passing Belinskij makes a favorable reference to Hoffmann and corrects those who accused the German of fatalism.

> In Germany there once was a special literary school, the *fatalist* school – one of the most unfortunate and pitiful errors of the human intellect. The fatalists deprive man of free will and make him the slave and plaything of some irresistable, inimical and menacing force, and eventually its victim. . . . Hoffmann does not belong to this school; the fatalistic and the fantastic are not one and the same thing. In Hoffmann man is often the victim of his own imagination, the plaything of his own delusions, a martyr to an unfortunate temperament, to an unfortunate brain structure, but not of a fate before which the ancient world trembled and at which the modern world laughs. (pp. 131–32)

Beginning early in the new year of 1836, translations of Hoffmann's works appeared again in the Russian press. Aside from the important *Serapionovy brat'ja,* the year produced four translations, [84] of which, however, three were reprints in *sborniki* and only one was published in a magazine. This was the "Nedobryj gost' " ("Der unheimliche Gast") in the *Teleskop* (T34). We recall that this story had been translated twice in 1831. The new version was good, despite minor errors, such as rendering *Donnerstag* as *vtornik.*

It was Naděždin again who included three Hoffmann texts in his *sbornik* called *Sorok odna povest'* (Forty-One Stories), the volumes of which were appearing in 1836. The third volume contained "Pesočnyj čelovek" ("Der Sandmann"), designated T35 in our Bibliography. It was reprinted from the good translation in *Teleskop,* 1831 (T26). Vol. 5 of the *sbornik* carried as its opening story a reprint (T36) of "Čto pena v vine, to sny v golove" ("Der Magnetiseur") from the defunct *Moskovskij vestnik* of 1827 (T6). This, we remember, was the abridged translation begun by Venevitinov. Finally, the eleventh volume of *Sorok odna povest'* contained "Ezuitskaja cerkov'" ("Die Jesuiterkirche in G."; T37), which was a reprint from *Moskovskij vestnik* of 1830 (T17). All three texts were reproduced essentially unchanged. A review of *Sorok odna povest'* in Nadeždin's own *Molva* for February (no. 6, p. 158) mentions Hoffmann ˙ only in the title of the book. The *Biblioteka dlja čtenija* (vol. 15, Lit. letopiš, p. 7) was predictably critical of the collection as a whole, saying that the translations were pedantic and without taste, but here too Hoffmann's name appears only in the title of the collection. Puškin's *Sovremennik* (vol. 1, pp. 314—15) praised the idea of publishing the stories in one *sbornik*.

Vol. 32 of the *Teleskop* contained a long article by Belinskij on the *Moskovskij nabljudatel'*. Referring to a statement in a review by that magazine to the effect that operas should be "fantastic," Belinskij remarked:

> If opera should be a fantastic creation, then undoubtedly it ought to have a meaning *(smysl)*, just as Hoffmann's to-all-appearances most meaningless stories have a meaning. [85)]

In the same article Belinskij gives a rather striking characterization of the German literary hero, with special application to Hoffmann:

> The German's hero sits in a poor garret and — a martyr to thought — now elicits from his own head a theory of sound and the secret of its influence on the soul; now — martyr to his unsettled imagination — imagines himself to be the victim of some inimical spirit; now creates the ideal of a woman and, inflamed by it, rises to great achievements in art; and then, having found the incarnation of this ideal not in a peri nor an angel but in a mortal woman and having possessed her, begins to hate her, his children and himself and ends all this with insanity. Recall Hoffmann's "Cremona Violin," "Sandman" and "Painter." (p. 153)

The three stories referred to are "Rat Krespel," "Der Sandmann" and

evidently "Die Fermate" (called "La vie d'artiste" in Loève-Veimars'
translation).

The young Aleksandr Gercen (Herzen) had worked on an article about
Hoffmann in 1833 and 1834. It took time, however, to find a publisher,
and the author's arrest caused further delay. Gercen carried the manuscript with him into exile, later sending it to Polevoj with a request to
see that it got printed. It actually was published in the *Teleskop* for
1836, vol. 33, evidently on the instigation of N. X. Ketčer and without
Gercen's knowledge (C6). The incident drew forth Polevoj's displeasure.[86]
Gercen's article, the first truly original study of Hoffmann in Russian, is
full of youthful enthusiasm. The section dealing with biography derives
from Hitzig and does not escape from the standard image of Hoffmann
the drunkard and eccentric; Gercen directly attributes his fantasies to
wine. But the major part of the article is a rather sensitive and balanced
treatment of Hoffmann's literary production, in which, according to
Gercen, there are three outstanding features: "the inner life of the artist,
marvelous psychological phenomena and supernatural effects." Not
dwelling exclusively on Hoffmann's sober side as other articles printed
in Russia had done, Gercen points to his "lively, sharp, stinging humor."
Furthermore, Gercen's study was the first in Russia to emphasize Hoffmann's musical side. It includes long quotations from "Beethovens In-
strumental-Musik" and "Ritter Gluck." The first is Hoffmann's comparison of the music of Haydn, Mozart and Beethoven, while the second is
"Gluck's" fantastic description of the creative state. (Gercen's translations are abridged but accurate on the whole.) The young Russian calls
Johannes Kreisler Hoffmann's finest creation. The article also traces the
theme of the artist in "Die Jesuiterkirche," describing the predicament
of the hero who finds he cannot live with the incarnate ideal he has
married.

It is clear that Gercen was familiar with a far greater number of Hoffmann's works than other Russian critics had known before him. He was

the first to call attention to the long masterpieces *Lebensansichten des Katers Murr* and *Die Elixiere des Teufels.* He does not overlook the (already familiar) hypnotism theme of "Der unheimliche Gast" and "Der Magnetiseur" and the psychological depths of "Der Sandmann." Unfortunately, his view of the *Märchen* was shallower. He finds "Meister Floh," "Prinzessin Brambilla," "Klein Zaches," and "Der goldne Topf" entertaining but totally lacking in ideas! In general Gercen's essay is a better introduction to Hoffmann's works than any of the translated articles which had appeared earlier, for it treats his production more broadly and gives a better-rounded impression. The young author ended with the statement that Loève-Veimars had made an excellent translation of Hoffmann into French. "*Sometime* or other they will translate him in our country too from the French." By this he probably was referring to the lack of lengthy and authoritative Russian translations as late as the beginning of 1836, and it is possible that he was taking a jab at the practice of translating foreign literature through the intermediary of French rather than directly from the original.

2

The need for better translations was partially filled later in the year with the issuing of *Serapionovy brat'ja: Sobranie povestej i skazok* (The Serapion Brothers: A Collection of Stories and Tales) in eight volumes, translated by Bessomykin (T38). All bear the date 1836, although the dates of the censor's approval range from January 14 to March 29, 1835. The lateness of the reviews confirms that the complete edition was not available until well into 1836. Ivan Ivanovič Bessomykin was the husband of Nikolaj Polevoj's younger sister and a contributor to the *Moskovskij telegraf.* In the early 1830's he worked as a teacher at the Damskoe Učilišče in Revel (Tallinn), and his removal to Moscow to become head of a school there in 1835 probably facilitated the publication of his *Serapionovy brat'ja,* which was supposedly ready some years earlier. [87]

We have had occasion already to refer to the Bessomykin translation several times in comparing it with other Russian versions of individual stories. Its inaccuracies are few and minor. There can be no doubt that in faithfulness to the letter of Hoffmann's texts it towers above virtually all other Russian translations of the first decades, and it was, therefore, a very substantial contribution. It is also true, however, that, sticking closely to Hoffmann's words, Bessomykin sometimes becomes pedantic and unnatural in his Russian and his vocabulary is a bit archaic at times. The translation could hardly be reprinted unchanged for Russian readers today, even though it was a considerable achievement at the time. V. P. Botkin's review of Bessomykin's translation, in *Molva* (č. 12, pp. 75–79), was a vicious attack on the quality of the Russian style. It is couched in highly sarcastic terms and insists that the translation is something apart from Hoffmann:

> But tell us by what right you have distorted, mutilated, killed for a second time Theodor? By what right have you disturbed his ashes? And for what? In order to forge him a close, stifling coffin out of the crude prose from Sumarokov's times. . . . Isn't it shameful? Isn't it sinful? For pity's sake, do you know what it means to kill a book?

Botkin runs on at length in this tone. His criticism of the translation is very personal – the expression of a passionate adherent of Hoffmann who could be satisfied with little less than the original German text.

In its first volume for 1837 (vol. 20, Lit. letopis', p. 9) the *Biblioteka dlja čtenija* included its review of this edition, written in a callous manner (the translator's name is even misspelled as "Bezžomynin"). Said the reviewer:

> Some insist that Hoffmann was insane; others that he was a first-

class genius. Germany and France at first went mad over him, and now Germany and France are beginning to scold him. We in the meanwhile shall say nothing, for we consider Hoffmann neither insane nor a genius. We see in him only one of the very remarkable phenomena of German literature, an absolutely isolated phenomenon, like Jean Paul Richter.

This is the same ambiguous attitude the magazine had displayed from the beginning. Its article continues to supply misinformation; it lists "Čelovek-ščelkuška" and "Myšinyj korolek" ("Nußknacker und Mausekönig") as *two* stories and says that some of the tales in *Serapionovy brat'ja* are familiar and others are new, mentioning among the "new" "Rasskazy Krespelja sovetnika" (sic), "Vybor nevesty," "Tainstvennyj gost'" and "Sčastie igrokov" − all of which had appeared in Russian before this, some more than once. The review ends by sarcastically calling the books "bolee dvux tysjac pjatisot stranic umstvennoj pišči, izgotovlennoj v Moskve" (more than two thousand five hundred pages of mental pabulum cooked up in Moscow).

A curious item from 1836 is the little book *Černyj pauk, ili Satana v tjur'me: Fantastičesko-volšebnaja povest' nebyvalogo stoletija, Soč. Gofmana, Peredelannaja s nemeckogo A. Pro − m* (The Black Spider, or Satan Imprisoned: A Fantastic Fairy Tale from an Imaginary Age, by Hoffmann, done over from the German by A. Pro −; M., 1836). Despite the title page, this tale has nothing to do with Hoffmann. It is a rather crude story of how the devil in the form of a black spider was freed from a tree in which he was trapped, and to which he was ultimately returned. The *Biblioteka dlja čtenija* objected:

Can this nonsense really be the work of the famous Hoffmann? We have never had occasion to read it in the original, but on the other hand even intelligent writers have sometimes written absurdities (vol. 17, Lit. letopis', p. 35).

Belinskij, reviewing the tale in *Teleskop*, did not challenge the authorship but allowed himself some sarcasm as regards the contents:

> Ten years or more ago this story was printed in the *Novosti russ-
> koj literatury* of blessed memory — a rather poor magazine pub-
> lished by Mr. Voejkov — and now is being issued as a cheap little
> book *(knižonka)* in the size of *two-and-a-half* signatures and with
> the price of *three* rubles. But don't be frightened. That's printed
> on it only for greater importance, and it probably sells for a silver
> *pjatak*, no more. (č. 33, p. 313)

"Černyj pauk" did indeed appear in the *Novosti literatury*, in 1825
(kn. 12, pp. 91–121), where it was simply subtitled "Nemeckaja narodnaja skazka'" (German Folktale) without any indication of an author.
The separate edition of 1836 changed some of the chapter titles and
further Russianized the story by renaming the hero Rudolf "Vladimir."
Otherwise the text is essentially unchanged. It is evident that the name
"Hoffmann" was put on the title page purely as an inducement to buy-
ers. It is testimony of Hoffmann's drawing power in Russia.

E. T. A. Hoffmann was considerably neglected by the Russian press
of 1837. No translations at all were published. We have already referred
to the *Biblioteka dlja čtenija*'s review of *Serapionovy brat'ja* at the beginning of the year. In January the *Syn otečestva* printed an article entitled "Goffman i ego fantastičeskie proizvedenija" (Hoffmann and His
Fantastic Writings; C7). It was a translation of an *étude* by Charles
Maignien de Cambrai taken from the French magazine *France Littéraire*
of 1836. As Teichmann points out (p. 158), the article contains nothing
original but is a repetition of things said earlier by other writers. Maignien praises Hoffmann's passion for the arts, which is given to be his
saving grace. He discusses superficially the author's unrealistic side and
passes off the truly fantastic stories as the inconsequential product of
a drunken state. The reader is asked to judge Hoffmann generously —

by his virtues and not his faults! The Frenchman also repeats Walter Scott's injunction not to try to imitate Hoffmann. A comparison with the original shows that the translation of the article was good.

About May of 1837 (č. 185, pp. 8–38) the *Syn otečestva* presented its readers with the story "Tri nemca: Gofman, Veber i neizvestnyj" (Three Germans: Hoffmann, Weber and an Unknown) over the name Berthoud, with the translator signing himself "K – n  S – v." This is the story "Trois hommes, aventure allemande" which S. Henry Berthoud interpolated into his novel *Mater dolorosa* (Paris, 1834) and which was subsequently reprinted in French magazines. The opening of the story finds Hoffmann in a tavern in Dresden, where he by chance makes the acquaintance of Carl Maria von Weber and invites him to his apartment to hear his wife Bettina sing. Weber is hoping desperately to get to Paris and make his fortune, and Hoffmann pawns his dear wife's organ to give Weber money for the trip. But on the way to the coach Hoffmann starts to tell his young friend the tale of Meister Floh, and they end up in another inn, where they encounter a poor elderly fiddler and discover a common bond with him in music. The old man has written an opera, and Hoffmann and Weber, enchanted by it, promise him fame and fortune. But the next day the fiddler is dead from overindulging at dinner. Weber takes the opera with him to Paris and from there to London, where he dies of starvation. A few days after Hoffmann has received this sad news, his beloved cat Murr dies. There is nothing left for Hoffmann but to pass away also from despair. A stranger then makes a fortune from the fiddler's opera.

The story is, of course, weak, but it contains certain Hoffmannesque features, in particular the boundless love for music and the sacred friendship through art. Weber's drive to reach Paris is like that of some of Hoffmann's heroes who want to travel abroad to study, but Hoffmann's artistic Mecca is Italy, not France. The impressive figure of the mysterious old fiddler endowed with genuine but unrecognized talent is appropriate. As for biographical fidelity, Hoffmann's wife is greatly idealized, and unnatural words are put into his mouth which betray a foreign attitude toward him contemporary with Berthoud:

"I am mad! . . . I consider myself to be above people, and maybe I am worse than all of them, the very last of them! I think that reading my creations they say, 'A great genius!' while at the same time they shrug their shoulders and toss away the book with a contemptuous smile, saying, 'Madman!' "

(Translation from the Russian; we did not have an opportunity to compare the French and Russian texts.)

Nikolaj Greč issued an offprint of the story, carrying censor's approval of May 10, 1837. It was reviewed by *Literaturnye pribavlenija* (no. 45, pp. 444), where it is said the tale will be enjoyed by readers who like to laugh at "literary absurdities." The reviewer says that the French author has made Hoffmann and Weber into some sort of *čudaki* worthy of contempt. He adds, quite properly, that Carl Maria von Weber did not die hungry and unacclaimed in London. This defense of Hoffmann against the charge of eccentricity is symptomatic of the reappraisal underway.

The last mention of Hoffmann which we encountered in the Russian press of 1837 was in a review of new children's books. The *Biblioteka dlja čtenija* (vol. 22, Lit. letopis', p. 21) was urging writers to give some attention to young readers, who deserve better quality stories. The reviewer states that Hoffmann and Goldsmith set a good example in this regard.


3


In 1838 Hoffmann became almost the exclusive possession of the *Moskovskij nabljudatel'*. The magazine, which had been founded in 1835,

was acquired by a new publisher in 1838 (N. S. Stepanov), and its un-
official editor became V. G. Belinskij. It began to attract collaborators
from the Stankevič Circle and took a stand for "right Hegelianism." The
*Moskovskij nabljudatel'* 's espousal of Hoffmann amounted to a revival.

Vol. 16 of the *Nabljudatel'* (first quarter, 1838) carried the stories
"Master Iogannes Vaxt" and "Don Žuan" ("Don Juan") and an article
entitled "Žizn' Gofmana," the latter containing further excerpts from
his writings. The translation of "Meister Johannes Wacht" (T39) is very
good, and we might make only minor objections. Chronologically the
second item was "Žizn' Gofmana" (Hoffmann's Life), acknowledged to
be "from the French" (C8). It is in fact a translation of *La vie de E.-
T.-A. Hoffmann* written by Loève-Veimars and published in 1833 as
vol. 20 of the *Oeuvres complètes* of Hoffmann in Renduel's edition. The
biography was lengthy (85 pages in Russian) and represented primarily
a résumé of Hitzig (see Teichmann, p. 123). Thus the *Moskovskij
nabljudatel'* performed a service by providing the longest biography of
Hoffmann available in Russian to date. Naturally it contains both the ad-
vantages and the faults of Hitzig's work. There is a considerable amount
of facts to outweigh such inaccuracies as the statement that Hoffmann
published nothing in the year 1816. On the other hand, there is much
fantasizing about the subject's emotional state at various points in his
life.

The text of "Žizn' Gofmana" includes excerpts from Hoffmann's
diaries and letters, some large enough that we have chosen to place them
in our bibliography of translations (T40). The article also contains a
short unnamed tale (T41) — which we may call "Theodors Erzählung" —
taken from the *Serapionsbrüder,* where it is recounted by Theodor in the
dialogue of the Sechster Abschnitt, immediately following "Spielerglück."
The translation is quite accurate, despite its secondhand nature. Interestingly enough, there is internal evidence that the translator worked only
from the French article and did not have the German text in front of

him. In the sentence "Um mich eines französischen Ausdrucks zu bedie-
nen — der Mann war durchaus amusable, ohne im mindesten amusant
zu sein" the translator retained too much of the French: "un homme
amusable et fort peu amusant."

Following the second installment of "Žizn' Gofmana," the *Nabljudatel'* printed, again in vol. 16, "Don Žuan; proisšestvie, slučivšeesja s
putešestvujuščim èntuzijastom" ("Don Juan . . ."; T42). It is a first-
class translation, avoiding even the very minor inadequacies of the version
in *Literaturnye listki* (1833; T32). [88] One should recall that the earlier
edition, in an Odessa publication, probably did not have a great circulation, and therefore the *Moskovskij nabljudatel'* may have introduced the
story to many Russian readers for the first time.

In the next volume of the *Nabljudatel'* (May, 1838) Belinskij referred
in passing to "Der Sandmann," [89] and in June we find him putting
Hoffmann's name among his nominations for Germans of genius —
Goethe, Schiller, Hoffmann, Jean Paul, Haydn, Mozart, Beethoven, listed
in that order. [90]

The *Nabljudatel'*'s vol. 18 (third quarter, 1838) carried two more Hoffmann texts, the first being "Krejsler" ("Kreisleriana"; T43). The translator signed himself "V. B — n." This was none other than the Vasilij Botkin who wrote the highly critical review of Bessomykin's *Serapionovy
brat'ja* in 1836 (see above). [91] We now have a chance to see how he
himself did as a translator; and the result is not to Botkin's credit. His
"Krejsler" is a very free, approximate translation with many omissions
and some interpolations. More than once one has the feeling that Botkin was undecided as between two Russian phrases and ended up putting
in both. For example, "Wie war meine Brust so beengt" becomes:
"Tjaželo bylo u menja na serdce, grud' byla stesnena." Sometimes this
leads Botkin beyond Hoffmann's meaning, as in the phrase "vom
Drucke aller der nichtswürdigen Erbärmlichkeiten," which is expanded

into: "pod tjažestiju vsex pošlostej, vsex protivorečij i nesčastij žizni."
Immediately following this addition Botkin omits the end of Hoffmann's
sentence. One phrase which was added to the original, "Ved' nigde na
naš vopl' netu otzyva," made a great impression on Belinskij, who naturally took it for Hoffmann's words. Furthermore, Botkin had earlier
made snide remarks about Bessomykin's knowledge of the German language, whereas his own could have been improved. As an example, compare the sentence "Man hat ganz recht, wenn man diesen Gottlieb erst
sechzehn Jahr alt schätzt," with Botkin's rendering: "Pravo podelóm
vse tak ljubjat šestidesjatiletnego Gotliba."

Botkin omitted part three of "Kreisleriana," the chapter "Gedanken
über den hohen Wert der Musik"; and the first (long) paragraph of part
five is left out, as well as other sections of that chapter. Finally, part
six ("Der vollkommene Maschinist") is totally omitted, and Botkin adds
only one chapter of the second set of "Kreisleriana," i.e., "Kreislers musikalisch-poetischer Klub." Like his review, this translation of Botkin's
shows a very personal, subjective view of Hoffmann. He was concerned
principally with the passages on music and omitted particularly the
anecdotes which were not relevant to this. His esthetic orientation is
made evident also by a translator's footnote which ecstatically describes,
à la Kreisler, the effect on the listener of a certain trio by Beethoven.

The second translation in vol. 18 of *Moskovskij nabljudatel'* (1838)
was "Neskol'ko otryvkov iz žizni kota Murra i biografii kapel'mejstera
Murra [ sic ]" (excerpts from *Lebensansichten des Katers Murr* . . .; T44).
The amusing mistake in the title ("Murr" for "Kreisler") was faithfully
repeated in the table of contents of the magazine. The excerpt begins
with the Zweiter Abschnitt of the book and continues for two sections
of Murr's story and two of Kreisler's. The translator, who was guilty of
only very minor inaccuracies, was N. X. Ketčer, and the excerpt is a
sample of his complete *Kater Murr (Kot Murr)* which was finally published as a whole in 1840 (T51). The only other periodical known to

have printed a Hoffmann translation in 1838 was *Literaturnye pribav-lenija*, the supplement to *Russkij invalid*. In August it carried "Kavaler Gljuk" ("Ritter Gluck"), the first time that story appeared in Russian (T45). The rendering of the German text is very good.

We might add to the chronicle of events for 1838 that V. N. Olin's book *Strannyj bal* mentioned Hoffmann in its preface (see Chapter X). And Belinskij made this remark in a letter to the editor of *Moskovskij nabljudatel'*: " 'What writers (English and German) have been translated and read by us? ' asks Mr. A. M. Yes, much is still not translated, although for the times much already has been — W. Scott complete (whether well or poorly), Schiller in greater part, Hoffmann also — in fact, enough for the present . . ." (*Polnoe sob. soč.*, vol. 2, p. 382). Despite Belinskij's opinion, many translations were yet to appear.

The *Nabljudatel'* itself presented one more Hoffmann work in its last year of publication, 1839. This was "Zolotoj goršok" ("Der goldne Topf"; T46). Unfortunately, the long text was marred by many added phrases and some distortions of the tone of the piece, which is so important to its total effect. The translation reads like Botkin's above, two variants often being given for one phrase. For example, at the opening of the Siebente Vigilie it is said: "Endlich klopfte der Konrektor Paulmann die Pfeife aus, sprechend: 'Nun ist es doch wohl Zeit, sich zur Ruhe zu begeben.' " This is expanded into: "Nakonec konrektor Paul'man dokuril i poslednjuju trubku i stal ee vyciščat', pogovarivaja: 'Kažetsja i spat' pora. Pora otpravljat'sja na pokoj.' " Veronika's simple answer, "Jawohl," becomes: "Už davno pora, papin'ka." Did Botkin perhaps in fact do this translation?

Mentions of Hoffmann which we have found in the press of 1839 are mostly connected with works of Olin and hence are discussed in Chapter X. The German is referred to in Belinskij's review of Olin's *Strannyj bal*, in Olin's new book *Rasskazy na stancii* and in a review of the latter

by *Otečestvennye zapiski.* Also, in the *Nabljudatel'* of 1839 V. G. Belinskij offered an analysis of "real" and "imaginary" worlds in fiction. He
said that the imaginary world *(mir voobražaemyj)* may be subdivided into the "real-imaginary" *(voobražaemyj dejstvitel'nyj)* and the "illusory-
imaginary" *(voobražaemyj prizračnyj).* The former type, which is "no
more subject to doubt than the world of nature and history," has been
successfully conjured up by Homer, Shakespeare, Walter Scott, Cooper,
Goethe, Hoffmann, Puškin and Gogol'. But the fictional creation of
Sumarokov, Ducray-Duminil, Radcliffe, Racine and Corneille, Belinskij
assures us, is illusory. "That is why it is now forgotten by the whole
world." [92)]


## 4

In terms of translations, 1840 was as busy as 1838. The publishing house
of A. Syčev issued under date of 1840 the little book *Podarok na Novyj
god: Dve skazki Gofmana dlja bol'šix i malen'kix detej* (A New Year's
Gift: Two Tales by Hoffmann for Big and Little Children; T52). This
gift volume bore censor's approval of Dec. 1, 1839, and probably went on
sale before the end of that year. The contents were "Neizvestnoe ditja"
("Das fremde Kind") and "Gryzun orexov i carek myšej" ("Nußknacker
und Mausekönig"). The subtitle was evidently suggested by a sentence in
"Nußknacker"; several woodcuts of a crude quality illustrated the tales.
Jurij Arnol'd mentioned in his memoirs that the translator of this book
was none other than Prince Vladimir Odoevskij. [93)] (Žitomirskaja *[p. 14]*
believes it was N. X. Ketčer.)

The rendering of "Nußknacker" suffers somewhat from abridgment.
In fact, more than two pages are omitted from the very end of the text,
the Russian version ending after the account of Marie's visit to the magical realm. To this the very last sentence of the story was appended: "Vot

vam i skazka pro gryzuna orexov i car'ka myšej." It is hardly necessary
to point out that *gryzun orexov* is not a very felicitous rendering of the
word *Nußknacker.* "Neizvestnoe ditja" is a distinctly better translation.
However, Odoevskij found himself in a corner when it came to convey-
ing into Russian the words of the "fremdes Kind" – whose sex (if any)
must remain unknown – in view of Russian gender distinctions in the
past tense. He chose to use the neuter, which is not even an adequate
compromise. Bessomykin, in his *Serapionovy brat'ja* of 1836, adroitly
sidestepped this pitfall. For example, where Odoevskij has the child say,
"Ja slyšalo," Bessomykin used, "Mne očen' slyšno bylo."

*Otečestvennye zapiski* carried a notice of *Podarok na Novyj god* without comment in vol. 8 (Bibl. xronika, pp. 28–30); then V. G. Belinskij reviewed the book at length in vol. 9 for 1840 (Kritika, pp. 1–35). Together
with the new book *Detskie skazki deduški Irineja* (Children's Tales of Grand-
pa Irinej; an original composition by the same V. F. Odoevskij), it served as
excuse for an extended lecture on the youth of the times and parental
responsibilities in bringing up children. Belinskij attacks the reading of
contemporary girls, saying ironically, ". . . Schiller, Goethe, Byron, Hoffmann, Shakespeare, Walter Scott, Puškin are dangerous for a young
maiden's heart. . . ." He recommends that children be given a feeling
for good art early. Only a great poet, we are told, can write good stories
for children. Hoffmann is such a one, "the fantastic poet, the painter of
the invisible internal world, the seer of the mysterious forces of nature
and the spirit." Fantasy is good for children – but such reading ought
to be balanced with Scott and Cooper. "Das fremde Kind" is praised for
the good psychological portrayal of the sexes (Felix and Christlieb) and
for the theme that the first educator of children is Nature. "Nußknacker"
Belinskij calls "the apotheosis of the fantastic as an essential element in
the human spirit." He finds the story very rich but without symbols or
allegories. Finally, in praising Odoevskij's own book he says, ". . . It
would not be surprising to see on it the name of Hoffmann himself."

*Literaturnaja gazeta* also reviewed *Podarok na Novyj god,* calling the format very bad and the translation very good.

> ... It is the best children's book in European literature. We congratulate the lucky children who will enjoy it; the fruits of that enjoyment will stay with them for life" (1840, no. 5, col. 110).

The writer adds that the book will be useful to grown-up children as well.

In 1840 *Otečestvennye zapiski* carried the article "È. T. A. Gofman, kak muzykant (stat'ja Ieron. Truna)" (C9). A publisher's footnote acknowledged that it was taken from a German magazine (it was, in fact, from *Der Freihafen* of 1839). The note reads, in part:

> Hoffmann has been known in our country until now as a great poet whose fantastic stories contain plots entertaining in the highest degree, profound irony, richness, diversity and strength of thought. But here he enters the stage with new claims to European fame — as musician and composer. ... The reader ... will see that Hoffmann the musician is the equal of Hoffmann the poet.

The author of the article comments:

> ... There are still people even today who try to prove at all costs that Hoffmann was a man of bad qualities and that his heart on every convenient occasion became filled with bitterness and hellish spite, which he so abundantly poured out in his writings.

The German critic assures his readers, however, that Hoffmann's music is quite another thing. He says it never reflects the fantastic and capricious character of the stories but rather is classical in the tradition of Mozart and Cherubini. Hoffmann is said to have followed mostly Mozart in his music, but not slavishly. Quotations from letters and conversations show that information on Hoffmann's biography for this article was taken from Hitzig. His life is recounted from the point of view of his musical activity, and this section is relatively factual, avoiding many subjective interpretations. The last pages of the article are devoted to an analysis of Hoffmann's opera *Undine* with principal attention given to the score, which shows that Truhn was a considerable musicologist. In general he does not exaggerate Hoffmann's virtues as a composer, and the claim that his music was the equal óf his stories is largely the invention of the Russian publisher.

Hoffmann is mentioned twice in an article on Chamisso in vol. 40 of *Biblioteka dlja čtenija* (Smes', pp. 86, 88). Recounting one of the incidents of Chamisso's *Peter Schlemihls wundersame Geschichte,* the writer remarks, ". . . Hoffmann never succeeded better in preparing the reader for impressions oi the wondrous and bringing him so gradually and vividly into the world of supernatural happenings." Later he states that Chamisso was flattered to see his Schlemihl adopted by Hoffmann in one of his stories (i.e., in "Die Abenteuer der Silvester-Nacht").

In May the *Literaturnaja gazeta* printed "Smert' kota Mucija i nadgrobnoe emu slovo (Otryvok iz knigi: *Vzgljad na žizn' kota Murra*)" (The Death of Tomcat Muzius and Eulogy to Him; Excerpt from the Book *Tomcat Murr's View of Life;* T47). A publisher's note explains that this is a sample of the translation of *Lebensansichten des Katers Murr* by N. Ketčer which was about to appear in book form. The footnote claims that the last part of the book was being printed at that moment. "It is a most pleasant gift to Russian literature." We shall discuss the translation as a whole below. In its issue for May 29, 1840, the *Literaturnaja gazeta* carried a Belinskij article in which he commented that N. A. Polevoj once wrote stories in imitation of Hoffmann ("but who remembers now those ephemeral phenomena of magazine literature? "). [94]

About September the story "Mejster Flo; Skazka o semi priključe-nijax dvux druzej" ("Meister Floh . . .") was included in *Otečestvennye zapiski* (T48). The author is identified only in the table of contents of the magazine. As for the quality of the translation, it seems complete and accurate, a professional piece of work. Although the translator did not sign himself, it is clear from the correspondence of Belinskij and others that it was once again N. X. Ketčer. [95] In a letter to Ketčer written March 1, 1841, Aleksandr Gercen congratulated him on a good translation of "Meister Floh." [96] Ketčer also completed a Russian text of "Klein Zaches" in 1840, but it was held up by the censor and evidently was printed only in 1844 (see T54).

A minor Hoffmann story made its appearance in *Literaturnaja gazeta* for October, 1840. It was "Videnie," an unnamed tale from the second volume of *Die Serapionsbrüder* called by editors "Eine Spukgeschichte" or "Schwebende Teller" (T49). It had been given two French translations in 1836 under the title "La vision," and it is possible the Russian title — if not the whole text — was derived from the French (which we have not seen). The heroine of the Russian version has her name changed from Auguste to Èl'zelina, and the translation is very free and slightly abbreviated.

A new magazine, devoted to the theater, was founded in 1840 — *Panteon russkogo i vsex evropejskix teatrov* (Pantheon of the Russian and All European Theaters). Its publisher was the bookseller V. P. Poljakov, who, we remember, translated a Hoffmann text back in 1823 (T2). Vol. 2 of the *Panteon* contained "Predstavlenie Don-Žuana: Artističeskaja fantazija Gofmana" ("Don Juan . . ."; T50). At the end of the text we read: "Per. E. D...Ja" (Translated by E. D.). The Russian version seems definitely to have been done from the French translation in *Revue de Paris* for 1829: "Une représentation de Don Juan — Souvenir musical" (vol. 6, pp. 57—69), although we have been able to examine the two only separately. The Russian, like the French, is free and omits certain small segments but manages to convey the sense of the original. The role of Theodor is nearly eliminated.

V. G. Belinskij makes reference to Hoffmann in three pieces written for *Otečestvennye zapiski* of 1840. Reviewing the magazine *Panteon*, he qualifies a statement in it about the fantastic nature of Shakespeare's *The Tempest*. He distinguishes Shakespeare's fantasy from that of Hoffmann, saying that it is never form without content or content without form. Thus he leaves the implication that Hoffmann's works sometimes have one or the other of those faults. [97] A further review by Belinskij of *Panteon*, in *Otečestvennye zapiski*, vol. 11, mentions the translation of Hoffmann's "Don Juan" which appeared there (i.e., T50). Belinskij calls the story an "old acquaintance" and praises *Panteon* for printing it even though it had appeared once in *Moskovskij nabljudatel'* (1838). It is so good that it deserves another edition, he continues. But Belinskij likens the translating of such a text to holding a beautiful butterfly in one's hands — it is difficult not to damage it, and in this case, says he, indeed some of the "irridescent poetic dust has been blown away." [98]

*Otečestvennye zapiski's* vol. 12 contained Belinskij's review of "Jarčuk, sobaka-duxovidec" (Jarčuk the Spirit-Seer Dog) by Aleksandrov.

> This time Mr. Aleksandrov brings his readers into the world of the fantastic, a world as enchanting as it is dangerous; it is a true underwater reef for every talent, even for a German poet — if he is not Hoffmann.

Belinskij feels compelled to inform Aleksandrov that the *fantastic* is not synonymous with the *absurd*, and that it takes a great talent to write fantasy successfully.

> Such a one was the genius Hoffmann. In his stories, which are to all appearances wild, strange, absurd, there is to be seen a most profound rationality. In his elementary spirits he personified poeti-

cally aspects of life, bright and dark sensations, desires and yearnings which live unseen in the depths of human nature. If you wish, we will undertake to show and prove the profoundly rational meaning of every element of any of Hoffmann's fantastic stories. But Hoffmann was unique, and up to now nature has not allowed anyone to strive with impunity to become a Hoffmann. [99]

The major event of 1840 of interest to us was the publication of the four-volume *Kot Murr (Lebensansichten des Katers Murr)* in the transla-tion of N. X. Ketčer (T51). In fact, the appearance of the complete *Kater Murr* in Russian must be considered second in significance only to that of *Die Serapionsbrüder* of 1836. Nikolaj Xristoforovič Ketčer (1809 — 1886), by profession a physician, was a member of the Stankevič Circle and a close friend of Gercen, Ogarev, Belinskij and other important literary fig-ures. He produced many translations from English and German, but he was best known for his complete dramatic works of Shakespeare. [100]

All four volumes of *Kot Murr* bore censor's approval dated April 18, 1839. Ketčer's translation seems complete and adequate, although occa-sionally the tone is not appropriate to the original. Also, the preface and the "editor's note" at the end are abbreviated. In the subtitle of the first part the words "Gefühle des Daseins" are not translated. At the end of the edition there is a two-page "Translator's Note" that explains Hoff-mann never set down the third part of the book.

> In that part, Kreisler, disillusioned in all his dreams, loses his reason, and the lucid moments of the mad musician were to con-clude the composition which Hoffmann himself considered the best of all his works. . . . Kreisler was, so to speak, the personi-fication of the author himself, and in none of his other works do we find so many hints of various events in his own life.

This is in fact taken from Hitzig. [101] The same passage was used in the biography "Žizn' Gofmana" which appeared in *Moskovskij nabljudatel'* in 1838 (C8), and the Russian wording of the two versions is so similar that Ketčer must have either adapted it from the *Nabljudatel'* or independently translated it from Loève-Veimars. The thoughts are expressed in a different order by Hitzig. Alternatively, this may be evidence that Ketčer was also translator of the article.

The critics were full of praise for *Kot Murr.* V. G. Belinskij, writing in *Otečestvennye zapiski,* [102] said that in 1840 the Russian reading public was fortunate to receive translations of "two most excellent works of German literature — the 'Roman Elegies' of Goethe and Hoffmann's *Tomcat Murr.*" Turning to the latter, he continues:

> This composition, which for its originality, character and spirit is unique in all literature, is a most important work of Hoffmann's wonderful genius. A high, endless and at the same time painful pleasure awaits the readers, for in no other of his compositions did Hoffmann's wonderful genius display so much depth, humor, sarcastic bitterness, poetic enchantment and despotic, whimsical, capricious power over the soul of the reader.

Belinskij promises to return to *Kot Murr* in a later article, saying, "budet o čem pogovorit' i mnogo, i ot duši!" (He never kept the promise.) Now he proceeds to attack the quality of the edition, claiming that it is extremely bad — on poor paper, with inferior type and ink and full of misprints.

> It is evident that poor Hoffmann has fallen into the hands of the most illiterate proofreader. We hasten to warn the public of this in order to save in time the translator (to whom be honor and glory for his good intention) from undeserved disgrace. The translator lives in Moscow, and his translation was printed out of his sight, in Petersburg, by a *zealous* and *efficient* publisher.

Belinskij criticizes the publisher, one Pesockij, by name. It should be recalled that the translator of *Kot Murr,* N. X. Ketčer, was a personal friend of Belinskij and the future publisher of his collected works.

Notice that Hoffmann, who a few years before was often called *čudak* (an eccentric) in Russian reviews, has now been assigned a *čudnyj genij* (wonderful genius).

The magazine *Galateja* (no. 17, pp. 294–95) interrupted a review of Schiller's *Die Räuber* to comment on the services of Ketčer as a translator. The writer said that although the edition of *Kot Murr* had not yet been received in Moscow he was willing to believe the remarks of the *Otečestvennye zapiski* (i.e., Belinskij's article above) to the effect that the publisher mutilated Ketčer's work. He quoted Belinskij on the subject and added:

> Apparently someone must have jinxed *(sglasil)* the *zealous* and *efficient* publisher, Mr. Pesockij. Otherwise, how can one reconcile such strange deeds on his part with the praises that have been heaped  on him as a publisher by certain magazines?

The *Galateja* writer criticizes Pesockij for cheap editions and expresses the hope that he will *not* print Shakespeare, as proposed!

P. A. Pletnev combined *Kot Murr* and Balzac's *Le Père Goriot* in one short notice for the *Sovremennik* (vol. 20, pp. 106–07), in its entirety as follows:

> Here are two contemporary writers, representatives of two schools — the German fantastic and the French romantic. Read both works to see whence comes the breath of true poetry. Neither language, nor color, nor gaiety, nor wit enchants our soul like that unclear yet palpable, mysterious yet understandable world, far away and yet close to the heart — where everything is life, beauty and truth.

The *Biblioteka dlja čtenija* concluded an ecstatic review of Lermontov's "Mcyri" with the words (vol. 43, Lit. letopis', pp. 11—12):

> Alas, in what I have yet to talk about no joy awaits you! Is it likely that you will start to read *Cat Murr* if you have not yet read it in German, which is even unlikely?

There then comes a notice of Ketčer's translation, complete as follows:

> The cat Murr, most intelligent of cats, entirely deserves your love and tenderness, and all the more since also the translation of this excellent tale, one of the best works of Hoffmann's fantastic imagination, is very satisfactory.

This praise for both the original story and the translation makes the preceding comment puzzling. As usual, the *Biblioteka dlja čtenija's* attitude toward Hoffmann is unclear, although here even this magazine seems more positive in its appraisal than earlier.

The *Syn otečestva* printed a review of *Kot Murr* which attained the proportions of an article (vol. 6, pp. 469—75). It is filled with praise and reverence for Hoffmann, but the ideas are not original and are expressed almost naively. Why are we attracted to Hoffmann's stories, asks the writer.

> Because they are given our soul, a human soul; because that soul consists of the profoundest, most elevated, if one may use the expression, true truths *(istinnyx istin)*.

We are reminded that Hoffmann knew how to combine the real and the fantastic so that they can no longer be distinguished.

> . . . Hoffmann is inimitable precisely because of this incomprehensible combination of a certain sick irritability of the mad genius with the careful mind of the philosopher-observer and the profound wisdom of the artist.

The reviewer quotes some passages from *Kot Murr* and recommends the book to readers, adding that the translation is "very good." It is worth noting that even the hard-to-please V. P. Botkin is known to have praised Ketčer's *Kot Murr.* [103)]

5

Bobrov once wrote that E. T. A. Hoffmann characterized a whole period in Russia, and of course he had in mind principally the 1830's. [104)] It is true in any case that the popular German's presence was very much felt in the reading public and in the literary circles of that time. Not only do the periodicals testify to this, as we have seen, but considerable evidence can be found in memoirs, private correspondence and other sources.

I. I. Panaev (1812 — 1862) wrote of the 1830's in his *Literaturnye vospominanija* (Literary Memoirs):

> In the period I am describing, aside from the literary meetings I have mentioned, there were small literary get-togethers — known only to a few — of amateurs who still, so to speak, engaged in literature in a domestic way *(domašnim obrazom)*. To such meetings belonged the evenings in the apartments of A. A. Komarov and Cadet Captain Kluge von Klugenau *[Kljuge fon Klugenau]*. They were called Serapion evenings (Hoffmann at that time had a great vogue here *[ Gofman u nas byl togda v bol'šom xodu ]*). At those evenings *our Serapions* read their compositions by turn. P. V. Annenkov was among them. . . . [105)]

In another place, Panaev says that on a certain occasion (evidently about 1840) Katkov asked him to accompany him to a wineshop *(pogrebok)* and drink wine as Hoffmann used to do in Berlin. When reminded that it was not the practice in Russia to drink the wine where it was bought, Katkov insisted that they should introduce the custom. He finally gave up the notion but went away angry at Panaev (p. 233).

D. V. Grigorovič (1822 – 1899) recalled that the first literary works he read in his youth were translations of Hoffmann's *Kater Murr* and DeQuincey's *Confessions of an English Opium-Eater,* both of which had been recommended to him by his young friend Fedor Dostoevskij. [106)]

The poet V. K. Kjuxel'beker (1797 – 1846) mentioned Hoffmann a number of times in his private diary (published 1929). Under date of January 11, 1833, we find:

> I haven't read any Hoffmann in a long time. In the *Herald* [i.e., *Vestnik Evropy,* 1823] is his story "Gambler's Luck," the beginning of which is masterful. Towards the end there are too many happenings; however, they might perhaps produce a strong effect if they were developed more, if they were not told exceedingly cursorily and somewhat confusedly. [107)]

In entries of 1833 and 1834 Kjuxel'beker remarked on similarities of style among Washington Irving, Hoffmann and Bestužev-Marlinskij (pp. 153 and 167). He also spoke of reading a fragment of "Der goldne Topf" (probably that in *Moskovskij telegraf,* 1831). "The imagination here too is wild and frightening, but powerful" (p. 181). In still another place he said that Hoffmann was superior to Irving and Bestužev, because, "I believe in Hoffmann's tales as he himself – with conviction" (p. 199). Kjuxel'beker's entire diary entry for November 18, 1834, reads:

> Today my little tomcat died. I understand very well Hoffmann's sorrow for his Murr. Shall never forget my Vas'ka (p. 222).

In 1840 he wrote in his diary that he saw an imitation of Jean Paul, Hoffmann and Bestužev-Marlinskij in Polevoj's story "Èmma" (p. 251), and the next year he noted that Aleksandr Vel'tman was apparently aiming to become a Hoffmann or a Jean Paul (p. 281).

Aleksandr Gercen not only wrote the long and appreciative article on Hoffmann which appeared in 1836, but he referred to him on several occasions in his other writings and correspondence. In "Pervaja vstreča" (First Encounter), set down in his notebook of 1836 but published in 1882, he remarked, " . . . I love Hoffmann in a tavern, but I hate most of all mystification and selfishness, whether in Goethe or Hugo" (*Sobranie sočinenij*, vol. 1, p. 118). A Gercen article entitled "Um xorošo, a dva lučše" (Two Heads are Better Than One), begun in 1843 and printed much later, said sarcastically that the journalist Senkovskij had divided himself into two "like Hoffmann's Medardus" (vol. 2, p. 116). Hoffmann even came up in the examination by the investigating committee after Gercen's arrest in 1834. The transcript of questions from June 24 shows that he mentioned the German writer among foreign authors he had read. He swore all these were quite innocent and that he had not acquired any forbidden books! (See vol. 21, pp. 414–15.) Nor did Gercen entirely forget Hoffmann in later years. We find him mentioned in a letter to Proudhon in 1856 (vol. 26, p. 15), and Gercen spoke of *Kater Murr* and its author in a *Kolokol* article of 1858 (vol. 13, p. 414).

The young student Fedor Dostoevskij wrote to his brother on August 9, 1838, in part as follows:

> I myself read in Peterhof at least no less than you. All of Hoffmann – Russian and German (i.e., the untranslated *Cat Murr*). . . . I have a plan – to go insane. Let people rage, let them cure me, make me sane *(umnym)*. If you read all of Hoffmann undoubtedly you remember the character of Alban. How do you like him? It is terrible to see a man who has in his power the inscrutable, a man who doesn't know what he is to do, who plays with a toy which is – God! [108]

The German scholar Arthur Sakheim interpreted this letter too literally and concluded that by 1838 all of Hoffmann's works with the exception of *Kater Murr* had indeed been translated into Russian. [109] In another letter to his brother, January 1, 1840, Dostoevskij mentions taking long walks with a friend and discussing Homer, Shakespeare, Schiller and Hoffmann (p. 57).

The historian T. N. Granovskij (1813 — 1855) also belonged to the generation which was nourished on Hoffmann in its youth. It is typical, however, that by 1840 he had recovered from this intoxication while still respecting Hoffmann's accomplishment. In that year Granovskij wrote to this sisters that he was sending them some books.

> Je ne sais si vous connaissez quelque chose de Hoffmann; je crois que ses contes fantastiques vous plairont. Il y a tant d'imagination dedans. Pour les mieux apprécier, vous devez les lire deux fois à quelques mois de distance. Vous verrez que la seconde lecture vous fera plus de plaisir que la première. C'est toujours le cas avec les productions de ce genre. Au commencement le monde bizzare de l'auteur vous étonne trop pour que vous puissiez vous y plaire, du moins c'est ce qui m'est arrivé, quand j'ai lu Hoffmann pour la première fois. Maintenant je ne le lis plus, parce que j'ai été trop fantastique moi-même et que je suis las des rêves. Cet ouvrage m'a été donné par un de mes amis, Botkine. De mon côté je vous envoie des romans de Bulwer. . . . [110]

After sending off the books, Granovskij offered his sisters this advice in another letter:

> Avant de lire les contes de Hoffmann, lisez, je vous en prie, une notice sur cet auteur par W. Scott. Elle se trouve dans le premier volume des oeuvres. Cette biographie vous fera comprendre plusieurs choses qui sans cela vous paraîtront obscurs. Je vous ai déjà dit que pour la première fois plusieurs contes vous paraîtront tout bonnement bizarres: par exemple la princesse Brambilla et le

chat Murr, mais je suis sûr que cela finira par vous plaire. Il y a
dans ce jeu d'une imagination, qui a pris le mord aux dents,
quelque chose d'entraînant. Et puis personne n'a compris mieux
que Hoffmann la vie intime de l'artiste de son côté maladif.
C'est un monde tout nouveau pour vous. Ce qu'il dit de la
musique est admirable. Il était grand musicien lui-même. Je vous
ai parlé de l'opéra de Mozart — Don Juan. Vous trouverez chez
Hoffmann une pièce sous ce titre, qui contient une profonde
analyse de l'oeuvre musicale. Cela vous donnera une idée des
caractères du drame et de la musique. (p. 91)

The reference to Walter Scott's "notice" of course proves that the edition Granovskij sent his sisters was the French translation by Loève-
Veimars.


6


Rodzevič put his finger on a key reason for Hoffmann's popularity
among the literary elite when he wrote that to the young Russian
"Schellingists" Hoffmann seemed Schelling's ideal of the poet-philoso-
pher.[111] Schelling had said that the true philosopher must look at the
world as at a poem. Thus for Botkin, Stankevič, Belinskij and the others,
in the period before Hegel was discovered, E. T. A. Hoffmann was more
than just a great fiction writer. P. N. Annenkov (1812 — 1887), in his
very informative memoirs, stated the case this way:

> The attitude of Stankevič, as well as that of Belinskij, resulted
> partly from the fact that they chose as their teacher of esthetics
> a man who never made even the slightest concessions to weakness,
> contemporary taste or fashion in his elevated theory of art (teorija
> izjaščnogo), namely Hoffmann. ... The burning, almost feverish
> love for art which distinguished Hoffmann came up to the level of

his Russian admirers' extraordinarily sharp critical inquisitiveness.
In him they found a passionate, almost ideal attachment to his
pursuit (cause), which they considered about the only *cause* in the
world worthy of that name. Hoffmann almost never mistook the
meaning of the subject of art; but he never portrayed it otherwise
than in a fiery and unbearable brilliance. . . . He had an electrify-
ing effect on serious young minds, who held his words to be a
poetical insight into the very depths of creativity. . . . His stories
and fantastic tales themselves found a sympathetic echo in Stankevič's circle; they corresponded so well to the dominant philosophical system with their powerful personification of lifeless nature.

Annenkov also suggested that Hoffmann had a very positive effect on the
development of Russian literary criticism. He pointed particularly to
Belinskij's theatrical critiques, in which the high standards of writing and
acting demanded may trace to the German's utterances about the theater.

According to Annenkov, Belinskij asked in a conversation in 1839
why Western critics did not place Hoffmann as high as the greatest poets.
This was at the time when Belinskij was undergoing the transition to
Hegelianism.

He was experiencing now the last days of that romantic-philosophical
attitude. On the same evening I am describing, a conversation began about some humorous manuscript story written jointly, as a
joke, in the manner of Hoffmann by some people at their get-to-
gethers − for the sake of passing the time. "Yes," said Belinskij
seriously, "but Hoffmann is a great name. I cannot understand at
all why to this day Europe does not put Hoffmann beside Shakespeare and Goethe. They are writers of equal ability *(sila)* and the
same order."
    This proposition and other similar ones Belinskij inherited and
still maintained from the era of the Schellingist outlook, accord-

ing to which, as is well known, the external world was a partici-
pant in the great evolution of the absolute idea and expressed in
its every phenomenon a moment and stage of its development.
So the fantastic element of Hoffmann's stories seemed to Belinskij
a fraction of the discovery or disclosure of this all-creating absolute idea and had for him the same reality as, for example, a faithful
portrayal of character or the rendering of any occurrence from life. [112]

We have seen the very numerous comments Belinskij made about
Hoffmann in the periodicals. It is true, as Annenkov indicated, that toward the end of the 1830's Belinskij's attitude began to change. We find
considerable wavering in his private letters, where he sometimes praises
the German very highly and at other moments is critical of him. A letter
to K. S. Aksakov of June 21, 1837, ends:

> Farewell and keep happy; preserve peace and harmony in your
> soul, because happiness is only in that. Dream, fantasize, be enrap-
> tured, be moved; only forget about two dangerous things which
> can destroy you — magnetism and fantasism. Those are stupid
> things. I am beginning to be strongly disillusioned in Hoffmann,
> because I just cannot explain for myself that mad and sickly poet-
> ry (*Polnoe sobranie sočinenij,* vol. 11, p. 133).

But less than a month later Belinskij wrote to Bakunin that he was
studying German and had looked for a text to read. "My choice fell on
that *čudak* Hoffmann. I want to take him up." He hesitated between
*Kater Murr* and the third part of *Die Serapionsbrüder,* finally selected
the latter and was particularly enchanted by "Der Kampf der Sänger."

> Here is Hoffmann's true side! His fantastic is a sickness of the
> spirit, an illusory life. Art as the subject of art — here Hoffmann
> is great, and he should be given to young people to develop their
> feeling for fine art. . . . It is decided. I'll read in German *The
> Serapion Brothers* (vol. 11, p. 204).

Again in a letter to Botkin of August, 1838, he refers to "Hoffmann's sickly subjectivism" (vol. 11, p. 264). And writing to Stankevič in 1839 he commented that Konstantin Aksakov "long ago began to emerge from the spectral world of Hoffmann and Schiller" (vol. 11, p. 366). But later in the year, August 24, 1839, he was outlining to Kraevskij the plan for a projected *Biblioteka dlja romanov* (Library of Novels), in which the first translations would be the *complete* works of Scott and Cooper and "Hoffmann entire (from the German)." Translators were to be Katkov and Ketčer (vol. 11, p. 375). Nothing came of the project. In 1840 Belinskij mentioned that Lermontov was reading Hoffmann while under arrest (vol. 11, p. 496). He wrote repeated appeals that Ketčer send off to him his "Klein Zaches" and also translate "Meister Floh." In March he reported to Botkin that he had just read "Meister Martin." "A great poet! Schiller, Goethe and Hoffmann – these three are one – the profound, inner and many-sided German spirit!" (vol. 11, p. 498). The following month he was telling Botkin to get Ketčer to translate all of Hoffmann which was not yet available in Russian. And in the same letter he said:

> I have read all of Hoffmann's *Serapion Brothers*. A wonderful and great genius is this Hoffmann! For the first time I understood his fantastic intellectually *(mysliju)*. It is the poetic personification of the mysterious inimical forces which are hidden in the depths of our spirit. With that in mind, Hoffmann's sickliness has disappeared for me; only poetry remains.

He became quite ecstatic and even said he wanted to reread "Der Magnetiseur." "Alban is not phantasmagoria, but reality; *now* I know that" (vol. 11, p. 507 f). We recall that Belinskij expressed some of these same impressions publicly in his review of Aleksandrov the same year. In a letter of August 16, 1840, to Ketčer, the critic complained that Bessomykin distorted the *Serapion Brothers* (vol. 11, p. 545).

It is clear that as his ideas evolved Belinskij had constant difficulty finding the proper place for Hoffmann in his gallery of talented writers. In December, 1840, he wrote to Botkin:

> I have decided for myself an important question. There is artistic poetry (the best is Homer, Shakespeare, Scott, Cooper, Byron, Schiller, Goethe, Puškin, Gogol'); there is religious poetry (Schiller, Jean Paul Richter, Hoffmann, Goethe himself); and there is philosophical poetry ("Faust," "Prometheus," in part "Manfred," etc.). Among them one cannot place definite boundaries (vol. 11, p. 582).

In letters to Botkin of December 16, 1839, and March 14, 1842, he quoted the line which had attracted him in "Kreisleriana" (actually interpolated by Botkin) — "Ved' nigde na naš vopl' netu otzyva!" (Nowhere is there an answer to our cry).

Belinskij's preoccupation with E. T. A. Hoffmann is of interest to us because he was a leading critic and because he may be taken as an illustration of the attitudes of a whole segment of the Russian literary world. It is particularly revealing to see that Belinskij's opinions had been based only on fragmentary reading of the German's works. He arrived at a new evaluation when he read him more systematically, but it seems unlikely that even this well-informed critic ever became acquainted with Hoffmann's total *oeuvre*. It is evident that Belinskij lost much of his interest in Hoffmann during his last years, for he mentions him only rarely after 1840. There is no proof, however, for the assertion of Soviet scholars that he rejected him completely.

# X

## Olin

### 1

We have indicated that for some Russians of the period E. T. A. Hoffmann remained nothing more than an exciting storyteller, a purveyor of ghost tales. On this superficial level he was taken up by third-rate writers who used the prestige of his name, if not elements of his literary style. The case of Olin will suffice as an example of this phenomenon.

Valerian Nikolaevič Olin was such a minor figure that he is rarely referred to in sources of the period, and very little is known about his biography. He was born about 1788 and evidently died at some time in the 1840's. Vengerov characterized him as an "extremely zealous and productive writer, but with exceedingly little talent." Olin tried nearly everything in literature, but he was equally unsuccessful in all genres, and his critical essays were also poor. More than once he "borrowed" literary material from other writers and published it with very little original added. Often in financial trouble, he polished many an apple over the years. He wrote poems in praise of the despicable Arakčeev and Czar Nicholas I. The latter himself was so disgusted at being called a "god" by Olin that he forbade the censors to pass such poems in future. [113] Olin contributed to literary almanacs at least as early as the 1820's, and he engaged in some publishing activities. The *Karmannaja knižka dlja ljubitelej russkoj stariny i slovesnosti na 1829 god* (Little Pocket Book for Lovers of Russian Antiquity and Literature, 1829) was published by him and contained his story "Kumova postelja" (The God-Parent's Bed) and an article by him on Goethe. But of particular

interest here is Olin's short story *Strannyj bal* (A Strange Ball) of
1838, [114] which formed part of his book *Rasskazy na stancii* (Stories
at the Station) of the next year. [115]

The 1838 edition of *Strannyj bal* was preceded by a preface which
began as follows: "This story *(povest')* — if I may use the expression —
in the manner of some of the *phosphoric* stories (*v rode nekotoryx iz
fosforičeskix povestej*) of Hoffmann and Washington Irving, is an excerpt from a fantastic novel *(fantastičeskogo romana)* entitled *Stories
at the Station* and divided into four parts. . . ." We shall see just how
much this tale was in the manner of the "phosphoric" stories of Hoffmann and Irving, but it is better to consider *Strannyj bal* in the context
of *Rasskazy na stancii,* where it makes up the second of three chapters
in part one, the first being "Stancionnaja beseda" (A Conversation at a
Station) and the third "Čerep mogil'ščika" (The Gravedigger's Skull).
For epigraph the book has: "Le réel est étroit, le possible est immense
(Lamartine)."

"Stancionnaja beseda" forms the frame for the remaining two stories
and opens with conventional motifs from popular adventure stories. The
narrator is traveling through the Russian countryside in bad weather.
His driver points out a spot along the road where the body of a merchant killed by robbers was found recently, adding the confession that
he forgot their weapons in Petersburg. They stop in a village and find a
whole company of travelers who have taken refuge from the weather
and are sitting about drinking punch and telling stories. All of them will
play a role, says the author, "in the phantasmagorical drama of our story." With the conversation at the station Olin manages to get in all those
jabs at women's styles, use of the French language, homeopathy and
other subjects which contemporary writers could not resist taking. Then
the talk turns to the supernatural. One traveler, Sergej Sergeevič, mentions a strange incident which happened to a certain general, and the
company persuades him to relate it. Before presenting the tale, how-

ever, Olin interrupts with a lengthy invocation of the poets of fantasy
that almost defies translation:

But before we begin Sergej Sergeevič's story, I must warn my readers that we will have to be carried away out of the circle of family
conversation at the station, or, to put it better, out of *ordinary*
life, and into the lofty sphere of *idealism,* or of the *possible,* and
at the same time ask gracious pardon from the great geniuses of
misty romanticism. O thou who wast drunk half of thy life; thou
whose entire life was a constant fever; thou who died in madness;
thou, finally, the patriarch of all frightful rustlings *(patriarx vsex
strašnyx šelestov),* of all fantastic images and figures — immortal
Hoffmann! And thou, noble viscount of stormy springs *(blagorodnyj
vikont burnyx istočnikov),* prince of phantasmagorias! And thou,
our illustrious coryphaeus of the mysterious world of witches,
spirits and ethereal dancers, [ who wast ] inspired by apparitions
and corpses that prepared your path to immortality and, what is
no doubt still more important, to the sources of the Ganges that
boil with life! And thou, our eternally youthful Shakespeare, who
only lately joined the banners of romanticism and who deluged the
temple of Melpomene and Thalia with bandits, murderers, sorcerers
and, in a word, with a confusion of times and tongues; thou, father
of the northern melodrama, gathering ears *(klassy)* like Ruth in
Boaz' field, after the great reapers of the recent school, who are
subjects of thy wonder and thy dithyrambic transports! And ye, all
ye romantic poets and prose-writers, living and dead, foreign and
domestic! graciously forgive my traveler, o fathers and brethren, for
having dared to follow you, or, to put it better, for wending his
way with his pilgrim's staff along the paths of that trail that disappears in mysterious darkness and that was beaten by the flashing
hooves of your hellish steeds, which are blacker than night and
breathe flame from their nostrils!

At the end of this rhetorical nonsense a superfluous footnote tells us:
"The reader will undoubtedly realize that all this is only a literary joke."
It is not a very successful one, and it certainly does not show a mature
understanding of literature.

   Sergej Sergeevič's story is "Strannyj bal," the adventure of a general,
who, sitting at home of an evening, finds himself bored by every pastime. "In a word, some sort of inimical influence seemed to surround
him and weigh down on him," remarks the narrator rather inappropriately. The general decides to go for a walk. "It seemed that some
mysterious power drew the general against his will into the street."
Outside during his wanderings he meets his friend Vel'skij, who is dressed in a Spanish cape and broad-brimmed hat and looks for all the world
like Satan. Vel'skij invites our hero to a masquerade party, but the general says he wants to return home and read the Bible. Vel'skij grimaces
at this, his face is temporarily obscured by a fog or smoke, and the
smell of sulphur is noticeable. When this diabolical individual resumes
his previous form he manages to persuade the general to go to the ball,
promising him that there will be beautiful women. Entering the brilliantly lighted hall, the general sees a large assembly of guests in costumes,
and he notices that their images in the wall-mirrors represent "a sort of
dream-like gallery of other fantastic guests with all of their movements,
or, it would be better to say, an animate cosmorama of optical or ideal
beings." When Vel'skij points out attractive women, the general calls
him "tempter" — but feels fifteen years younger. He watches the strange
guests in their fantastic and even frightening costumes and joins the
dance. His head begins to spin, and he imagines the statues to come
down from their pedestals and start to dance also. When he is drawn into a game of forfeits *(fanty),* he is required to jump off from a chest of
drawers. He hesitates to do this but is derided by the others for his fear.
Suddenly he wakes up and finds himself standing alone on scaffolding
at the fourth floor of an unfinished house. In other words, it was all a
dream which would have cost him his life had he jumped.

When "Strannyj bal" appeared separately in 1838 it was reviewed by
V. G. Belinskij in the *Moskovskij nabljudatel'* (1839, č.1, otd.5, pp. 74–79):

> ... We find strange only the fact that you associate your story with
> the genre of *phosphoric* stories by Hoffmann and Washington Ir-
> ving. First, in our opinion those two writers have nothing in com-
> mon, and one should by no means place the talented storyteller
> Washington Irving on the same plane as that great genius of an
> artist Hoffmann. Secondly, in the *phosphoric* stories of Hoffmann
> there is included not only phosphorus, devils and apparitions, but
> also ideas *(mysl')* which produce that magical, fascinating power
> over the human spirit. Thirdly, we cannot understand at all what
> connection there is between the *phosphoric* stories of Hoffmann
> and Mr. Olin's phosphoric story.

Belinskij also says that Olin made a mistake in printing an excerpt of his
book first, because if people read the sample they will certainly shun the
novel itself. Recounting the plot, he finds nothing Hoffmannesque about
it and concludes that, if Mr. Olin is right, it is easy to become a Hoffmann by merely retelling in bad style any absurd anecdote which is making the rounds. "No, gentlemen, the fantastic is not that at all. It is one
of the most important and profound elements of the human spirit. A
great thought glimmers in the mysterious dusk of the realm of the fantastic *(mysl' velikaja mercaet v tainstvennom sumrake carstva fantastičeskogo)*. . . ." Belinskij felt constrained to correct Olin about the confusion of romanticism with the supernatural: "Why this incessant talk
about romanticism as the poetry of cemeteries, devils, witches, sorcerers
and apparitions? They understood romanticism like that only in the
twenties. . . ." In the *Sovremennik* (1838, vol. 10, pp. 61–62) Pletnev
said that this new work by Olin was as disappointing as all the other
forms he had tried. The *Biblioteka dlja čtenija* (1838, vol. 28, otd. 6,
p. 21) treated "Strannyj bal" summarily and added the final insult by
saying that "Olin" was evidently a pseudonym. It seems likely

that was meant ironically, for his name had been in print a number of years.

Naturally we must concur in the negative appraisal of the story and in Belinskij's observation that it has nothing to do with Hoffmann. The plot, as the critic said, is no more than an anecdote, and the fantastic elements are for the most part inserted artificially. The narrator *tells* us that things seem diabolical when he ought to let them speak for themselves. We should be tempted to consider "Strannyj bal" a parody, if it were not that the critics who were in a better position to judge seem to have thought that it was meant seriously. The use of Hoffmann's name in connection with this tale shows very well the superficial view of his works in minds such as Olin's.

And then there is an interesting sidelight on "Strannyj bal." In 1831 Orest Somov printed his story "Videnie na javu" (A Vision While Awake) in the magazine *Girlanda* (The Garland; no. 4, pp. 93—103). It begins with a monologue in which the narrator goodheartedly speaks about the Germans' attempts to revive "belief in miracles" and regrets that nineteenth-century people find it hard to accept the fantastic. "Da zdravstvujut nemcy! da procvetaet ix Wunderland!" (Long live the Germans! May their Wunderland flourish!) The story itself concerns a poetic young dreamer, who, strolling through the city one April night, comes to a brightly lighted house where a party is going on. Men on the balcony recognize him and wave to him to come in. He declines, but servants finally persuade him by repeated invitations from the host and hostess. The guests are rather strange; they are very "free" in their manners, are all dark-complexioned and unfriendly looking. He goes out on the balcony to find the friend who had motioned to him, and there he becomes involved in a game of forfeits with some young people. When he dares to kiss one of the girls, the kiss seems to make his lips burn. He is given the penalty of jumping off a flower stand. The young people gather round to watch this, but he crosses himself before jumping, and suddenly the whole scene disappears and he finds himself alone "in an unfinished and empty house, on the fourth floor, on the edge of an unfinished balcony," from where he had nearly jumped onto the pavement below!

The similarity of this story to "Strannyj bal" is too great to be a coincidence. Olin certainly composed his tale with *Girlanda* open in front of him, or at least with the memory of Somov's story. We may add that his version suffers still more by comparison with Somov's polished tale. "Videnie na javu" bears the subtitle "Improvizacija odnogo vesel'čaka v svetskom krugu" (A Jovial Fellow's Improvisation at a Social Occasion), and for the style of an improvisation it is quite passable. It is irrelevant whether Somov or anyone else actually improvised the story in company; the marks of the genre are unmistakable. "Videnie na javu" might serve as commentary to Puškin's "Uedinennyj domik na Vasil'evskom." It tends to confirm the idea that the fantastic improvisations of the period drew on traditional horror devices and owed little if anything to Hoffmann, even when they were associated with his name.

## 2

We return now to the remainder of Olin's *Rasskazy na stancii*. Part one concludes with the story "Čerep mogil'ščika," which makes use of several ideas current in magazine literature. The traveler Lenskij tells how he once came into possession of the skull of a former gravedigger. Staring at it one evening he sees it become filled with tiny lights, and little demons *(besenjata)* come out of it — "from the organ or the capacity for wisdom *(glubokomyslie)*, . . . the organ of *fantasy.*" They are the demons of contemplation, politics, poetry, mysticism, vanity, ambition, etc. The author makes it clear that this was only a dream. In a fever Lenskij imagines that he goes out into a "Salvator landscape," is chased by a giant bird and ends up in a cemetery, where he sees the dead rise and perform a dance. The dead gravedigger comes to demand his skull back — but obligingly sits down on a step to tell his life story. (He was an intelligent and talented man who had constant misfortune on this earth.) Again when Lenskij is in a fever the ghost comes to demand his skull, but, as luck would have it, a friend has misplaced it and it cannot be found. The company offers Lenskij various advice as to how he might have freed himself of the spook, but he replies that someone gave him a good dose of medicine and he never saw the gravedigger again. Lenskij makes it plain that the story his naive listerners take so seriously is just a tall tale.

Out of a clear blue sky Lenskij asks, "I should like to know what, in your opinion, is injurious to the success of our literature?" Sergej Sergeevič answers him confidently:

> It is very understandable and clear. . . . It is the excessive spirit of imitation, a certain conventional determinateness *(kakaja-to uslovnaja opredelennost'),* a strange necessity for adjusting to the demands of the time, as though the masses should refine taste, when it ought to be the other way around; perhaps some short-coming in the constant striving — in love of art solely for love of art; maybe coldness; finally, perhaps also calculation *[* i.e., a view to profits *]* prescribed by circumstances — to avoid calling it by another name — which is, however, forgivable and very sensible due to the necessity.

In this obtuse monologue it is as though Olin were trying to justify his own unoriginality by his tight circumstances and need to publish. We should add that "Čerep mogil'ščika" and the monologue are couched in an ironic tone.

Part two of *Rasskazy na stancii* is the story "Pan Kopytínskij, ili

Novyj Mel'mos." The subtitle (The New Melmoth) reveals the apparent connection with Maturin's novel. The story is close to the Mephistopheles-Faust theme, for the supernatural character Pan Kopytinskij uses his special abilities to help the hero and heroine and bring them to a happy state and then try to gain their souls. Aside from the figure of Kopytinskij, the fantasy is mostly limited to atmosphere, such as "Salvator landscapes."

The *Otečestvennye zapiski* (1839, vol. 4, otd. 6, pp. 16–20) recounted part of Olin's literary career in its review of *Rasskazy na stancii*, pretending at first to sympathize with him for the bad treatment he had received from critics – and then saying that the new book would also not retrieve his name! "These new stories of his will still find readers among people who have been fed on the mystical stories of Clauren and brethren." The journalist then made great fun of Olin's style, quoting some of his unintelligible passages. Of the statement on foreign literary influences he said: "So that's how they discuss Russian literature at stations. With this opinion all stationmasters, postmen, conductors and literate drivers would agree. The illiterate ones would agree too, but probably they didn't catch what the author was saying to them." A review of *Rasskazy na stancii* in *Syn otečestva* (1839, vol. 9, otd. 4, pp. 146–47) was brief and also negative.

3

Valerian Nikolaevič Olin was an ambitious writer whose works are hardly redeemed by any literary qualities. In his fantastic tales we find no trace of the direct influence of E. T. A. Hoffmann, but they have a small part in our history because their author's claim of affinity with the masters of fantasy demonstrates the shallowness with which such people viewed the foreign models. And Olin's case is another bit of evidence of the drawing power which Hoffmann's name was felt to have in the 1830's. In a sense Olin was behind the times, because, when he published these stories at the end of the decade, at least the more sophisticated readers and critics had arrived at a new and profounder understanding of fantasy and of Hoffmann.

# XI

## The Declining Years, 1841 – 1845

### 1

For a period of eleven years (1830–40) E. T. A. Hoffmann was an almost constant object of attention on the part of the Russian press and reading public, with peaks of publishing and criticism at the beginning and the end of the decade. But after 1840 there was a very sharp drop of interest, and the content of our present chapter is in the nature of an aftermath. Only three translations appeared in the whole five years from 1841 to 1845, one in 1843 and two in 1844. Those of the latter year, however, were important additions to the available texts of Hoffmann in Russian – "Klein Zaches" and "Prinzessin Brambilla." Hoffmann also seems to have been mentioned less often than in the preceding years in the magazines. The few references we have are almost exclusively from the pen of V. G. Belinskij, who was not as enthusiastic about the German writer as earlier but by no means had forgotten him.

Belinskij mentioned Hoffmann twice in his article "Russkaja literatura v 1840 g." in *Otečestvennye zapiski* (1841, vol. 14, otd. 5, pp. 2–34). He referred to the translations "Mejster Flo" and *Podarok na Novyj god,* as well as the essay "È. T. A. Gofman, kak muzykant," all of which had appeared in 1840. The children's stories of *Podarok* (translated by V. F. Odoevskij) he calls a better translation than that by Bessomykin in *Serapionovy brat'ja,* although as regards accuracy at least he was certainly mistaken. One wonders to what extent Belinskij relied on the appraisal of Bessomykin made by his friend Vasilij Botkin. A little later in the year Belinskij was listing Hoffmann among the greatest novelists *(romanisty),* together with Cervantes, Walter Scott,

Cooper and Goethe, and saying that he produced an original genre of the fantastic. [116) But in another article Belinskij seems to have contradicted himself with the statement that Hoffmann was not as great as Goethe or Schiller because he remained too narrow. Here he once more applied the epithet "genial'nyj sumasbrod" (madcap genius) to the German. [117) Belinskij referred to Hoffmann once more in 1841 in his review of *Upyr'* by Krasnorogskij (A. K. Tolstoj). (See Chapter XII.)

In 1842 a review (evidently not by Belinskij) of Chamisso's *Peter Schlemihls wundersame Geschichte* appeared in *Otečestvennye zapiski* (vol. 20, Bibliog. xronika, p. 74). Quoting at length from a German article which valued Chamisso very highly, the reviewer takes issue with it and sees in *Schlemihl* only a good children's story. And even then he says that it is not as good as Hoffmann's "Fremdes Kind," despite the fact that Hoffmann himself liked Chamisso's story and imitated it by creating a character who had lost his mirror image (i.e., in "Abenteuer der Silvester-Nacht").

2

One Hoffmann translation is known from 1843. It seems to be the first to have appeared since 1840, and then it is not new but a reprinting of the *Skazka o ščelkune* which had been published separately in 1835 (T33). The present edition (T53) was in a children's magazine, *Biblioteka dlja vospitanija* (Library for Education).

Again in 1843 we find several mentions of E. T. A. Hoffmann in articles written by Belinskij for *Otečestvennye zapiski*. His "Russkaja literatura v 1842 g." (vol. 26, no. 1, otd. 5, pp. 1–26) included a characterisation of the Russian romantic prose of the preceding years:

To your misfortune you *[* kind and innocent romanticism *]* got to know a madcap genius *(genial'nyj sumasbrod)*, the German Hoffmann, started to rave over the "fantastic" and shook it up with the "ideal," adding to this amalgam some sentimental water from the novels of August Lafontaine which you remembered from childhood. And you saw stretching out in a long line ugly stories and novels with heroes living in the bliss of insanity, sleep-walkers, somnambulists, hypnotists, idealized cooks, bourgeois poets, dreamers, gingerbread Abbaddonnas, saccharine love, mouse-like heroism and all sorts of like nonsense.

Of course the attack here is on Nikolaj Polevoj and similar writers. In Belinskij's article "Russkij teatr v Peterburge" (The Russian Theater in Petersburg; vol. 26, no. 2, otd. 8, pp. 100–03) we read:

... *[* The German writers *]* turned reality into phantasmagoria with that madcap genius Hoffmann, whose genius suffocated in the closeness of ideal and "Hofrat" reality.

Still later, in an article on Puškin (vol. 30, no. 9, otd. 5, pp. 1–60), Belinskij compared his knight Togenburg with Hoffmann's Nathanael ("Der Sandmann") and Vadim with Anselmus ("Der goldne Topf"), without of course implying any historical connection.

The year 1844 saw the last two Hoffmann translations which appeared in our period. "Kroška Caxes, po prozvan'ju Cinnober" ("Klein Zaches genannt Zinnober") was published in *Otečestvennye zapiski,* vol. 34 (T54). The source of the translation is something of a puzzle. On the one hand, it is certain that N. X. Ketčer prepared "Klein Zaches" for that magazine as early as 1840 and that it was held up by the censor. In letters of March 14 and April 16, 1840, to V. P. Botkin Belinskij asked why Ketčer had not sent him "Zaches" yet. [118] And on August 16, 1840, he wrote to Ketčer, saying that he would hold the translation until it could be passed by the censor:

> But I am not sending you "Zaches"; there is nothing for him to
> do at your place or at Botkin's; let him lie here for a while – sit
> by the sea and wait for good weather. Maybe he'll get printed,
> and Kr[aevskij] wants to take all possible measures to that end
> (p. 545).

Žitomirskaja and the editors of the recent complete works of Belinskij
believed that the "Kroška Caxes" of 1844 was Ketčer's text. On the
other hand, this translation has many small inaccuracies, including paraphrases, so that it does not seem to be up to the quality of Ketčer's
*Kot Murr.* Furthermore, Levit stated that it was the work of M. N. Katkov. [119]

A review of *Antologija iz Žan Polja Rixtera* (Anthology from Jean
Paul Richter) in vol. 34 of *Otečestvennye zapiski* gave Belinskij an excuse to discuss Hoffmann as well. Goethe and Schiller, he said, were
able to rise above their environment,

> But such people as Hoffmann and Richter, while bearing brilliant
> and strong talents, could not but submit to the harmful influence
> of the bad sides of society which surrounded them like the air.
> In talent Hoffmann is on the whole greater and more remarkable
> than Richter. Hoffmann's humor is much more vital, substantial
> and biting than Jean Paul's, and the German Hofrats, philistines
> and pedants must feel to their very bones the power of the Hoff-
> mann humoristic scourge. How masterfully Hoffmann portrayed
> Prince Irenäus, his comical court and his microscopic state! How
> profound is his excellent story "Meister Johannes Wacht"! How
> many wonderful and new thoughts about the deep secrets of art
> this man expressed who was endowed with such a rich artistic
> nature! And all this did not stop him from engaging in the most
> absurd and monstrous phantasm in which, like a priceless pearl in
> the slime, his brilliant and powerful talent drowned! What drove

him into the foggy realm of fantasizing, into that kingdom of
salamanders, spirits, dwarfs and monsters, if not the stinking
atmosphere of *Hofrat*ism, philistinism and pedantry, in a word,
the boredom and mediocrity of a social life in which he was
suffocating and from which he was ready to escape – if only
to a madhouse?

Shortly afterwards, Belinskij reviewed Odoevskij's *Sočinenija* [120] and
in passing chided him for borrowing Hoffmann's fantasy:

> But Hoffmann's phantasm comprised his nature, and Hoffmann,
> even in the most absurd tomfoolery of his fantasy, managed to be
> true to ideas. Therefore, it is extremely dangerous to imitate him.
> You can borrow and even exaggerate his failings without borrow-
> ing his merits. Moreover, fantasy comprises the weakest side of
> Hoffmann's works. The great and true side of his talent is his deep
> love for art and his rational understanding of its laws, his biting
> humor and his ever-lively ideas.

The last translation for 1844, and the last for the entire period, was
*Princessa Brambilla: Fantastičeskaja povest'* ("Prinzessin Brambilla"),
issued in Petersburg with censor's approval of November 23, 1843 (T55).
It lacks the "Vorwort" altogether and has a number of small omissions
but seems to be adequate. The council scene of Hermod is put into
good and appropriate poetic prose. The edition includes illustrations,
some, at least, by Callot. *Princessa Brambilla* must have been placed on
sale at the end of the year, for all the reviews were dated 1845. The
*Otečestvennye zapiski* said that the story would appeal only to those
who like art for art's sake. The reviewer added that both translation and
format were bad (vol. 38, Bibliog. xronika, pp. 26–27). The *Biblioteka
dlja čtenija*, as usual, wrote enigmatically of Hoffmann but called the
work an "entertaining little book, even if a little bit belated" (vol. 68,
Lit. letopis', p. 13). The review in *Literaturnaja gazeta* says *Princessa*

*Brambilla* may please those readers who like uncontrolled flights of fancy.

> We think that much in Hoffmann's fantastic works has genuine poetic quality and real content and is distinguished by profound irony and humor, but there is little or none of that in his *Princess Brambilla.* Here you will find only a lot of wonders, entanglements and strange adventures . . . (no. 4, Bibliografija, p. 73).

The reviewer, who by the way is not very consistent in his interpretation of the story, assures us more than once that he does not reject fancy altogether. He cites Gogol' 's "Nos" as a story where fantasy is intertwined with reality. The translation he considers good but the format of the book poor.

Finally, the *Sovremennik's* reviewer (perhaps Pletnev) joined those who considered the Russian version a disservice to its author. His notice read  in full (vol. 37, p. 324):

> One cannot but feel sorry when a great writer is translated without respect for his genius. Hoffmann represents an amazing phenomenon of insight, wonderful humor and original poetry. All this he put inseparably into each of his creations. But what does the common reader or translator see in him? Words – sometimes funny ones, but more often incomprehensible ones – a plot and a dénouement which satisfy childish curiosity. What is understood that way is transmitted (translated) that way. And what will the foreign reader find of genius here? Nothing.

Closing our chronicle of E. T. A. Hoffmann in the Russian press is the 1845 article by Belinskij in *Otečestvennye zapiski* on Russian literature of the preceding year, where he refers to Hoffmann twice in passing. In one of the passages he mentions the translation of "Klein Zaches." [121])

3

The tone of published comments on Hoffmann in the years 1841 to 1845 is like that of a backward look at a thing of the past. For once the *Biblioteka dlja čtenija* probably was right when it called the translation of "Prinzessin Brambilla" "belated." The infatuation with Hoffmann on the part of critics and serious readers was clearly over and felt to belong to the preceding decade. New developments were taking place in native Russian literature, criticism and philosophical thinking which tended to exclude the master of fantasy. Belinskij began noticeably to downgrade him, at least in his public pronouncements, no longer placing him on a par with Goethe and Schiller.

During the span of years from 1846 to 1872 very few Hoffmann translations appeared in Russia. In 1873 a complete Russian edition of his works was undertaken but attained merely four volumes, covering *Die Serapionsbrüder*. A revival really started only about 1893 with major editions of Hoffmann's writings and his espousal by the symbolists. This period — which extended into the 1920's — would make interesting material for a separate study. Until recently Soviet publishers tended to consider Hoffmann primarily a children's storyteller, to judge by the repeated editions of "Nußknacker," "Der goldne Topf" and other "skazki" (fairy tales). (For details see Žitomirskaja.) That attitude has changed, and he is now treated as a classic of world literature. In 1962 appeared a three-volume collection of selected works, printed in 100,000 copies, [122] and in 1967 an attractive edition of *Kater Murr* and selected stories, issued in 300,000 copies. [123] These publications testify to enduring love of the Russian reading public for Hoffmann, even though he could never again be such a major figure in their eyes as he was in the 1830's.

It remains to examine the traces of Hoffmann's influence in the writings of two Russians of a somewhat younger generation: Aleksej Tolstoj and Mixail Lermontov.

# XII

## Aleksej Tolstoj

1

The poet Aleksej Konstantinovič Tolstoj (1817 – 1875) passed through
his formative years in the 1830's when E. T. A. Hoffmann was fashionable reading in Russia, and it is not surprising that the German had an
effect on him. Tolstoj's preoccupation with fantastic literature and with
Hoffmann in particular is all the more understandable when we recall
that his uncle, in whose house he grew up, was none other than A. A.
Perovskij (Pogorel'skij). Young Aleksej, according to his own testimony,
started writing compositions at the age of six, and from an early time
his diet of reading included much supernatural literature – and E. T. A.
Hoffmann. [124]

By no means all of Aleksej Tolstoj's youthful pieces have been preserved, but those which have include prose stories in which the influence
of his uncle and of his reading in the horror tales and the "genre
frénétique" is obvious. For our purposes the most interesting of his early
stories is the tale *Upyr'* (The Vampire). It was published as a separate
edition in St. Petersburg, 1841, under the pseudonym "Krasnorogskij"
and was Tolstoj's first appearance in print. In later years he did not recall the youthful work with favor and omitted it from his collected
works. Only in 1900 did Vladimir Solov'ev, a friend of the Tolstoj
family, republish it – together with a very complimentary preface.

The plot of *Upyr'* is complex, but only certain parts of it need concern
us here. The hero Runevskij is told by a half-insane man named Rybarenko that an old couple attending a ball, Sugrobina and Teljaev, are in
reality vampires, and that Sugrobina is plotting to lure her beautiful grand-

daughter Daša to a country house where she can suck her blood. Runevskij, who falls in love with the girl, passes through a series of terrifying
and puzzling encounters with ghosts and vampires that finally end in the
dispersion of the supernatural forces and his wished-for marriage to
the heroine. In the course of all this, Tolstoj cleverly leaves open the
question of whether the supernatural really exists or is merely in the
nightmares and feverish imagination of the hero, fed by insane tales of
Rybarenko's.

The contents of *Upyr'* owe something to both E. T. A. Hoffmann
and to Tolstoj's uncle, Antonij Pogorel'skij. One source of inspiration
seems to have been Hoffmann's tale that is inserted in *Die Serapionsbrüder* after "Der Zusammenhang der Dinge" and usually called either
"Graf Hyppolit" or "Vampirismus." It is preceded by a brief discussion of
vampires, during which we learn: "Diese scheußlichen Kreaturen erschei-
nen oft nicht in eigener Gestalt, sondern en masque." There is also reference to the "roter Fleck" left on the victim by a vampire (as in Tolstoj). Of course these ideas are common in the lore of vampires and
need not come from Hoffmann. However, the story itself bears a certain
resemblance to "Graf Hyppolit." Hoffmann's story – which, along with
"Ignaz Denner" and perhaps "Der Sandmann," is one of the few truly
terrifying pieces he wrote – has a young hero, Count Hyppolit, who
falls in love with the beautiful Aurelie. The girl's mother is a frightening
old woman who seems to have some mysterious designs for her. In this
there is an obvious similarity to Runevskij, Daša and the grandmother
Sugrobina. In Hoffmann's version, though, the death of the old woman
does not result in the happiness of the young couple, because the
diabolical mother triumphs even after death. Hyppolit goes mad when
he discovers his young wife in a cemetery at night feeding on a human
body with other ghouls.

While a guest at Sugrobina's country estate Runevskij occupies a room
in which hangs a portrait of Praskov'ja Andreevna, an aunt of Sugrobina

who died there from sorrow when her fiancé disappeared the day before
their wedding. In the middle of the night the woman of the picture —
who strongly resembles Daša — seemingly comes alive and orders the hero
to marry her portrait (meaning Daša). The theme of the portrait is already known to us from Gogol', where it serves a different function. In
*Upyr'* it seems that the picture itself does not come alive, but rather the
ghost of its subject appears. Here the parallel of the portrait in "Ein
Fragment aus dem Leben dreier Freunde," rejected by scholars as a
source for Gogol''s "Portret" precisely for this circumstance, is relevant.
And in the Hoffmann it is also a likeness of an old maiden aunt who
was "stood up" on her wedding day. [125] The resemblance of Daša to
her great-grandaunt is also a Hoffmannesque trait (cf. "Das öde Haus").
And consider in this connection *Die Elixiere des Teufels,* where much is
made of the resemblance of Aurelie to the painting of St. Rosalia. Hoffmann's novel, moreover, shares with *Upyr'* the idea that one generation
can put to rest the souls of ancestors by its actions. Both stories make
the intrusion of the devil into everyday life an important moving force,
although the young Tolstoj presented this more naively. It is the mad
Rybarenko who in the Russian story propagandizes the supernatural explanation of events. In his tragic preoccupation with this idea he reminds
us of Nathanael in "Der Sandmann," and perhaps it is not by chance that
he, like Nathanael, ends precisely by jumping from a bell tower.

Finally, inserted in the story is Rybarenko's account of adventures he
experienced three years earlier in Como, Italy, including a terrifying and
mystifying night spent inside the Villa d'Urgina or "Casa del Diavolo."
This episode is somewhat Hoffmannesque in spirit if not in details. We recognize here the same tendency as in his works to treat Italy as *the* distant
and exotic land and to use it as a poetic counterpart to one's native city.
The mystifications of the Casa del Diavolo are in the Hoffmann manner,
and Antonio's dream of Jupiter's court reminds one of scenes from "Prinzessin Brambilla" and other tales, although it is not as rich in imagination.

Despite the overly elaborate plot, in which not all the threads are
tied up at the end, Tolstoj's youthful attempt at fiction has much to
commend it, particularly the deft blending of the real and supernatural.
In praising *Upyr'* Vladimir Solov'ev said that the best fantastic tales
leave room for some natural explanation, while at the same time the
writer manages to make such an interpretation seem unlikely. Tolstoj
accomplished this, skillfully interjecting hints and doubts that make the
reader want to conclude in favor of the existence of vampires.

V. G. Belinskij was quick to see that, with all its shortcomings,
*Upyr'* revealed in its author a remarkable young talent "which promises
something for the future." He added: "*The Vampire* is a fantastic work,
but its fantasy is only external. There are not noticeable in it any ideas
*(mysl'),* and therefore it is not like Hoffmann's fantastic creations. ..."
He complimented the novice author for skillful handling of a complex
plot and for his excellent Russian style. [126] The other reviews in 1841
were quite unfriendly. *Syn otečestva* (no. 38, pp. 437–54) recounted
the whole story in great detail and included long quotations, ending,
"Whether you have understood anything of this or not, we cannot know"
*(ne mogim znat').* The reviewer blamed the entire story and its composition on opium. *Biblioteka dlja čtenija,* it is not surprising to find, was
equally sarcastic about *Upyr'* and insisted the reader keep in mind the
essential fact that Rybarenko is touched in the head (vol. 48, Lit. letopis',
pp. 6–12).


2


The traces of Hoffmann in Aleksej Tolstoj's other youthful stories are fewer
and less obvious. He wrote two fantastic tales in French: "La famille du
vourdalak" and "Le rendez-vous dans trois cents ans," the first of which
is known in Russian in a translation by Markevič, "Sem'ja vurdalaka.[127]

The other was first printed by Lirondelle in 1912 from a manuscript
(Lirondelle, pp. 579–601).

"La famille du vourdalak" is of interest because it is another treatment
of the theme of vampirism which had been used in *Upyr'*. The plot itself
is set in Serbia and bears no external relationship to *Upyr'* and no
particular similarity to Hoffmann. In an introductory explanation, however, the narrator d'Urfé defines *vurdalak* in a manner very reminiscent
of a passage from Hoffmann's "Vampirismus" (we translate from the
Russian version):

> It is appropriate to tell you, mesdames, that *vurdalaki* – the vam-
> pires of the Slavic peoples – are, according to local opinion,
> nothing but the bodies of dead people which come out of the
> grave to suck the blood of the living. Generally speaking their
> customs are the same as those of vampires in other countries,
> but they have in addition a peculiarity which makes them still
> more dangerous. *Vurdalaki,* mesdames, prefer to suck out the
> blood of their closest relatives and best friends, who, dying, in
> turn are transformed into vampires, so that they say in Bosnia
> and Hercegovina there are whole villages whose inhabitants are
> *vurdalaki.*

Hoffmann quotes Michael Ranfft's book on vampires (1734).

> ". . . Du wirst daraus entnehmen, daß ein Vampir nicht anders ist,
> als ein verfluchter Kerl, der sich als Toter einscharren läßt und
> demnächst aus dem Grabe aufsteigt und den Leuten im Schlafe
> das Blut aussaugt, die dann auch zu Vampirs werden, so daß nach
> den Berichten aus Ungarn, die der Magister beibringt, sich die Be-
> wohner ganzer Dörfer umsetzten in schändliche Vampirs."

Both Hoffmann and Tolstoj follow these passages with supposedly doc-
umented cases in which a vampire was exhumed and burned. In each

instance the corpse let out an audible moan when a stake was driven through its heart. However, Hoffmann's example is from Ranfft and Tolstoj's from Dom Calmet (*Dissertation*, 1746), and the similarities may result from a common, conventional depicting of vampires. Lirondelle has shown that Tolstoj read several sources on vampires, only one of which was *Die Serapionsbrüder*.

"Le rendez-vous dans trois cents ans" contains nothing of direct relevance to our study. It does, however, make use again of the resemblance of the heroine to an ancestress and to a portrait of the latter — a motif which may possibly trace to Hoffmann (see above concerning *Upyr'*). Both "La famille du vourdalak" and "Le rendez-vous dans trois cents ans" are more successful than the earlier *Upyr'*, and for ghost stories they are very readable even today.

Lirondelle saw some influence of Hoffmann in the text of "Amena" (fragment of an unfinished novel called *Stebelovskij*). The hero Āmvrosij is seduced by the temptress Amena but eventually rejects her and her pagan gods with the words: "I renounce you and your gods; I renounce Hell and Satan!"

> Hearing these words, Amena let out a piercing screech, the features of her face became distorted in a monstrous way, and blue flame started to issue from her mouth; she rushed at Amvrosij and bit him on the cheek.

Lirondelle points out that a similar experience happened to Erasmus Spikher in "Die Geschichte vom verlornen Spiegelbilde." At the critical moment he finds strength to reject Giulietta:

> Funkelnde Blitze schossen aus Giuliettas Augen, gräßlich verzerrt war das Gesicht, brennende Glut ihr Körper. "Laß ab von mir, Höllengesindel, du sollst keinen Teil haben an meiner Seele. In des Heilandes Namen, hebe dich von mir hinweg. Schlange — die Hölle

glüht aus dir." — So schrie Erasmus und stieß mit kräftiger Faust
Giulietta, die ihn noch immer umschlungen hielt, zurück.

As a further parallel we might mention the witch in *Die Elixiere des
Teufels,* who on dying is changed from a beautiful young woman into
a hideous monster. The theme of the novel is closer to that of "Amena,"
for there too the seductress is an incarnation of Venus and the spirits
are pagan.


3


We have seen how well demonstrated is the effect of fantastic literature
on the sensitive young Aleksej Tolstoj in the 1830's and early 1840's.
Probably through his uncle, A. A. Perovskij, he was led to read E. T. A.
Hoffmann, and the German helped to form the vision of some of Tolstoj's early prose stories. *Upyr'* is the clearest example, but a few elements of other texts (including the two composed in French) also suggest Hoffmann.

A. K. Tolstoj is known in Russian literary history almost exclusively
as a poet and dramatist. His youthful prose works were an experiment in
writing, and no great importance can be attached to them within his
total *oeuvre.* His early preoccupation with fantasy was not carried over
into his mature work. It is interesting, however, that he remembered
Hoffmann even in later years. He himself acknowledged that the conception of Don Juan in his dramatic poem of that name was indebted to
Mozart and E. T. A. Hoffmann.

# XIII

## Lermontov

### 1

Among the prose writers who grew up during the period of Hoffmann's vogue in Russia was the major figure of Mixail Jur'evič Lermontov (1814 – 1841). And yet it is remarkable that, despite the many foreign influences he experienced and his early inclination to nonrealistic literature, there is almost no trace of Hoffmann in Lermontov's production and the German certainly did not touch any of his principal works. For our purposes, attention is limited almost exclusively to a prose fragment from the last months of Lermontov's life, the supposed beginning of a novel to be called *Štoss.*

Lermontov cannot have been unexposed to E. T. A. Hoffmann in the 1830's when he was the center of so much interest in Russia. And we recall the letter written by Belinskij to V. P. Botkin on March 14, 1840, in which he reports that Lermontov is reading Hoffmann while under arrest. [128] The earliest work by the young Russian that may owe a small debt to Hoffmann is the poem "Tambovskaja kaznačejša" (The Tambov Treasurer's Wife; 1836), the climax of which is a gambling scene with an outcome similar to that of "Spielerglück." The old treasurer of Tambov, Mr. Bovkovskij, is host at a party on his nameday. He himself serves as banker for the card game, and as it progresses he loses very heavily. His house and all his belongings are gambled away. It is after midnight when the treasurer, who has sat for a while pale and silent, asks for attention and declares that he wants to bet once more to regain his estate, and as his last stake he offers his beautiful young wife! An officer accepts this challenge, the play continues, and in a few moments the treasurer's wife has been gambled away. She throws her wedding ring in the old man's face and faints, only to be carried away by the victorious officer.

In discussing Puškin's "Pikovaja dama" (see Chapter IV) we called attention to the scene in Hoffmann's "Spielerglück" in which Chevalier Menars, reduced to poverty by his gambling, accepts the challenge of the banker Duvernet to bet his wife against the restoration of his fortune in the amount of ten thousand ducats. He loses, and Duvernet goes to take possession of his prize. Admittedly, the incidents in Hoffmann and Lermontov are dissimilar in nearly all the details. It is Lermontov's banker who loses his wife, and not one of the players at the table, although in both cases the banker is the one who proposes the bet. In "Spielerglück" the deal is made secretly, while the effect of Lermontov's climax is enhanced by a public scandal which the bet provokes. Moreover, the tone of the works is utterly different. "Tambovskaja kazna-čejša" is a humorous parody of a love theme, whereas Hoffmann's story is earnest and tragic (the wife is found dead when Duvernet comes to claim her). In short, the two stories have little in common except the gambling away of an attractive wife by her desperate husband. One is inclined to believe that Lermontov took this theme from "Spielerglück," which, as we know, was printed in Russian repeatedly by this time – in the *Vestnik Evropy* (1823; T2), the *Sankt-Petersburgskij vestnik* (1831; T20) and in *Serapionovy brat'ja* (1836; T38). However, considering the lack of further similarities of text or relevant biographical information, the comparison remains inconclusive.


## 2

The idea of a woman as stake in a card game was used by Lermontov again in the unfinished *Štoss*. In the spring of 1841 during the author's last visit to Petersburg he summoned a select group of friends together one evening for the avowed purpose of reading to them a serious new novel, saying that it would require at least four hours. Countess E. P. Rostopčina, who was present, left this account in her memoirs:

> He [Lermontov] insisted that we gather early in the evening and that the doors be locked against outsiders. All of his wishes were carried out, and about thirty selected people gathered. Finally Lermontov came in with a huge notebook under his arm, a lamp was brought, the doors were locked, and then the reading began. In a quarter of an hour it was finished. The incorrigible practical joker had enticed us with the first chapter of some frightening story which he had begun the day before. About twenty pages were written, and the rest of the notebook was blank paper. The novel stopped there and was never finished. [129]

The text of this reading survived after Lermontov's death a few months later, but we have only Rostopčina's word for it that the title was to be *Štoss.* Commentators agree that this seems likely, because much is made in the story of a three-sided pun on the proper name Štoss, the card game *štos* and the answer "Čto-s?" to a question by the hero.

The content is as follows. At a "musical evening" held by Count V. a sophisticated society woman named Minskaja talks to the guest Lugin, who is in a melancholy mood and eventually tells her he is going mad. He says that recently everyone seems to him to have a yellow face as though he had a lemon for a head. She suggests coquettishly that he cure himself by falling in love, but he confides that he is aware of his own unattractiveness and thinks he cannot be happy in love. Lugin has, he says, recently been followed by a mysterious voice which repeats in his ear a certain address — "Stoljarnyj Lane, by Kokuškin Bridge, house of the Titular Councilor Štoss, Apartment 27." Minskaja advises him to get rid of the voice by actually going to the address and satisfying himself that no Štoss lives there.

Lugin has some trouble finding Stoljarnyj Lane, but when he does
he also locates a house recently bought by a certain Štoss. He learns
from the janitor that Apartment 27 is empty and has been so for years;
even though several tenants have let it, they never moved in. Shown the
apartment, Lugin decides on the spot to rent it and has some of his
belongings brought from the hotel. Only after saying he will take the
apartment does he notice a strange portrait on one of the walls. It is
the likeness of a middle-aged man, whose face is especially life-like. At
the bottom of the picture is written the one word "Wednesday"
("sereda"). Lugin feels that there is some mysterious significance to the
picture and the word, but it is Monday, and with Wednesday more than
twenty-four hours off, he settles down to sleep.

On the next day the remainder of Lugin's things are moved to the apartment. He is a painter, and among his canvases is one bearing several studies
of a woman's head. The author repeats that Lugin, due to his unattractiveness, is uncertain of his success in love. And "such an attitude of spirit
excuses a rather fantastic love for an ethereal ideal, a love very harmful
for a man of imagination." On Tuesday evening Lugin remains in his
room and becomes immersed in sad thoughts, recalling his youth which
is past. About midnight he sits down to draw and suddenly realizes that
the face in his sketch is that of the strange portrait on the wall. A noise
is heard beyond the door, which slowly opens, and an old bent man in
dressing gown and slippers enters. It is the figure of the portrait! To
Lugin's horror this apparition seats himself at the table, draws out two
packs of cards and after a frightening pause invites Lugin to play at
štos with him. The hero decides that if this is a ghost he will not give
in to it and be intimidated. He bets against him, and the old man names
his stake by pointing to something "white, unclear and transparent"
next to him. Lugin loses and demands another game, but the apparition
simply says, "On Wednesday." Lugin demands that it be tomorrow or never, to which the mysterious old man reluctantly agrees.

On the following night the apparition comes again in the same manner and prepares to play. But the hero insists on knowing his opponent's name, to which he receives the answer, "Čto-s? " (What, Sir?) Understandably, he misinterprets this to be the proper name Štoss. On this occasion Lugin looks over his shoulder and sees that the transparent something he has been playing for is a beautiful woman, the image of his "ethereal ideal." She is "colors and light instead of form and body, warm breath instead of blood, thought instead of feelings." The author warns us, moreover, that the vision is "also an empty and false apparition." Having seen the figure, Lugin resolves to play until he wins her. The game continues on many consecutive days, but the hero consistently loses. His resources are running low, and a crisis is approaching. Finally he makes an important decision . . . and here Lermontov's fragment ends!

In addition to the text of *Štoss* as outlined above, there are extant two notes of Lermontov's which clearly relate to the conception of the story. In an album of 1840—41 we find:

> A plot: at a lady's house: yellow faces. Address. House: old man with a daughter invites him to deal *[ cards ]*. Daughter is in despair when old man wins. Sharper: old man lost daughter *[* in game *]* in order to . . . Doctor; little window . . .

And an album given to Lermontov by V. F. Odoevskij (apparently in 1841) contains these words:

> But who are you, for God's sake? — What, sir? *(Čto-s?)* answered the little old man, winking slightly with one eye. — Štoss! Lugin repeated with horror. Sharper has intelligence *(razum)* in his fingers. [130)]

There are two or three additional words at the end of the latter note, which some editions call "illegible" but others report to be "bank" and "skoropostižnaja." The first word can either refer to the bank in a card game or can be an abbreviation for *bankrotstvo* 'bankruptcy'; and the second word ("sudden"), in the feminine gender, invites a completion as "sudden death." How Lermontov intended to continue the story, if at all, can be of course only the subject of guesswork.

It has been pointed out more than once that the atmosphere and some details of *Štoss* are Hoffmannesque. The intrusion of supernatural agents into real life and the fateful interconnections of phenomena *(Zusammenhang der Dinge)* were, as we know, themes very dear to our German writer. The motif of the card game played for possession of a beautiful woman may well trace through "Tambovskaja kaznačejša" to Hoffmann's "Spielerglück." And, most importantly, *Štoss* takes up the subject of the artist and his ideal woman, one of the major themes of Hoffmann's works. It is possible, however, that relatively little of this came directly from E. T. A. Hoffmann, despite the fact that Lermontov was reading him in 1840. Rather, it seems clear that much of *Štoss* depends on Gogol' (especially "Portret") and possibly Puškin as well ("Pikovaja dama"), in which case the Hoffmannism is secondhand.

A considerable parallel between Lermontov's tale and the first part of "Portret" is undeniable. Two young painters, both inclined to dreaming, find mysterious portraits of men in their apartments. The pictures have in common that the faces are very life-like, and in each instance we are told that it is difficult to avert one's gaze from the face. In Gogol' the portrait seems to come alive and leave its frame; in Lermontov's story the original of the picture (or his ghost) appears. Both figures greatly influence the fates of the heroes. Moreover, there is a doubt as to whether the strange men really exist or are hallucinations or dreams.

Having noted the essential connection of *Štoss* with the tradition of the fantastic artist story which derives in some measure from Hoffmann,

it is important, to determine what Lermontov's intention was in com-
posing such a tale as late as 1841. Not only had Gogol' and others re-
pudiated the genre by this time but Lermontov himself had entered a
mature stage of writing and shown an inclination to realistic prose.
Countess Rostopčina's anecdote suggests that, since the reading of the
text was a practical joke, the story itself may not have been taken
seriously by the author. But even if this is true, his attitude at the time
of the original conception of the plot could have been different. This
puzzle was discussed by Professor John Mersereau Jr. of the University
of Michigan in his recent article "Lermontov's *Shtoss:* Hoax or Literary
Credo?" [131] He points out that Rodzevič treated the story as a serious
offspring of the fantastic school. [132] Mersereau himself seems inclined
to consider it ironical; but he leaves open the question of Lermontov's
full intent in writing it. It seems clear to us that *Štoss*, at least in the
form in which it has been preserved, is not a serious production but a
whimsical treatment of romantic themes – in effect, a parody. An
attentive reading of the text reveals a consistently ironic use of familiar
motifs, which are often introduced so inappropriately that they are
comical. This can hardly have been unintentional on the part of the
mature Lermontov. Let us examine some of the features which give
that impression.

The very figure of Lugin is almost a caricature of the romantic
dreamer. First of all, he is quite unattractive in appearance. Says the
author, "He was awkwardly and coarsely built, spoke sharply and
curtly; the sickly and thin hair on his temples, the uneven complexion
of his face, signs of a chronic and secret illness, made him older in
appearance than he actually was. . . ." Minskaja is described as a beautiful
and intelligent woman, but Lugin does not treat her with the politeness
which a proper young gentleman in literature should show. In fact, he does
not even answer her when she first speaks to him. " 'Hello, Monsieur Lugin,'
said Minskaja *to someone.* 'I am tired . . . say something!' " With virtually
no preface, Lugin abruptly tells her:

"Imagine what a misfortune is following me; what could be worse for a man who, as I, has dedicated himself to painting! For two weeks now everybody looks yellow to me — and only people. If it were all objects it would be all right; then there would be a harmony in the general coloring; I would think that I was walking through a gallery of the Spanish school. — But no! Everything else is as before; only faces have changed. Sometimes it seems to me that people have lemons instead of heads."

Then he tells her he is going mad and describes the voice he hears repeating the address. She replies to this "absentmindedly" ("rassejanno"), as though little were amiss. But when Lugin takes her advice to visit the address, she looks after him "with surprise." Naturally it is possible to explain away Lugin's actions and words in this section as resulting from his disturbed mental condition, but this does not alter the fact that the passage is written so as to produce a humorous effect (cf. the lemons) and represents an inversion of literary conventions.

The Apartment number 27 in the house of Štoss shares with many haunted places the fact that a series of people have been unable to live there. The description of the rooms makes them unappealing; they are damp and full of cobwebs, and the wallpaper has a green background with red parrots and golden lyres! Lermontov comments with ironic understatement, "Overall the rooms had a certain strange, out-of-date appearance." Nevertheless, "Lugin, I don't know why, took a liking to it [the apartment]." Lugin himself remarks on the odd coincidence that he noticed the portrait on the wall only after saying he would rent the apartment (a trite motif). Already anticipating some mysterious significance to the picture, he seems not too surprised at the absurd inscription "Wednesday." Mersereau notes that the apparition of the old man has a farcical side, but we cannot agree with him that it consists in his dress. Ghosts are often described as attired in nightclothes, a motif which emphasizes that the apparition is at home on the premises. What is funny is the excessive idea of the little old man's figure growing tall or short, fat or thin at will. Lugin, himself mocking the traditional view of ghosts, tells him that he does not intend to bet his soul on the turn of a card. Other conventional motifs used include the description of the old man as a "dead figure." Lermontov forgets to say the apparition looks like the portrait until the episode is over.

The combination of details such as these tends to demonstrate that Lermontov wrote the story rapidly and somewhat carelessly and was consciously parodying the conventions of the horror story. *Štoss* shows nearly every evidence of having been written "off the top of his head," and it reads rather like an improvisation throughout. Indeed, it might find a place in the history of improvisations of the period, for its tone is light and its chief virtues are the surprise and suspense that might hold the attention of a listening audience, such as that to which Lermontov in fact read it. Where *Štoss* differs from the genre of the fantastic improvisation, as far as we know it, is in some passages of realistic description unnecessary to the action.

Mersereau believes that *Štoss* owes a lot to Puškin's "Pikovaja dama," in that they are both "anti-romantic" works. Without becoming involved in a reinterpretation of "Pikovaja dama," it is only necessary to point out that that story is, at least artistically, a serious and carefully constructed work. And while Puškin's sympathies were not wholly with the fantastic, "Pikovaja dama" cannot be said to be a parody, while the hastily written *Štoss* certainly is. It appears to us rather that the "anti-romantic" (that is, anti-fantastic) character of Lermontov's fragment comes almost wholly from Gogol', who, as we know, abandoned the supernatural side of his original "Portret," showed the tragic consequences of dreams in "Nevskij prospekt" and parodied the fantastic genre in "Nos." It is likely that Lermontov's artist, deceived by his madness, would have to pay dearly for his illusions, as do Gogol''s heroes. In this connection the manuscript word "skoropostižnaja" is very suggestive. Whether Lermontov intended to complete *Štoss* and revise it for publishing is really irrelevant; his ironical attitude toward the genre of writing is clear.


### 3


Rodzevič wrote that Hoffmann cannot be said to have left large traces in Russian literature, because the very greatest prose-writers were not deeply affected by him. [133)] Whether we like this as a criterion or not, we must recognize that in the cases of Puškin and Lermontov — but perhaps not Gogol' — this appraisal is correct. And of the three it was Lermontov who was least of all influenced. Despite his affinity for the mystical vision of the German poets, Lermontov never seems to have become preoccupied with the ideas of Hoffmann. In both instances where we suspect direct or indirect connections of Lermontov works with Hoffmann's, the themes are degraded and treated humorously. "Tambovskaja kaznačejša" is a burlesque of literary representations of love, and *Štoss,* following in the steps of Gogol', parodies the fantastic school and the artist's feminine ideal.

261

# Notes

1.  E. G. Gudde, "E. Th. A. Hoffmann's Reception in England," *PMLA*, vol. 41 (1926–27), p. 1005. See also H. Zylstra, "E. T. A. Hoffmann in England and America," Harvard diss., 1940.

2.  Elizabeth Teichmann, *La fortune d'Hoffmann en France* (Paris, 1961), p. 17 ff. Henceforth this book will be referred to as "Teichmann."

3.  Franz Schneider, "E. T. A. Hoffmann en España: Apuntes bibliográficos e históricos," in *Festschrift Bonilla y San Martín* (Madrid, 1927), p. 279 ff.

4.  Michel Gorlin, "Hoffmann en Russie," *Revue de Littérature Comparée*, vol. 15 (1935), pp. 60–76.

5.  S. I. Rodzevič, "K istorii russkogo romantizma: È. T. A. Gofman i 30–40-e gody v našej literature," *Russkij filologičeskij vestnik*, vol. 27 (1917), pp. 194–237.

6.  Teodor Levit, "Gofman v russkoj literature," in È. T. A. Gofman, *Sobranie sočinenij*, vol. 6 (M., 1930), pp. 335–371. Levit mentions other Russians he thinks were touched in one degree or another by Hoffmann: Katkov, K. Aksakov, Ju. Samarin, Karolina Pavlova, A. Grigor'ev. Other scholars add people such as Bestužev-Marlinskij, Vel'tman, Kukol'nik, Baron Brambeus (Senkovskij), Kireevskij, Družinin. Writings of some of these are outside our period; and in any case it would be impossible to treat all of them.

7.  Charles E. Passage, *The Russian Hoffmannists*, Slavistic Printings and Reprintings, 35 (The Hague: Mouton, 1963). Hereafter cited as "Passage."

8.  *Dostoevski the Adapter: A Study of Dostoevski's Use of the Tales of Hoffmann*, University of North Carolina Studies in Comparative Literature, 10 (Chapel Hill: University of North Carolina Press, 1954).

9.  Mention should be made also of Vincenzo Gibelli's book *E. T. A. Hoffmann: Fortuna di un poeta tedesco in terra di Russia* (Milano: Giuffrè, 1964). It is a slight and superficial piece of work, undocumented and lacking in specifics, which can serve only to acquaint Italian readers with some general information about Hoffmann's influence in Russian literature. Gibelli included A. F. Vel'tman among the earliest writers affected by the German; but he only asserted the connection without trying to make a case.

10. Passage's "Chronology of Hoffmannia in Russia" (pp. 248–252) is quite in-

complete and full of errors. That the compiler was limited to data in secondary sources is evident from his note 7 on page 72, where he is unable to confirm that "Očarovannyj bumažnik" ("Die Irrungen") appeared in *Moskovskij telegraf* in 1829.

11. *Russkaja periodičeskaja pečat' (1702–1894): Spravočnik* (M., 1959), p. 175.

12. *Russkij biografičeskij slovar'*, vol. 14 (1905), pp. 479–480.

13. The error "Irving Washington" for Washington Irving was common in the Russian press of the period.

14. In D. V. Venevitinov, *Polnoe sobranie sočinenij* (M.-L., 1934), ed. B. V. Smirenskij. Venevitinov's letter is given on p. 338 and the manuscript text on pp. 176–183.

15. /Walter Scott/, "On the Supernatural in Fictitious Composition, and Particularly on the Works of Ernest Theodore William Hoffmann," *Foreign Quarterly Review*, vol. 1 (July, 1827), pp. 60–98.

16. A note attached to the article cites "Oeuvres complettes /sic/ de Sir Walter Scott, Paris, 1829," as though that were the source for the translation. However, as far as I can determine the Defauconpret translation of Scott in French did not include by 1829 his essay on Hoffmann; and Teichmann mentions no such French edition. The first part of Scott's article appeared under the title "Du merveilleux dans le roman" in *Revue de Paris*, vol. 1 (April 12, 1829), pp. 25–33, bearing the exact equivalent of the Russian title and breaking off precisely where the first Russian installment does; the second part was made the introduction to Loève-Veimars' translation of Hoffmann. Pierre-Georges Castex wrote on this subject but seemed confused about the publishing facts. See "Walter Scott contre Hoffmann: Les épisodes d'une rivalité littéraire en France," in *Mélanges d'histoire littéraire offerts à Daniel Mornet* (Paris, 1951), pp. 169–176.

17. D. S. Mirsky, *A History of Russian Literature From Its Beginnings to 1900* (N. Y., 1958), p. 119.

18. V. Gorlenko, "A. A. Perovskij," *Kievskaja starina*, vol. 21 (1888), no. 4.

19. Pogorel'skij's works were collected in the posthumous *Sočinenija* in two vols. (SPb., 1853). References in the present chapter are to this edition.

20. S. S. Ignatov, "A. Pogorel'skij i È. Gofman," *Russkij filologičeskij vestnik*, vol. 72 (1914), pp. 249–278.

21.  Evgenij Degen, "Èrnest-Teodor-Amadej Gofman (Istoriko-literaturnyj ètjud)," *Mir Božij*, 1901, no. 12, otd. 1, pp. 113–145.

22.  Arthur Sakheim, *E. T. A. Hoffmann: Studien zu seiner Persönlichkeit und seinen Werken* (Leipzig, 1908).

23.  A. I. Kirpičnikov, "Antonij Pogorel'skij: Èpizod iz istorii russkogo romantizma," *Istoričeskij vestnik*, 1890, no. 10; reprinted in his *Očerki po istorii novoj russkoj literatury* (SPb., 1896), where the reference appears p. 101.

24.  Passage tries to see "Der goldne Topf" as source for the general idea of "Izidor i Anjuta" but in effect admits that this is farfetched (p. 50).

25.  *Syn otečestva*, 1828, č. 118, pp. 274–276.

26.  *Severnye cvety na 1829 g.* (1828), Proza, pp. 85–93.

27.  Dal' indicates that *sten'* is a dialect form for *ten'* 'shadow' and also for a household spirit (*domovoj, domašnjaja nežit'*). See his *Tolkovyj slovar'*, vol. 4 (1882), pp. 350–351.

28.  *Moskovskij vestnik*, 1828, č. 10, pp. 160–164.

29.  *Moskovskij telegraf*, 1828, č. 20, pp. 358–362.

30.  See the comparisons made by Passage, p. 60.

31.  Mirsky, p. 120.

32.  A. I. Kirpičnikov, "Nemeckij istočnik odnogo russkogo romana," *Russkaja starina*, 1900, no. 12, pp. 617–619.

33.  "Zacharias Werner," *Le Globe*, March 24, 1830.

34.  Note that V. Praxov was also translator of a French article on Hoffmann in 1830 (C3).

35.  "Werner: De sa vie et de ses écrits," *Le Globe*, 1828, pp. 513–515, 531–533.

36.  From *Morgenblatt*, Jan., 1831.

37.  *Teleskop*, 1831, č. 6, pp. 482–483.

38.  The 1819 and 1824 editions of *Allgemeine deutsche Real-Encyclopädie* (Leipzig: Brockhaus) carried the incorrect date of birth 1778.

39.  Quoted from I. I. Zamotin, *Romantizm 20-x gg.* (Varšava, 1903), vol. 1, p. 212.

264                                     Notes

40.  Jules Janin, "Hoffmann et Paganini," *Contes fantastiques et contes littéraires* (Paris, 1863).

41.  X. Marmier, "Hoffmann," *Nouvelle Revue Germanique*, vol. 13 (1833), pp. 12–29. On April 14 the article was reprinted in *Cabinet de Lecture*. (Teichmann, p. 113.)

42.  V. G. Belinskij, *Polnoe sobranie sočinenij* (M., 1953–59), vol. 1, p. 288.

43.  Janin was popular in Russia in this period. Teichmann mentions (p. 95 ff.) that in the preface to the 1832 edition of *Contes fantastiques et contes littéraires* he admitted that his stories have no real claim to the designation "fantastic" and he refers to Hoffmann as "maître fantastique."

44.  A. Končeozerskij, "Gofmanskij večer: Povest'," *Literaturnye pribavlenija*, 1835, no. 83, pp. 659–662; no. 84, pp. 667–670.

45.  Further research might prove that still more of the Russian versions of Hoffmann's tales were done from the French rather than directly from German. It may seem an easy matter to determine this, but in practice confronting the texts is often complicated by the fact that no one library has all the required editions. In some cases I saw French editions when the Russian ones were no longer available to me.

46.  "Schicksale eines Livländers in St. Petersburg von 1833 bis auf die Gegenwart," *St. Petersburger Zeitung*, 1878, no. 23–69. Quoted from Štejn.

47.  Sergej Štejn, *Puškin i Gofman: Sravnitel'noe literaturnoe issledovanie* (Derpt, 1927), Acta et Commentationes Universitatis Tartuensis/Dorpatensis, B. Humaniora, 13 (Tartu, 1928).

48.  Štejn took information on Puškin's library from B. L. Modzalevskij, *Biblioteka A. S. Puškina* (SPb., 1910).

49.  Tit Kosmokratov /V. P. Titov/, "Uedinennyj domik na Vasil'evskom," *Severnye cvety na 1829 god* (SPb., 1828), Proza, pp. 147–217.

50.  I was indebted to Professor Passage for calling my attention to "Datura fastuosa" in this connection.

51.  A. Veselovskij, *Zapadnoe vlijanie v novoj russkoj literature*, 5th ed. (M., 1916), p. 184.

52.  Sakheim, p. 63.

53.  In the cited article on Pogorel'skij and Hoffmann.

54. N. A. Polevoj, "Èpilog Abbaddonny," *Syn otečestva*, 1838, vol. 4, Russkaja slovesnost', pp. 17–82; vol. 5, Russkaja slovesnost', pp. 101–156.

55. Passage indicates (p. 87) that the story has more of Klopstock and Schiller in it than Hoffmann.

56. A. I. Kirpičnikov, "Meždu slavjanofilami i zapadnikami: N. A. Mel'gunov; Istoriko-literaturnyj očerk, po neizdannym dokumentam," *Russkaja starina*, 1898, no. 11. The article was reprinted in his book *Očerki po istorii russkoj literatury*, 2nd ed., vol. 2 (M., 1903), pp. 148–220.

57. N. A. Mel'gunov, *Rasskazy o bylom i nebyvalom*, 2 vols. (M., 1834; censor's approval dated March 15, 1833).

58. N. A. Mel'gunov, "Putevye očerki," *Moskovskij nabljudatel'*, 1836, č. 8, pp. 5–47 and 143–193.

59. "Kto že on? Povest'," *Teleskop*, 1831, č. 3, pp. 164–187, 303–326, 446–462 (signed "M.").

60. "Otryvok iz povesti: Da ili net? Glava III, Podsudimyj," *Teleskop*, 1834, č. 19, pp. 144–162.

61. *Moskvitjanin*, 1844, no. 1, Izjaščnaja slovesnost', pp. 39–94; no. 6, pp. 197–231.

62. *Moskvitjanin*, 1845, no. 10, pp. 175–200.

63. *Literaturnye pribavlenija*, 1839, vol. 1, nos. 18–21, pp. 395, 414, 434 and 456.

64. P. N. Sakulin, *Iz istorii russkogo idealizma: Kn. V. F. Odoevskij, myslitel'-pisatel'*, č. 2 (M., 1913), p. 343.

65. M. Gorlin, *N. V. Gogol und E. Th. A. Hoffmann,* Veröffentlichungen des Slavischen Instituts an der Friedrich-Wilhelms-Universität Berlin, 9 (Leipzig, 1933). Cf. Ad. Stender-Petersen, "Gogol und die deutsche Romantik," *Euphorion*, vol. 24 (1922), pp. 628–653.

66. *Moskovskij nabljudatel'*, 1835, č. 1, p. 404.

67. *Molva*, 1835, č. 9, no. 17; quoted here from Belinskij, *Polnoe sobranie sočinenij*, vol. 1, p. 181.

68. Gorlin mistakenly says that neither Odoevskij nor Polevoj used the device of the diary. He overlooked the journal of the (mad) hero in Odoevskij's "Sil'fida."

69. In effect acknowledged by Hoffmann in his "Nachricht von den neuesten Schicksalen des Hundes Berganza" in *Fantasiestücke in Callots Manier.*

70. An attempt was made by Charles Passage (p. 174 f.) to connect "Šinel'" (The Overcoat) also with Hoffmann. He thought that the ghost owes something to the ghost in "Das Majorat," though that is farfetched. In this connection Passage makes a comment that illustrates his method of using the unprovable to prove a point: "The echo from Hoffmann is remote admittedly, and undemonstrable, but it is there. The influence of Hoffmann had pervaded Gogol's artistic mind more thoroughly than he knew."

71. *Literaturnye salony i kružki: Pervaja polovina XIX v.* (M.-L., 1930), p. 179.

72. A common remedy named for the famous Dr. Friedrich Hoffmann (1660–1742).

73. *Literaturnye salony,* p. 450 f.

74. *Literaturnye salony,* p. 445 f.

75. A. Veselovskij, *Zapadnye vlijanija v novoj russkoj literature* (M., 1910), p. 235.

76. V. Žirmunskij, *Gete v russkoj literature* (L., 1937), p. 193.

77. Especially vol. 2, pp. 342–363, for his views of Odoevskij's relation to Hoffmann and Jean Paul.

78. Quoted in the magazine *Ljubov' k trem apel'sinam,* 1915.

79. V. F. Odoevskij, *Russkie noči* (M., 1913), p. 14.

80. *Literaturnye salony,* p. 458.

81. V. F. Odoevskij, *Muzykal'no-literaturnoe nasledie* (M., 1956), p. 244.

82. Belinskij, vol. 8, p. 314 f. An undeniable connection with Hoffmann, however, is the title of one of Odoevskij's tales for children, "Pis'ma k ljubeznejšemu djadjuške Gospodinu Kateru fon Muru ot ego počtitel'nogo plemjannika Kotovas'ki" (Letters to Most Kind Uncle Mr. Kater von Murr from his Respectful Nephew Kotovas'ka), published in part 1 of *Detskaja biblioteka* issued by A. Bašuckij and A. Očkin, 1836. See Sakulin (part 2, pp. 358–359), who says there is nothing of Hoffmann in the contents of the story.

83. Odoevskij had earlier planned a cycle of stories with the collective title *Dom sumasšedšix* (Madhouse) but abandoned it and partly merged the project with *Russkie noči.* Passage perversely suggests (p. 103) that Odoevskij gave up the

first plan because it would be too obviously "Hoffmannian." And then Passage sidesteps the question of the form of *Russkie noči* by saying that only its predecessor, *Dom sumasšedšix*, was suggested by *Die Serapionsbrüder*.

84. Sergej Štejn lists in his bibliography (p. 326) an additional translation for 1836, "Krejsler," said to have been printed in *Moskovskij nabljudatel'*. This evidently is an error for the "Krejsler" which appeared there in 1838 (T43).

85. Belinskij, vol. 2, p. 164.

86. See details of this incident in A. I. Gercen, *Sobranie sočinenij*, vol. 1 (M., 1954), pp. 487–488.

87. *Nikolaj Polevoj: Materialy po istorii russkoj literatury i žurnalistiki 30-x godov* (L., 1934), p. 508.

88. In a letter of July 10, 1838, to Panaev Belinskij stated that the translation of "Don Juan" in *Nabljudatel'* was done by Botkin. However, on comparing its accuracy to the looseness of Botkin's "Kreisleriana" one finds this hard to believe. Perhaps Belinskij made a mistake for "Kreisleriana," or for the later "Goldner Topf," which does have the characteristics of Botkin's work. (Žitomirskaja accepted that Botkin was the translator of T42.)

89. Belinskij, vol. 2, p. 43.

90. Belinskij, vol. 2, p. 505.

91. See P. Morozov, "È. T. A. Gofman v Rossii," in È. T. A. Gofman, *Fantastičeskie p'esy v manere Kallo* (M.-L., 1923), vol. 1, p. 45.

92. Belinskij, vol. 3, p. 85.

93. *Literaturnye salony*, p. 458.

94. Belinskij, vol. 4, p. 186.

95. Belinskij, vol. 11, pp. 496, 507 f., 545.

96. Gercen, vol. 25, p. 102.

97. Belinskij, vol. 4, p. 165.

98. Belinskij, vol. 4, p. 292.

99. Belinskij, vol. 4, pp. 315, 318.

100. *Ènciklopedičeskij slovar'* (SPb., 1895), vol. 15, p. 32.

101.  /J. E. Hitzig/, *Aus Hoffmanns Leben und Nachlaß*, vol. 2 (Berlin, 1823), pp. 144–146.

102.  1840, vol. 12, Bibliog. xronika, pp. 6–7.

103.  Cf. V. P. Botkin, *Sočinenija*, vol. 3 (SPb., 1893).

104.  Evg. Bobrov, *Filosofija i literatura*, vol. 1 (Kazan', 1898), p. 132.

105.  I. I. Panaev, *Literaturnye vospominanija* (M., 1950), p. 105.

106.  D. V. Grigorovič, *Literaturnye vospominanija* (M., 1961), p. 47 f.

107.  *Dnevnik V. K. Kjuxel'bekera* (L., 1929), p. 87.

108.  F. M. Dostoevskij, *Pis'ma*, vol. 1 (M.–L., 1928), p. 47.

109.  Sakheim, p. 56.

110.  *T. N. Granovskij i ego perepiska* (M., 1897), vol. 2, pp. 89–90.

111.  *Russkij filologičeskij vestnik*, vol. 76 (1917), p. 196.

112.  P. N. Annenkov, *Literaturnye vospominanija* (L., 1928), pp. 186–189.

113.  S. A. Vengerov, "V. N. Olin," in V. G. Belinskij, *Polnoe sobranie sočinenij*, vol. 4 (SPb., 1901), pp. 513–519.

114.  V. N. Olin, *Strannyj bal: Povest' iz rasskazov na stancii; i vosem' stixotvorenij* (SPb., 1838).

115.  V. N. Olin, *Rasskazy na stancii*, 2 parts, 1839.

116.  "Razdelenie poèzii na rody i vidy," *Otečestvennye zapiski*, vol. 15, pp. 13–64.

117.  "Russkaja narodnaja skazka," *Otečestvennye zapiski*, vol. 18, no. 10, otd. 5, pp. 19–32.

118.  Belinskij, vol. 11, pp. 496, 507 f.

119.  Passage attributed the translations of both "Meister Floh" and "Klein Zaches" to Katkov, but he is clearly wrong in the first instance. R. I. Sementkovskij in his *M. N. Katkov: Ego žizn' i literaturnaja dejatel'nost'* (SPb., 1892), p. 11, states that Katkov in his youth made rather "unsuccessful" translations of Heine, Hoffmann and Shakespeare for the *Nabljudatel'*, but he does not name the works.

120.  *Otečestvennye zapiski*, vol. 36, no. 10, otd. 5, pp. 37–54.

121. "Russkaja literatura v 1844 godu," *Otečestvennye zapiski*, 1845, vol. 38, no. 1, otd. 5, pp. 1–42.

122. Ėrnst Teodor Amadej Gofman, *Izbrannye proizvedenija v trex tomax*, 3 vols. (M.: Xudožestvennaja literatura, 1962).

123. Ėrnst Teodor Amadej Gofman, *Žitejskie vozzrenija kota Murra vkupe a fragmentami biografii kapel'mejstera Iogannesa Krejslera, slučajno ucelevšimi v makulaturnyx listax: Povesti i rasskazy*, Biblioteka vsemirnoj literatury, Serija vtoraja: Literatura XIX veka (M.: Xudožestvennaja literatura, 1967).

124. André Lirondelle, *Le poète Alexis Tolstoï: L'homme et l'oeuvre* (Paris, 1912), p. 11.

125. I think, however, that Margaret Dalton somewhat overemphasizes the relevance of "Leben dreier Freunde" in her *A. K. Tolstoy* (New York: Twayne, 1972), pp. 42–43.

126. *Otečestvennye zapiski*, 1841, vol. 18, otd. 6, pp. 37–38.

127. A. K. Tolstoj, *Polnoe sobranie sočinenij*, vol. 3, (SPb., 1907), pp. 81–108.

128. Belinskij, vol. 11, p. 496.

129. *Russkaja starina*, 1882, no. 9, p. 619.

130. M. Ju. Lermontov, *Polnoe sobranie sočinenij*, vol. 4 (M.-L., 1948), pp. 468–469.

131. John Mersereau Jr., "Lermontov's *Shtoss:* Hoax or Literary Credo? *Slavic Review*, vol. 21 (1962), pp. 281–295.

132. *Russkij filologičeskij vestnik*, vol. 77 (1917), p. 197. We were unable to consult Rodzevič's book *Lermontov kak romanist* (Kiev, 1914).

133. *Ibid.*, p. 195.

# Bibliography

*Russian Translations of Hoffmann's Works, 1822 – 1845*

## 1822

T1.    "Devica Skuderi (Povest' veka Ljudovika XIV)." *Biblioteka dlja čtenija*, 1822, kn. 3, pp. 14–50, 51–86, 95–138. At the end: "K. G. Gofman."

("Das Fräulein von Scuderi")

T1a.   *Devica Skuderi. Povest' veka Ljudovika XIV.* Per. s nem. SPb., 1822. Offprint of T1.

("Das Fräulein von Scuderi")

## 1823

T2.    "O sčastii igrokov. (S. Gofmana)." *Vestnik Evropy*, 1823, no. 13, pp. 97–140. At the end: "S nemec. Vas. Poljakov."

("Spielerglück")

T3.    "Dož i dogaressa. (Povest' soč. Gofmana)." *Biblioteka dlja čtenija*, 1823, kn. 12, pp. 49–138. Signed: "K – n."

("Doge und Dogaresse")

## 1825

T4.    "Beloe prividenie." *Moskovskij telegraf*, 1825, Pribavlenija, č. 6, no. 22, pp. 435–453; no. 23, pp. 458–470; no. 24, pp. 479–490. Note: "Povest', soč. Gofmana." At the end: "(S nemeckogo.)." Cf. T18.

("Die Marquise de la Pivardiere")

## 1826

T5.    "Botanik. (Povest', soč. Gofmana)." *Moskovskij telegraf*, 1826, t. 8, Slovesnost', no. 5, pp. 11–37; no. 6, pp. 48–76; no. 7, pp. 89–121.

("Datura fastuosa")

1827

T6. "Čto pena v vine, to sny v golove. Povest'." *Moskovskij vestnik,* 1827, t. 5, pp. 244–301. At the end: "(Iz Gofmana). V." /Tr. D. Venevitinov et al./ Cf. T36.

("Der Magnetiseur")

1829

T7. "Očarovannyj bumažnik. (Povest', soč. Gofmana)." *Moskovskij telegraf,* 1829, č. 25, pp. 343–361, 461–489.

("Die Irrungen")

T8. "Sin'or Formika. Povest', soč. Gofmana." *Syn otečestva i Severnyj arxiv,* 1829, (nos. 13–21), t. 2, pp. 321–336, 385–400; t. 3, pp. 3–24, 65–90, 129–144, 193–203, 257–272, 321–337; t. 4, pp. 3–27. Cf. T31.

("Signor Formica")

1830

T9. /A tale/, *Syn otečestva,* 1830, č. 131, no. 4, pp. 219–228, in the text of the article "Poslednie dni žizni i smert' Gofmana." Tr. from French. Cf. C2.

("Die Abenteuer der Silvester-Nacht, Die Gesellschaft im Keller")

T10. "Vospominanija osady Drezdena, v 1813 godu. Soč. *Gofmana.*" *Slavjanin,* 1830, č. 14, pp. 677–692. At the end: "L – n." In table of contents: "per. Laxmana." /Tr. from French./

("Erscheinungen")

T11. "Pustoj dom. (Iz soč. Goffmana)." *Literaturnaja gazeta,* 1830, no. 31, pp. 245–250; no. 32, pp. 253–258; no. 33, pp. 261–264. At the end: "S nemec. V. Langer."

("Das öde Haus")

T12. "Zaxarij Verner." *Moskovskij vestnik,* 1830, č. 3, pp. 118–136 (Proza). At the end: "Iz *Globe.* R." In table of contents: "(iz Gofmana)."

("Zacharias Werner")

T13.  "Maiorat. (Povest' Gofmana)." *Moskovskij telegraf,* 1830, č. 34, pp. 307–339, 439–471; č. 35, pp. 42–73, 196–223.

("Das Majorat")

T14.  "Sanctus. (Povest' soč. Gofmana)." *Vestnik Evropy,* 1830, t. 5, nos. 19–20, pp. 220–249. At the end: "Okt. 8. 1830 goda." /Tr. V. Praxov? (Žitomirskaja)./

("Das Sanctus")

T15.  "Kremonskaja skripka. (Povest' Gofmana.)." *Vestnik Evropy,* 1830, t. 6, nos. 21–22, pp. 3–45. Note: "Per. V. Praxov."

("Rat Krespel")

T16.  "Domovoj-pesočnik. Povest' Gofmana." *Moskovskij telegraf,* 1830, č. 36, pp. 302–337, 464–489.

("Der Sandmann")

T17.  "Ezuitskaja cerkov'. (Iz Gofmana.)." *Moskovskij vestnik,* 1830, č. 6, pp. 33–78. At the end: "Per. V. D." /From French of Loève-Veimars./ Cf. T37.

("Die Jesuiterkirche in G.")

T18.  "Beloe prividenie." In *Povesti i literaturnye otryvki,* ed. N. Polevoj, č. 5, pp. 5–91. M., 1830. Censor's approval of May 5, 1830. Reprint from *Moskovskij telegraf,* 1825; cf. T4.

("Die Marquise de la Pivardiere")

1831

T19.  "Ignac Denner. Povest'. (Gofmana.)." *Žurnal inostrannoj slovesnosti,* 1831, č.1, no. 1, pp. 3–40; no. 2, pp. 105–127. Two parts only.

("Ignaz Denner," fragment)

T20.  "Sčast'e igroka. (Povest' Gofmana)." *Sankt-Peterburgskij vestnik,* 1831, t. 2, no. 15, pp. 25–34; no. 16, pp. 45–50; no. 17, pp. 65–76; no. 18, pp. 89–100. At the end: "Per. N. Ju." /N. Jungmejster?/.

("Spielerglück")

T21.  "Majorat. Povest'." *Sankt-Peterburgskij vestnik*, 1831, t. 3, no. 30, pp. 59–74; no. 31, pp. 79–99; no. 32, pp. 115–133; no. 33, pp. 143–154. At the end: "S nemec. *A*."

("Das Majorat")

T22.  "Vybor nevesty. Povest'." *Syn otečestva*, 1831, č. 143 (Izjaščnaja slovesnost'), no. 30, pp. 193–212; no. 31, pp. 257–286; no. 32, pp. 321–347; č. 144 (Izjaščnaja slovesnost'), no. 33, pp. 3–15. Note: "Per. Ju – č."

("Die Brautwahl")

T22a.  *Vybor nevesty. Povest' Gofmana.* SPb.: N. Greč, 1831. 87 pp. Censor's approval of Aug. 1, 1831. At the end: "Perev. Ju – č." Offprint of T22.

("Die Brautwahl")

T23.  "Pjatyj i sed'moj večera, iz povesti: Zolotoj goršok. Sočinenie Gofmana." *Moskovskij telegraf*, 1831, č. 40, pp. 33–63.

("Der goldne Topf," excerpts)

T24.  "Tainstvennyj gost'. (Povest' Gofmana.)." *Literaturnye pribavlenija k Russkomu invalidu*, 1831, Slovesnost', no. 60, pp. 466–470; no. 61, pp. 474–477; no. 62, pp. 482–487; no. 63, pp. 490–495; no. 64, pp. 497–502. Note: "S nem. *V. Tilo.*"

("Der unheimliche Gast")

T25.  "Skazka." *Literaturnye pribavlenija k Russkomu invalidu*, 1831, no. 77, Slovesnost', pp. 604–606. At the end: "(Iz Gofmana.)."

("Nachricht aus dem Leben eines bekannten Mannes")

T26.  "Pesočnyj čelovek. Povest'." *Teleskop*, 1831, č. 6, no. 22, pp. 196–232; no. 23, pp. 335–360. Cf. T35.

("Der Sandmann")

T27.  "Čerty iz žizni kota Murra i otryvki biografii kapel'mejstera Ioganna Krejslera. Soč. È. T. A. Goffmana." *Moskovskij telegraf*, 1831, č. 42, pp. 255–286, 385–410.

(*Lebensansichten des Katers Murr*, excerpts)

T28. "Tainstvennyj gost'. Povest' Gofmana." *Syn otečestva,* 1831, č. 146, Izjaščnaja slovesnost', no. 50, pp. 321–343; no. 51, pp. 385–404; no. 52, pp. 457–478.

("Der unheimliche Gast")

1832

T29. "Žizn' trex druzej. Povest' Goffmana." *Moskovskij telegraf,* 1832, č. 44, pp. 495–532; č. 45, pp. 30–69. At the end: "Revel'. Dekabr'1831. S nemeckogo I. Bzsmkn" /I. I. Bessomykin/. Cf. T38.

("Ein Fragment aus dem Leben dreier Freunde")

T30. /Excerpts from *Serapionovy brat'ja/. Raduga,* 1832, kn. 6, pp. 483–486, in the text of the article "Russkij perevod povestej Gofmana." Tr. I. I. Bessomykin. Cf. T38.

(*Die Serapionsbrüder,* excerpts)

T31. "Sin'or Formika. (Soč. Gofmana)." In *Rasskazčik, ili Izbrannye povesti inostrannyx avtorov,* č. 4, pp. 1–157. SPb.: Nikolaj Greč, 1832. Reprint from *Syn otečestva i Severnyj arxiv,* 1829; cf. T8.

("Signor Formica")

1833

T32. "Don Žuan. (Povest' Gofmana)." *Literaturnye listki, Pribavlenija k Odesskomu vestniku,* 1833, no. 12, pp. 95–98; no. 13, pp. 103–105. At the end: "Perev. M. Ivanenko."

("Don Juan")

1835

T33. *Skazka o ščelkune: sočinenie Gofmana. (Perevod s nemeckogo).* M.: Lazarevyx Institut vostočnyx jazykov, 1835. 135 pp. Censor's approval of March 19,1834. Cf. T53.

("Nußknacker und Mausekönig")

Bibliography

T33a. "Kukla g-n Ščelkuška. (Fantastičeskaja skazka iz kukol'nogo mira)." In *Detskaja knižka na 1835 god, kotoruju sostavil dlja umnyx, milyx i priležnyx malen'-kix čitatelej i čitatel'nic Vladimir Burnašev*, pp. 247–313. SPb.: Dep. vnešn. torgovli, 1835. /Žitomirskaja, p. 43./

("Nußknacker und Mausekönig")

1836

T34. "Nedobryj gost'. Povest' Gofmanna." *Teleskop*, 1836, č. 31, pp. 114–142, 299–340.

("Der unheimliche Gast")

T35. "Pesočnyj čelovek. Povest'." In *Sorok odna povest' lučšix inostrannyx pisatelej*, ed. Nikolaj Nadeždin, č. 3, pp. 105–202. M.: N. Stepanov, 1836. Reprint from *Teleskop*, 1831; cf. T26.

("Der Sandmann")

T36. "Čto pena v vine, to sny v golove. Povest' Gofmana." In *Sorok odna povest' lučšix inostrannyx pisatelej*, ed. Nikolaj Nadeždin, č. 5, pp. 1–85. M.: N. Stepanov, 1836. Reprint from *Moskovskij vestnik*, 1827; cf. T6.

("Der Magnetiseur")

T37. "Ezuitskaja cerkov'. Povest' Gofmana." In *Sorok odna povest' lučšix inostrannyx pisatelej*, ed. Nikolaj Nadeždin, č. 11, pp. 189–251. M.: N. Stepanov, 1836. Reprint from *Moskovskij vestnik*, 1830; cf. T17.

("Die Jesuiterkirche in G.")

T38. *Serapionovy brat'ja. Sobranie povestej i skazok*. Sočinenie È. T. A. Goffmana. Perevod s nemeckogo I. Bessomykina. 8 čč. M.: N. Stepanov, 1836. Cf. T29, T30.

(*Die Serapionsbrüder*)

Čast' pervaja. 240 pp. Censor's approval of Jan. 14, 1835. Contents: "Razgovor i kratkie rasskazy druzej," "Rasskaz o mnimom Serapione," "Rasskaz o sovetnike Krespele," "Fermata," "Poèt i kompozitor."

Čast' vtoraja. 418 pp. Censor's approval of Jan. 14, 1835. Contents: "Razgovor druzej," "Otryvok iz žizni trex druzej," "Dvor Artusa," "Falunskie rudokopni," "Čeloveček-ščelkuška i myšinyj korolek."

Čast' tret'ja. 387 pp. Censor's approval of Feb. 19, 1835. Contents: "Razgovor i rasskazy druzej," "Sostjazanie pevcov," "Razgovor i rasskazy druzej," "Avtomat," "Dož i dogaressa."

Čast' četvertaja. 296 pp. Censor's approval of Feb. 19, 1835. Contents: "Razgovor druzej," "Mejster Martin," "Čužoe ditja."

Čast' pjataja. 348 pp. Censor's approval of March 18, 1835. Contents: /"Razgovor druzej," "Vybor nevesty," "Tainstvennyj gost'"/.

Čast' šestaja. 297 pp. Censor's approval of March 22, 1835. Contents: "Soedinenie i razgovor druzej," "Devica Skjuderi," "Razgovor druzej," "Sčastie igrokov," "Razgovor i kratkie rasskazy druzej: O starike-prokaznike, O ljubitele prekrasnyx vidov, O strannom znatoke muzyki."

Čast' sed'maja. 314 pp. Censor's approval of March 26, 1835. Contents: "Razgovor i kratkie rasskazy druzej," "Sin'or Formika," "Razgovor i kratkie rasskazy druzej," "Javlenija," "Razgovor druzej."

Čast' os'maja. 321 pp. Censor's approval of March 29, 1835. Contents: "Razgovor druzej," "Sceplenie veščej," "Razgovor druzej," "Rasskaz Kipriana o grafe Ippolite," "Razgovor druzej," "Rasskaz Otmara ob èstetičeskom večere," "Carskaja nevesta."

### 1838

T39.  "Master Iogannes Vaxt. (povest' Gofmana.)." *Moskovskij nabljudatel'*, 1838, č. 16, pp. 206–267.

("Meister Johannes Wacht")

T40.  /Excerpts from diaries and letters/, *Moskovskij nabljudatel'*, 1838, č. 16, pp. 345–384, 497–541, in the text of the article "Žizn' Gofmana" (cf. C8). Translation from French.

(Tagebuch und Briefe, excerpts)

T41.  /Theodor's story/, *Moskovskij nabljudatel'*, 1838, č. 16, pp. 361–365, in the text of the article "Žizn' Gofmana" (cf. C8). Translation from French.

(Theodor's story, end of Book Three of *Die Serapionsbrüder*)

T42. "Don Žuan. Proisšestvie, slučivšeesja s putešestvujuščim èntuzijastom. (Iz Gofmana.)." *Moskovskij nabljudatel'*, 1838, č. 16, pp. 546–564.

("Don Juan")

T43. "Krejsler. (Iz Gofmana)." *Moskovskij nabljudatel'*, 1838, č. 18, kn 2, pp. 144–189. At the end: "S nemeckogo V. B – n" /V. P. Botkin/. In table of contents by error: "Kresler. Iz Gofmana."

("Kreisleriana," excerpts)

T44. "Neskol'ko otryvkov iz žizni kota Murra i biografii kapel'mejstera Murra /sic/." *Moskovskij nabljudatel'*, 1838, č. 18, pp. 364–411. At the end: "(s nemeckogo)." In table of contents: "Iz Gofmana." /Tr. N. X. Ketčer./ Cf. T51.

(*Lebensansichten des Katers Murr*, excerpts)

T45. "Kavaler Gljuk. Vospominanie iz proisšestvij 1809 goda. (Soč. Goffmanna.)." *Literaturnye pribavlenija k Russkomu invalidu*, 1838, no. 34, Slovesnost', pp. 661–665. /Also published in *Moskovskie vedomosti*, no. 70, pp. 573–575 (Žitomirskaja)./

("Ritter Gluck")

1839

T46. "Zolotoj goršok. (povest' Gofmana)." *Moskovskij nabljudatel'*, 1839, č. 1, Proza, pp. 35–194.

("Der goldne Topf")

1840

T47. "Smert' kota Mucija i nadgrobnoe emu slovo. (Otryvok iz knigi: *Vzgljad na žizn' kota Murra*, soč. Goffmana)." *Literaturnaja gazeta*, 1840, no. 37, cols. 848–858. At the end: "Perev. N. Ketčer." Cf. T51.

(*Lebensansichten des Katers Murr*, excerpt)

T48. "Mejster Flo. Skazka o semi priključenijax dvux druzej." *Otečestvennye zapiski,* 1840, t. 13, Slovesnost', pp. 117–221. /Tr. N. X. Ketčer/ Author identified in table of contents.

("Meister Floh")

T49. "Videnie. (Rasskaz, iz Gofmana)." *Literaturnaja gazeta,* 1840, no. 79, cols. 1779–1787.

("Eine Spukgeschichte")

T50. "Predstavlenie Don-Žuana. Artističeskaja fantazija Gofmana." *Panteon russkogo i vsex evropejskix teatrov,* 1840, č. 2, kn. 6, pp. 65–72. Note: "Per. E. D.. .Ja."

("Don Juan")

T51. *Kot Murr. Povest' v 4-x č. Soč. È. T. A. Gofmana.* Perevod s nem. *N. Ketčera.* 4 čč. SPb.: I. Pesockij, 1840. Censor's approval of April 18, 1839, Cf. T44, T47.

(*Lebensansichten des Katers Murr*)

T52. *Podarok na Novyj god. Dve skazki Gofmana dlja bol'šix i malen'kix detej.* SPb.: A. Syčev, 1840. 320 pp. Censor's approval of Dec. 1, 1839. Contents: "Neizvestnoe ditja," "Gryzun orexov i carek myšej." /Tr. V. F. Odoevskij./

("Das fremde Kind," "Nußknacker und Mausekönig")

1843

T53. "Skazka o ščelkune, sočinenie Gofmana. (Perevod s nemeckogo)." *Biblioteka dlja vospitanija,* 1843, otd. 2, č. 3, pp. 1–135. Reprint of the 1835 edition; cf. T33.

("Nußknacker und Mausekönig")

1844

T54. "Kroška Caxes, po prozvan'ju Cinnober. Povest' È. T. A. Gofmana." *Otečestvennye zapiski,* 1844, t. 34, no. 3, Slovesnost', pp. 149–219. /Tr. N. X. Ketčer?/

("Klein Zaches genannt Zinnober")

T55.  *Princessa Brambilla. Fantastič. povest' È. F. A.* Goffmanna. S politipažnymi
       ris. SPb.: X. Gince, 1844. 229 pp.

       ("Prinzessin Brambilla")


                    *Russian Articles on Hoffmann, 1822 – 1845*

C1.   "O čudesnom v romane. Soč. Val'tera Skotta." *Syn otečestva i Severnyj arxiv,*
       1829, t. 7, pp. 229–245, 288–309, 355–365. Note: "Oeuvres complettes de
       Sir Walter Scott. Paris 1829."

       Cf. /Walter Scott/, "On the Supernatural in Fictitious Composition; and Par-
       ticularly on the Works of Ernest Theodore William Hoffmann," *Foreign Quar-
       terly Review,* 1827, vol. 1, pp. 60–98.

C2.   "Poslednie dni žizni i smert' Gofmana. (Otryvok)." *Syn otečestva i Severnyj
       arxiv,* 1830, č. 131, no. 4, pp. 217–236 (Izjaščnaja slovesnost'). At the end:
       "Iz Revue de Paris – A. O." Cf. T9.

       Loève-Veimars, "Les dernières années et la mort d'Hoffmann," *Revue de Paris,*
       vol. 7 (Oct. 25, 1829), pp. 248–263.

C3.   "O fantastičeskix povestjax Gofmanna." *Vestnik Evropy,* 1830, t. 6, nos. 23–
       24, pp. 146–158. At the end: "S franc. V. Praxov."

       Cs. /Philarète Chasles/, "*Contes fantastiques* de E. T. A. Hoffmann, traduits
       de l'allemand par Loève-Weimar /sic/ et précédés d'une notice historique par
       W. Scott," *Journal des Débats,* May 22, 1830.

C4.   "Kratkoe žizneopisanie Gofmana." *Raduga,* 1832, kn. 3, pp. 214–215.

C5.   "Goffman." *Teleskop,* 1833, no. 13, pp. 93–115 (Znamenitye sovremenniki).
       At the end: "Ks. Marm'e."

       X. Marmier, "Hoffmann," *Nouvelle Revue Germanique,* vol. 13 (Jan., 1833),
       pp. 12–29; reprinted in *Cabinet de Lecture,* April 14.

C6.   Iskander /A. I. Gercen/, "Goffmann. Rodilsja 24 janvarja 1776. Umer 25
       ijunja 1822. (N. P. O–u)." *Teleskop,* 1836, č. 33, pp. 139–168 (Znamenitye
       sovremenniki). At the end: "Iskander. 1834. aprelja 12."

C7. "Goffman i ego fantastičeskie proizvedenija." *Syn otečestva*, 1837, č. 183, pp. 63–81 (Nauki i iskusstva). Note: "France Littéraire."

Maignien /de Cambrai/, "Hoffmann, Contes fantastiques," *France Littéraire*, 1836, vol. 24, pp. 71–82.

C8. "Žizn' Gofmana." *Moskovskij nabljudatel'*, 1838, č. 16, pp. 345–384, 497–541. At the end: "(s francuzskogo)." Cf. T40, T41.

/A. Loève-Veimars/, *La vie de E.-T.-A. Hoffmann, d'après les documens originaux* (Paris: Renduel, 1833).

C9. Ieron. Trun. "È. T. A. Gofman, kak muzykant." *Otečestvennye zapiski*, 1840, no. 3, pp. 1–34 (Nauki i xudožestva).

H. Truhn, "E. T. A. Hoffmann als Musiker, mit Beziehung auf die Herausgabe seines musikalischen Nachlasses," *Der Freihafen*, 1839, no. 3, pp. 66–105.

\* \* \*

To this list may be added two items noted by Žitomirskaja that appeared during our period in reference books:

"Gofman" and "Sočinenija Gofmana." In *Kartiny sveta*, č. 2, cols. 369–378 and 395–399. M., 1837.

F. N. M/encov/, "Gofman." In *Ènciklopedičeskij leksikon*, vol. 15, pp. 51–53. SPb.: Pljušar, 1838.

# Index

298                              Index